JOHN DONNE:
LANGUAGE AND STYLE

THE LANGUAGE LIBRARY

EDITED BY ERIC PARTRIDGE AND DAVID CRYSTAL

A. C. Partridge

JOHN DONNE:
LANGUAGE AND STYLE

ANDRE DEUTSCH

First published 1978 by
André Deutsch Limited
105 Great Russell Street London WC1

Printed in Great Britain by
W & J Mackay Limited, Chatham

British Library Cataloguing in Publication Data

Partridge, Astley Cooper
  John Donne – (The language library).
  1. Donne, John – Criticism and interpretation
  I. Series
  821'.3   PR2248

ISBN 0-233-97030-4

FOR ERIC
EMINENCE GRISE OF LEXICOGRAPHERS

Contents

🐍🐍🐍🐍🐍

Preface

DONNE was a transitional but influential figure in the later English Renaissance. He is credited with leading the revolt against Petrarchism in England, and deflating the Elizabethan tradition of fluidity and sweetness in poetry. He certainly headed an intellectual movement that culminated in a new mode of verse writing. This movement, though it was adumbrated by Wyatt, did not really emerge until the last eight years of Queen Elizabeth's reign – a critical period, not only for Donne and Shakespeare (who was eight years Donne's senior), but for the development of the English language. T. S. Eliot, in spite of reservations about the preacher's emotional temperament, regarded Donne as 'one of the few great reformers and preservers of our tongue' ('Donne in our Time', *A Garland for John Donne*, p 19).

Born into a zealous Catholic family, which yielded several martyrs, Donne was not himself a thinker of doctrinaire habits. He was well taught by private tutors in mathematics, theology, rhetoric and classical languages, and is said to have had some understanding of Spanish, as well as Italian. That he was a precocious pupil is shown by his matriculation at Hart Hall, Oxford, at the age of twelve years. He does not, however, seem to have questioned the tenets of his family's religious beliefs until after his admission as a law student at Lincoln's Inn in 1592. He served in naval expeditions to Cadiz and the Azores, and his ambitions seem to have been secular, until his clandestine marriage to Ann More in 1601.

A decade of humiliation, when he had squandered his inheritance, induced him to find refuge in the state religion. His conversion to Anglicanism was gradual, however, and not entirely due to self-interest. The casuistry of his immature style, which first appears in *Paradoxes and Problems* (not printed until 1633), seems to have been unrelated to his change of heart. On the advice of

9

King James I, Donne took Anglican orders in 1615, at the age of 43. His letters show that he was little troubled by the current theological conflict. He felt it, rather, his mission to preach, and to spread the gospel of salvation, as he had personally experienced it. His decision to reject Catholicism was made after long study of the Christian Fathers, especially St Augustine, whose spiritual progress resembled his own. The *De Doctrina Christiana, De Trinitate* and *Confessions* were his favourite reading, after the Psalms and the Pauline epistles.

Being one of the royal chaplains, Donne was honoured on the King's visit to Cambridge in 1616, with the degree of Doctor of Divinity, and he preached his first sermon at Court in April of that year, the month of Shakespeare's death. His reputation as an impassioned orator, fascinating a spellbound audience, was confirmed in 1640 by the admiration of his first biographer, Izaak Walton, who was a personal acquaintance. But more is known about Donne than most of his contemporaries, through some 160 surviving letters, written in a medieval epistolary form, that resemble familiar essays.

As early as 1620, John Cave, an Anglican divine of Lincoln College, wrote that the ideal interpreter of Donne was a man whose 'minde might be made see as far as th'eye' (Dyce MS, Victoria and Albert Museum). Cave appraised the 'well plac'd words' and 'more pure mind', and likened the 'splendor' of Donne's imagery to 'rays out of a cloud'. Most of the funeral elegies in Donne's honour commemorate his masculine language, and wit, using the latter word in the original sense of 'alert intelligence'. What appeals to modern readers, however, seems to be Donne's intense naturalism.

Speculation was a feature of Donne's prose as well as his poetry; he was too intrigued by the working out of new ideas to be either a thorough-going mystic or a sceptic. The intellectualism and the wit had their origin, not in scholasticism only, but in the independence and dialectical skill of Reformation thinkers. Dramatic presentation of ideas, originality of phrasing and disregard of formal syntax overshadow other considerations of style. It is likely that the passion for verse argument proceeded from Donne's spell at Lincoln's Inn, and training as a lawyer. Donne's delight in squeezing the utmost meaning from words is different from Shakespeare's, but stems from the same source: curiosity of mind.

Preface

Perhaps Donne's greatest contribution to aesthetic speculation in the English Renaissance was the baroque assimilation of thought to feeling, coupled with the semantic teasing of words, still a logical priority in the rational process of theologians. Analysing the diverse forms of writing, when the author is as idiosyncratic as Donne, raises special problems, partly because theological implications are not those with which the language critic has normally to deal. My objectives have been to adapt linguistic expositions to the merits of style, and to minimize the risk of monotony for the reader by varying the technique of analysis on each occasion. In the method of *explication de texte* the second aim is as important as the first; each analysis should be appropriate to the content of the piece selected. The integration of biographical considerations with editorial facts and literary interpretation needs no excuse; it adds to the interest of an author-language study. With this in view, the thematic material was so organized as to cover every aspect of Donne's writing; there is only a slight preponderance in favour of the poetry. But fulness of treatment in any chapter need not imply the relative importance of the genre; rather it suggests that some aspects of Donne's writing have been neglected.

In presenting this essay, I wish to thank Eric Partridge, one of the editors of the Language Library, who suggested the topic to me. Without his encouragement, the editorial care of Professor David Crystal and the guidance of the late Professor Simeon Potter, such a difficult study could not have been undertaken. To Mr Piers Burnett, of André Deutsch Ltd, I am especially indebted for the opportunity of participating in what promises to be a fruitful author-language series.

But my principal debt is to my wife, who, by second-sight, deciphered the manuscript from papers in disarray, helped with the proof-reading and checked the index. Any student who seeks to explicate the writings of Donne must be prepared to amend his judgements repeatedly.

A.C.P.
JOHANNESBURG
JANUARY 1978

🔲🔲🔲🔲🔲🔲

I AM no great voyager in other mens works: no swallower nor devourer of volumes nor pursuant of authors. Perchance it is because I find borne in my self knowledge or apprehension enough, for (without forfeiture or impeachment of modesty) I think I am bond to God thankfully to acknowledge it . . .

To know how to live by the booke is a pedantry, and to do it is a bondage. For both hearers and players are more delighted with voluntary than with sett musike . . . Yet I read something. But indeed not so much to avoyd as to enjoy idlenes. . .

So say I of authors that they thinke and I thinke both reasonably yet posibly both erroniously; that is manly. . .

(Donne's Letter to Sir Henry Wotton, *c* 1600)

CHAPTER I

Donne's Use of Language:
The *Elegies* and *Paradoxes*

𝕚𝕚𝕚𝕚𝕚𝕚

JOHN DONNE's conversational tone and employment of natural speech rhythms had forebears in English literary history, but no earlier writer combined these tendencies with the confidence that heralds a poetic revolution. Like most reformers, Donne was not altogether conscious of what he was changing; nor is self-assurance a necessary guarantee of sincerity. Donne's authoritative style was an effective screen for knowledge of his own limitations. In the criticism, silence and adulation of successive periods, Donne remains an enigmatic figure.

T. S. Eliot commended Donne's ingenuity in stanza forms and rhythmic variation, contending that he was the first to make it possible 'to think in lyric verse'. ('Donne in our Time', *A Garland for John Donne*, p 16). Eliot did not rebut Johnson's charge, in the Life of Cowley, that Donne's imagery was too fragmentary, and the style too analytical. He was concerned with another aspect of communication, the problem of what is natural and what artificial in a poetic style. He believed that Donne achieved more in the *Songs and Sonets, Elegies* and *Satyres* than in the *Sermons*; and he is not alone in that opinion.

Johnson's view of Donne, of course, reflected a change of sensibility, after the Restoration, which Eliot was one of the first to recognize; he ascribed it to the writings of Hobbes, Dryden and Pope, who inducted the Neo-classical era. Dryden first applied the term 'metaphysics' to the Donne genre in the *Discourse Concerning the Original and Progress of Satire* (1693), regretting the elaboration of figures in love poetry, because it perplexed 'the minds of the fair sex with nice speculations of philosophy, when he [the poet] should engage their hearts'.

Donne's poems were circulated in manuscript, and not published until after his death. Apart from the textual problems, dating is a subject of debate. For the purpose of this study, I accept the order established by Helen Gardner in editions of *The Divine Poems* (Clarendon, 1952) and *The Elegies and the Songs and Sonnets* (1965), which generally accords with the findings of W. Milgate in the companion edition of *The Satires, Epigrams and Verse Letters* (Clarendon, 1967).

When Donne, the aspiring lawyer of 1592–4, began to write, he was a realist and psychologist, aptly described by the Elizabethans as an 'anatomist'. Paradox and serious wit were his dominant characteristics, in verse and prose, the traditional rhetoric being adapted to both media. Observation and a taste for trenchant criticism are the principal features of this experiment:

> Though all her parts be not in th'usuall place,   15
> She'hath yet an Anagram of a good face.
> If we might put the letters but one way,
> In the leane dearth of words, what could wee say?
> When by the Gamut some Musitions make
> A perfect song, others will undertake,   20
> By the same Gamut chang'd, to equall it.
> Things simply good, can never be unfit.
> She's faire as any, if all be like her,
> And if none bee, then she is singular.
> All love is wonder; if wee justly doe   25
> Account her wonderfull, why not lovely too?
> Love built on beauty, soone as beauty, dies,
> Chuse this face, chang'd by no deformities.
>
> (*The Anagram, lines 15–28*)

These pentameter couplets, based on classical analogues of Horace and Ovid, are couched in a rugged diction, known as 'strong lines'. They have not yet the 'rich and pregnant phansie' Thomas Carew admired in line 38 of his *Elegie upon the death of the Deane of St. Pauls*. Donne seems here to be attracted by the shock technique of Ovid's *Amores,* and suggests a similar rejection of conventional values. The early *Elegies* were much indebted to Berni's Italian paradoxes in *terza rima,* referred to as *capitoli.* J. B. Leishman in *The Monarch of Wit* (pp 74–81) shows also that *The Anagram* consciously imitates 'compressed syllogisms' of Tasso's *Sopra La Bellezza,* a spirited encomium in which the poet defends his paradoxical manner.

According to the OED, the word *Anagram* (line 16) was used by Puttenham in *The Arte of English Poesie* (1589), meaning 'a transposition of the letters of a name, word or phrase, to fashion another word or phrase'. Donne's exercise is subtly metonymical. Proposing the paradox that 'beauty is skin-deep', he argues that Flavia has all the physical attributes a woman should possess, but that they are unusually disposed. Poverty of expression, the analogy runs, arises from ultra-conventional use of the alphabet's potential (16 and 17). Using the same notes, a musician could devise an alternative melody from the most perfect of songs (19–21). Each couplet is an analogical plea for diversity, the poet's message being: 'Content yourself with a homely woman, if she has no physical handicaps' (28).

The couplet style depends for its concision on rhetorical devices, e.g. rhetorical question (*erotema*) and aphorism (*sententia*), the latter especially in lines 22, 25, 27. An example of antithesis through syntactic inversion of an adverbial phrase is 'Love built on *beauty*, soone as *beauty*, dies;' this employs the repetitive scheme of words named *ploce*. Such sophistication all poets had learnt from the art of the rhetoricians, and adapted to the needs of poetry.

Donne may not have been responsible for all the contractions (*metaplasms*) in the first edition of his poems. Some are colloquial, some metrical, and some rhythmical signals, e.g. *th'*usuall (15), She'hath (16), She'*s* (23), chang'*d* (28). Every example here reflected appears, however, in holograph manuscripts (see *John Donne's holograph of 'A Letter to the Lady Carey and Mrs. Essex Riche'* ed. H. Gardner). The marks of elision in *th'usuall* and *She'hath* are metrical fictions, designed to point the rhythm; in neither case did Donne intend that a syllable should be suppressed by the reader. Rather, the marks suggest the desirability of retaining the extra-metrical syllables for colloquial realism.

The words *Anagram, Gamut* and *Musitions* are capitalized, not for emphasis, but because they are status words adopted by the various professions; some had only recently been naturalized. *Gamut* (19 and 21) is of interest, since only two earlier uses were recorded by the editors of the OED, the first being Skelton's in 1529. The *hexacord,* or musical scale of classical times, had six notes, beginning with *Ut* (A). But the Middle Ages introduced a seventh note, one tone lower, which they called *gamma* (G), from the Greek alphabet. The word *gamut* is therefore a contraction of *gamma* + *ut.* All the common names of the hexacord were, in fact, derived from the sapphic stanza in the Hymn of St John the Baptist's Day: '*Ut* queant laxis *re*sonare fibris *Mi*ra gestorum *fa*muli tuorum *Sol*ve polluti *la*bu reatum, Sanc*te* Iohannes.' (*Doh* for *ut* was an innovation of the tonic *sol-fa* system in the mid nineteenth century.)

The elegy of Donne is a secular exercise in the scholastic mode, whose subtlety entertains the poet as well as the reader. The poet at the centre, by the ingenuity of his argument and figurative expressions, works his way to the surface, whose rough exterior is invariably barbed with some amoral purpose.

Donne's prejudicial masculinity, and *energeia* of immoderate assertions enabled him to make play with the reasonableness of his mentors. The rhetoric is contentious and functional, never ornamental, and hyperbole is quite consistent with it. Argument through sustained image constitutes Donne's fanciful fusion of rhetoric and poetry. The appeal is partly to sensory experience, partly to a recondite order of nature, philosophically acceptable to his age. In the love poems, egocentric isolation is avoided by the public involvement of his ideas.

When Donne undertook the prose *Paradoxes and Problems,* from which the next passage is taken, he was familiar with Erasmus's *Apothegms,* but probably had in mind Anthony Munday's *The Defence of Contraries* (1593), a translation of a French version of Ortensio Lando's *Paradossi* (1543). The study of classical rhetoric led Donne to the anti-Ciceronian camp, which favoured *figurae sententiae,* figures of wit and thought, whose staple was antithesis, aphorism, metaphor and paradox ('opinion contrary to expectation'). Donne's versatile knowledge and verbal dexterity were admirably fitted for this liberated style. The passage is from the proposition 'That Nature is our Worst Guide' (*Selected Prose,* ed. E. Simpson, H. Gardner and T. Healy):

> *Nature though oft chased away, it will returne*; 'tis true, but those *good motions* and *inspirations* which be our guides must bee *wooed, courted,* and *welcomed,* or else they abandon us. . . . That poore knowledge whereby we conceive what *raine* is, what *wind,* what *thunder,* wee call *Metaphysicke, supernaturall*; 5 such *small* things, such *no* things doe we allow to our pliant *Natures* apprehension. Lastly, by following her, we lose

the pleasant, and lawfull commodities of this life, for wee shall drinke water and eate rootes, and those not sweet and delicate, as now by Mans *art* and *industry* they are made: we 10 shall lose all the necessities of *societies, lawes, arts* and *sciences,* which are all the workemanship of *Man*: yea we shall lack the last *best refuge* of misery, *death*; because no death is naturall.

(*Paradoxes and Problems,* p 14)

Note: The word *Metaphysicke* in line 5 is here used adjectivally, not as a noun (see OED, vol. VI, p 385).

The inspiration for this is the *Epigrams* of Martial, but the germ of the eloquent *Sermons* is already present. Observe (a) the cumulative effect of rhetorical devices in '*wooed, courted* and *welcomed*'; in 'what *raine* is, what *wind*, what *thunder*'; in 'such *small* things, such *no* things'; (b) the colloquial realism of '*tis* and *yea* in the first and penultimate lines; (c) the economy of qualifiers, which are commonplace, but appropriate adjectives; (d) the slender employment of subordination in the sentence structure; (e) the dextrous use of punctuation to point the argument. The passage is one of easy deliberation, and the vocabulary not overburdened with Renaissance latinity. This is a style neither aureate nor extemporaneous. In a letter to Sir Henry Wotton (*c* 1600) Donne indicated that the *Paradoxes* were merely 'alarums to truth', logical exercises of a student of Lincoln's Inn.

One of Coleridge's marginal notes preserved by A. J. Smith in *John Donne, the Critical Heritage* runs as follows:

Donne was a poor Metaphysician; he never closely questioned himself as to the absolute meanings of his words.
(p 278)

The heretical thesis of Donne's defence is that the works of man, though the product of artifice, are congenial to the humanist, and less dangerous than Nature's uncurbed instincts. Donne seems mistakenly to regard the study of natural phenomena ('poore knowledge') as supernatural (i.e. metaphysical). The distinction between natural science (physics) and metaphysics was, however, understood in England by the late sixteenth century, as Bacon shows in *The Advancement of Learning* (1605).

19

When the *Paradoxes and Problems* were first printed from manuscript in 1633, there were only twenty-one, and they were entitled *Juvenilia*. In the third edition of 1652, they were increased to twelve Paradoxes and seventeen Problems, an eighteenth Problem being added in the Nonesuch Edition of Donne in 1929, bringing the total to thirty. The manuscripts, many in different hands, reveal important variants, and no satisfactory text of the *Juvenilia* is yet available.

Besides the variant readings, there are considerations of capitalization, punctuation and italics. Donne's principle in using capital letters in the body of a line or sentence can only be guessed at from holograph letters, and is not as consistent as the practice of printers. Only the words *Metaphysicke, Nature* and *Man* (in the sense of mankind) are capitalized in the above prose passage. Donne's punctuation differs from the modern practice chiefly in the use of dual-purpose stops (time pauses and grammatical signals), such as commas, semicolons, colons and full-stops; notice the comma after *pleasant* (line 8), and the colons in lines 10 and 12. The absence of an apostrophe in the possessive *Natures* in line 7 accords with the Elizabethan practice. There were two methods of indicating italic function in manuscript: either words were underlined, or they were written in Italian hand, where the rest of the matter was in English hand. Proper names, alien words and quotations were commonly treated in this fashion. The liberal use of italics in the *Paradoxes and Problems,* e.g. in *good motions* (2), *inspirations* (2), *supernaturall* (5), *best refuge* (13), is inexplicable, unless it has some rhetorical or allusive purpose.

The Paradoxes are witty essays, argued from dubious premises, and relate to the cynical poems; but they substitute rational coherency for passionate intensity.

The Problems are shorter, more sardonic, and probably of later composition than the Paradoxes; one of them, 'Why was Sir Walter Raleigh thought the fittest Man, to write the Historie of these Times?' (containing no italics), did not appear in print until Gosse's edition of the *Life and Letters* (1899). The brief ¦discussion, 'Why do Women delight much in Feathers?', is typical of the Donne genre:

They think that Feathers imitate wings, and so shew their restlessness and instability. As they are in matter, so they would be in name, like *Embroiderers, Painters,* and such *Artificers* of curious *vanities,* which Varro and the vulgar edition call *Plumarios.* Or else they have feathers for the 5 same reason, which moves them to love the unworthiest men, which is, that they may be thereby excusable in their inconstancy and often changing.

The unusual feature here is the quite modern orthography; the reason is that this Problem was not printed until the 1652 edition of the *Juvenilia,* after the Civil War, when English spelling was, for practical purposes, standardized.

Witty essays, argued from dubious premises, may resemble cynical poems in their thematic ideas, but the poetry of Donne has a different conception of imagery. Thought-generated tropes and figures have a potent function in the conceptual pattern of the poem, and the line that separates nature and artifice is largely spurious. For instance, omnipresence of the word *all,* a positive, if hyperbolic feature of Donne's poetry, has a sonantal and emphatic value that more specific qualifiers could not supply. Word irony of this kind is, indeed, Donne's strength. Tropes change the semantic significance of words; schemes communicate the acoustic properties of phrase and sentence rhythm.

Donne's early verse in small compass is distinguished from the prose by the development of an elliptical colloquial technique to match the astringent wit and lightning illumination of the imagery. These are the principal sources of his poetic energy. He is most challenging when the rhythm is modulated freely, to suit the subtle progression of the thinking, which is often in conflict with the feeling. The movement adapts to the sense; and the emphasis, or lack of it, follows the intonation of the living voice. Juxtaposing two or more stressed syllables is one of the prime causes of dissonant effects. In a verse letter *To Mr T. W.* (Grierson, I, p 205), Donne confessed to 'harsh verse', 'lame measure' and 'weake feete'; the ruggedness was helped by the mingling of commonplace words with technical jargon from the arts and sciences. Donne's power to associate emotively ideas from different fields of learning was immense and startling.

A large proportion of Donne's poetry was composed in robust pentameter couplets, different in technique from those of Jonson and the unmelodious translators of the epigrams of Horace and

Martial. Jonson's diction is urbane and traditionally classic; Donne's is personal and imaginative. Both kinds attracted seventeenth century audiences, among whom Donne's elegy, *The Bracelet* (written *c* 1593–4) was one of the wittiest and most ingenious examples. In this poem of 114 lines the obscurity associated with tortuous syntax in metaphysical poetry is minimal. The true wit of it resides, as Coleridge saw, in Donne's 'wonder-exciting vigour, intenseness and peculiarity of thought' (*John Donne, the Critical Heritage,* ed. A. J. Smith, p 275).

T. S. Eliot in *The Sacred Wood* (1920) and George Williamson in *The Donne Tradition* (1930) drew attention to Donne's affinity to Chapman; but if one examines the 'affectation of words and indigested conceits' to which Chapman refers in the preface to *Ovids Banquet of Sence* (1595), it becomes evident that the likeness lies in the facility of Chapman and Donne to extract poetry from the prosaic. Chapman has no couplets or quatrains to compare in flexibility with this extract from *Loves Progress,* another of Donne's elegies:

> Perféction is in únitie; | Preférre
> Óne wóman fírst, | and thèn oñe thíng in hér.　　　　10
> Í, | when I válue góld, | may thínke upòn
> The dúctillness, | the àpplicátiòn,
> The whólesomeness, | the iǹgenúity,
> From rúst, | from sóyle, | from fýre éver frée,
> But if I lóve it, | 'tis becaúse 'tis máde　　　　15
> By our néw Náture, | úse, | the sóule of tráde.
> 　　Áll these in wómen wee might thínke upòn
> (If wómen hád them) | but yet lóve but óne.
> Can mén more ínjure wómen than to sáy
> They lóve'them for thát by which they áre nót théy?　　　　20
> Mákes vírtue wóman? | Múst I cóol my blóod
> Till Í both bée, | and fínd one, | wíse and góod?

In these fourteen lines the reflection is not bound in neat epigrammatic bundles. The rhythm is capable of expanding by enjambement, as in the four couplets 9/10, 11/12, 15/16, 19/20; or of contracting by the superflux of internal pauses. The fifteen pauses here are cunningly varied. The metrical rhythm of the pentameter is repeated in two lines (12 and 13), where balanced words of three and five syllables appear in the same order. Most effective is the modulation of primary stresses, varying from two in lines 12 and 13, to six in lines 10 and 21. Lines 14 and 22 are the only normally structured pentameters. Caesural pause falls in the middle of a foot in lines 15, 16, 18, 21 and 22, which simulate unstudied vocal delivery. Two lines (20, 22) are wholly monosyllabic, and it is notable that Donne's evocative language abounds in words of one syllable that denote action or value.

The rhetorical effect of *ploce* is quite unobtrusive, because the words repeated are commonly relational ones (*from*, *'tis*, *but*). *Woman* or *women*, and the first personal pronoun, occur five times, where the *ploce* has thematic relevance. *One*, *her* and *they* are rhetorically significant pronouns in lines 10, 18, 20 and 22, with weight of emphasis according to sense. Rhyme words are usually strong monosyllables, the vowels in *blood* and *good* being well matched in Donne's time. The periphrastic subjunctive *may/might thinke upon*, which terminates lines 11 and 17, gives rise to imperfect rhymes, but the deliberate weakness at the ends of 11–13 ensures rhythmic variation.

Being an unmelodious poet, Donne employs alliteration sparingly, the one exception being line 14. A debater like Donne has to rely heavily on *erotema*, which occurs three times, in lines 19 to 22. The poet starts with an aphorism, 'Perfection is in unitie,' and substantiates his thesis by assertion and counter-argument. One trope alone is favoured, in line 16: 'use, the *soule* of trade'; though this may be fortuitous, it is *prima facie* evidence that the elegy was an early one.

The orthography of the passage has some notable features:

LINE 9   *Preferre* – capital letter after a semicolon. This is frequent in Donne's verse and prose.
LINE 18 (If women had them) – conditional clause in parentheses. Donne was partial to such interpolations.
LINE 20 They *love'them* for that by which they are not they? – a typical metrical device, consistently used by the editor of the 1633 edition, to suggest that the two words are to be theoretically regarded as one syllable.

Donne's metric is indispensable to the understanding of his poetry; its arrestive ingenuity results from practice and experience. The revolt against symmetry in euphonious verse sought to avoid

monotonous cadence, and began with the couplet. Cadence originally meant the fall of the voice at the caesura or line-end; and
Samuel Daniel thought that uniformity marred the English couplet,
with 'a kind of certaintie which stuffs the delight rather than inter-
taines it.' ('A Defence of Rhyme', *Elizabethan Critical Essays,* ed.
Gregory Smith, II, p 382). The cadence in Puttenham and other
critics came to be associated with rhyme, and in particular with the
matching of masculine and feminine varieties. Donne's practice in
the *Elegies* differs from that in the *Satyres,* which belong to the same
years. His boldest innovations of stress-shift and inversion were
still to come in stanza forms; they were not invoked for jolting
novelty, but to deny the ear the full return of rhyme-sounds.
Delaying the caesura, as in line 9 of *Loves Progress,* was a modulation of which Donne was fond, but not the inventor.

The only authoritative edition of Donne's poems is the first
assembled by his son, and published in 1633. During the poet's
lifetime the texts that appeared in print were the lines prefaced to
Coryats Crudities (1611); *An Anatomie of the World* (1611); the *First
and Second Anniversaries* (1612); and the *Elegie upon the Death of
Prince Henry* (in Sylvester's *Lachrymae Lachrymarum,* 1613). Donne
was writing fitfully during the last decade of Queen Elizabeth's
reign, but the manuscripts were circulated secretly, as though he
were still uncertain about a literary career. The received texts belong entirely to the Jacobean and Caroline eras, with important
complications for their orthography when in print. The only holograph manuscript of a poem extant is the verse letter to Lady Carey
and Mrs Essex Riche, written about 1611–12. Scribal manuscripts,
such as the one of *Epithalamion made at Lincolnes Inne,* contain
variant readings, and sometimes alien practices of punctuation. It
is difficult to know whether verbal improvements were made by
author or transcriber. Donne himself circulated revised manuscripts, e.g. of the *Satyres,* written some forty years before they
were printed. The first printed edition (1633) named several poems
that had no titles in the manuscripts; the second edition (1635)
added twenty-eight new poems, several of which have since been
shown to be the work of contemporaries.

Orthography preserves not only spelling and punctuation, but
also aspects of accidence, prosody and colloquial contraction,
which it is the business of a language study to recognize. Grierson

preserved Donne's original punctuation, except (he said) where it was wrong or misleading, and caused the poet to be misunderstood. In most cases, however, the standard was the edition of 1633, or that of a textually reliable copyist, and not necessarily Donne's. Punctuation is central to principles of elision, to correct reading, and to the scansion of Donne's lines. He was addicted to the metaplasmic device of *synaloepha,* or fusion of contiguous vowels, the one ending and the other beginning adjacent words. In *Loves Progress* (line 20) *love'them* seems to imply that the personal pronoun was visualized as *'em.* It is most unlikely that Donne himself disapproved of trisyllabic substitution, which Helen Gardner compares with grace-notes in music (*The Elegies and the Songs and Sonnets,* p 109).

The editor of the first edition must have remembered Ben Jonson's comment to Drummond of Hawthornden, 'that Donne for not keeping of accent deserved hanging'. Syllable-count became an editorial fetish, ignoring the liberal attitude of Elizabethan accentual verse. Yet in the 1633 edition of Donne's poems, many pentameter lines contain twelve syllables, in which the medial vowels in words of three or more syllables, such as *desperate,* are not suppressed.

Analysis of *A Letter to the Lady Carey, and Mrs. Essex Riche,* now in the Bodleian Library, is the only reliable way of determining Donne's orthographic practice in verse. The manuscript, found in 1970, was among the Duke of Manchester's papers in the Public Record Office, where it had lain for nearly a century, awaiting identification by the Historical Manuscripts Commission (see facsimile edition, ed. H. Gardner). The ladies addressed by Donne from Amiens in France in 1612 were daughters of Sir Robert Rich, Earl of Warwick, and Penelope Devereux, his second wife, whom Sidney celebrated as 'Stella'. Donne made two MS corrections: *scarse* replaces *but litle* in line 41 and *I see* is deleted after *extasye* at the end of line 53: these are regarded as evidence of *currente calamo.* There are other scribal copies of Donne's letter in manuscript collections which, collated, show that the versions are not homogeneous. The holograph differs from the first edition (1633) in three places: *are* for *is* in line 13 (correct); *nor* for *or* in line 14 (incorrect); and *thys* for *their* in line 30 (correct). But as Helen Gardner observes (p 5), the discovery is more important for accidentals than for substantive readings.

Here is the text of Donne's holograph. I have preserved the customary scribal abbreviations of *you, your, our, which* and *with,* which occur eighteen times.

Madame/
Here, where by all, all Saints invoked are,
T'were too much Scisme to bee singulare,
And gainst a practise generall to war;
Yett, turninge to Saints, should my Humilitee
To other Saint, then yo^w, directed bee,   5
That were to make my Scisme Heresee.
nor would I bee a Convertite so cold
As not to tell ytt; If thys bee to bold,
Pardons are in thys Market cheaply sold.
where, because Fayth ys in too lowe degree,   10
I thought yt some Apostleship in mee,
To speak things wch by Fayth alone I see:
That ys, of yo^w, who are a firmament
Of vertues, where no one ys growen, nor spent;
Thay'are yor Materialls, not yor Ornament.   15
Others, whom wee call vertuous, are not so
In theyr whole Substance, but theyr vertues grow
But in theyr Humors, and at Seasons show.
For when through tastles flatt Humilitee,
In Doe-baked men, some Harmelesnes wee see,   20
Tis but hys Flegme that's vertuous, and not hee.
so ys the Blood sometymes; who ever ran
To Danger unimportund, hee was than
no better then a Sanguine vertuous man.
So Cloystrall Men who in pretence of fear,   25
All Contributions to thys Lyfe forbear,
Have vertu in Melancholy, and onely there.
spirituall Cholerique Critiqs, wch in all
Religions, find faults, and forgive no fall,
Have, through thys Zeale, vertu, but in theyr Gall.   30
we'are thus but parcell-gilt; To Gold we'are growen,
when vertu ys our Soules Complexione;
who knowes hys vertues Name, or Place, hath none.
vertu ys but Aguishe, when tis Severall;
By'Occasion wak'd, and Circumstantiall;   35

True vertu ys Soule, allways in all deeds all.
Thys vertu, thinkinge to give Dignitee
To yor Soule, found there no infirmitee;
for yor Soule was as good vertu as shee.
shee therfore wrought upon that part of yo^w 40
    scarse
wch ys ~~but litle~~ lesse then Soule, as shee could doe,
And soe hath made yor Beauty vertue too;
Hence comes yt, that yor Beauty wounds not harts
As others, wth prophane and sensuall darts,
But, as an Influence, vertuous thoughts imparts.   45
But if such frinds, by the'honor of yor Sight
Grow capable of thys so great a light,
As to partake yor vertues, and theyr might,
what must I thinke that Influence must doe,
where yt finds Simpathy, and Matter too,   50
vertu, and Beauty, of the same stuffe, as yo^w:
w^{ch}ys, yor noble worthy Sister; shee,
Of whom, if what in thys my extasye ~~I see,~~
And Revelation of yo^w both, I see,
I should write here, As in short Galleryes   55
The Master at the end large glasses tyes
So to present the roome twice to o^r eyes,
So I should give thys letter length, and say
That wch I sayd of yo^w; There ys no way
From eyther, but by th'other, not to stray.   60
May therefore thys bee'inough to testify
My true Devotion, free from flattery.
He that beleevs himselfe, doth never ly.

To the Honorable lady
    the lady Carew.

MORPHOLOGY AND SYNTAX

A. 28 spirituall Cholerique Critiqs, *which* in all/ Religions, find faults. (*Which* was the general relative for persons and things from the twelfth century; Butler's *English Grammar,* as late as 1634, still approved it.)

B. Donne retained *hath* and *doth*, as the recognized literary forms in

33, 42 and 63, where they are used as notional and auxiliary verbs. *Doth* (63) is an instance of *do* employed as a periphrastic auxiliary verb, a practice discontinued in the eighteenth century, except for emphasis.

c. 48 As to *partake your vertues*. (This verb was used transitively, without preposition, from the sixteenth to the nineteenth century.)

D. The inflexional subjunctive, in spite of its decline in the sixteenth century, is used by Donne four times (2, 5, 6, 8), twice in conditional and twice in main clauses, giving an archaic, formal flavour to the constructions.

E. Inversion of the normal order of words is resorted to sixteen times, especially for the sake of metre, rhyme, rhythm or rhetorical effect, i.e. in lines 1, 5, 9, 12, 18, 20, 26, 29, 31, 35, 36, 38, 43, 45, 54 and 56.

PROSODY

A. It should be noted that Donne does not use the tercet-scheme of stanza grouping adopted by editors. The stanza lends itself to run-on lines, enjambement occurring 14 times, at the end of lines 4, 11, 13, 16, 22, 23, 28, 37, 52, 53, 55, 58, 59 and 61, although occasionally it is disguised by commas, for example:

11/12 I thought yt some Apostleship in mee,/ To speak things which by Fayth alone I see:

52/3 which ys, your noble worthy Sister; shee,/ Of whom, if what in thys my extasye

B. Elizabethan resources in expanding or reducing syllables of words, according to metrical need, were abundant. The licence could seldom have been observed in reading.

1 Here, where by all, all Saints *invokèd* are,

23 To Danger *unimportund,* hee was than (a spelling that dispenses with elision)

3 And *gainst* a practise generall to war;

15 Thay'are your *Materialls,* not your Ornament. (trisyllabic)

16 Others, whom wee call *vertuous,* are not so (dissyllabic, similarly in lines 21 and 24)

28   *spirituall Cholerique* Critiqs, which in all (trisyllabic and
     dissyllabic, respectively)

32   when vertu ys our Soules *Complexione*; (four syllables)

34   vertu ys but Aguishe, when tis *Severall*; (trisyllabic)

35   By'Occasion wak'd, and *Circumstantiall*; (five syllables)

c. Donne's elisions are inconsistent, if the design is metrical
regularity. It is marked ten times, in lines 2, 15, 21, 31 (twice),
35 (twice), 46, 60 and 61, but not on the following six occasions:

20   In Doe-bak*ed* men, some Harmelesnes wee see,

21   *T*is but hys Flegme that's vertuous, and not hee. (So 34)

27   Have vert*u i*n Melanchol*y, a*nd onely there.

32   when vert*u y*s our Soules Complexione;

36   True vert*u y*s Soule, allways in all deeds all.

51   vertu, and Beaut*y, o*f the same stuffe, as you:

The deficiencies are supplied in Milgate's edition of the poem.

d. Eye-rhymes are favoured in all tercets, with exceptions in lines
3, 16, 27, 31, 40–42, 49–51 and 53.
In lines 1–3, 55–57, 61–64 one at least is a pseudo-rhyme, i.e.
dissonant, except by poetic licence; the rhyming was probably
strained in Donne's time.

e. Lines 8, 41 and 59 consist of monosyllabic words. Resonance
and rhythm in Donne seem to depend largely on the placing of
latinate polysyllables, e.g. *Convertite* (7), *Apostleship* (11), *unimportund* (23), *Contributions* (26), *Melancholy* (27), *Cholerique*
(28), *Circumstantiall* (35).

f. Donne's surest means of preventing the dislocation of verse
structure, with his vagaries of stress modulation, was the use of
the end-stopped line. He was an English accentualist, who tried
to preserve through elision the habits of an Italian syllabist, and
like Jonson, was in advance of his time.

CONTRACTIONS

Donne's language being in the high (or dignified) style of epistles,
the colloquial contractions are only three in number. All were
regarded in the sixteenth century as licences convenient for metrical
ends; for example:

A. Proclitic *t* for it. *T'were* appears in line 2 (mark of elision wrongly placed), and *Tis* (without elision) in lines 21 and 34.

B. Proclitic *th'* for *the*: 60 by *th'*other (but cf by *the'*honor, in line 46)

C. Enclitic *'s* for *is*: 21 Tis but hys Flegme that*'s* vertuous

SPELLING

A. Donne's practice contains a few examples of the ubiquity of alternative spellings, e.g. *ytt* (8) and *yt* (11, 43, 50); *so* (16, 22) and *soe* (42); *wee* (20) and *we* (31); *vertu* (27, 30, 32, 34, 36, 37, 39, 51) and *vertue* (42)

B. *y* and *i* are interchangeable, but Donne prefers the former in everyday words, e.g. *Fayth* (10, 12); *thys* (8, 9, 26, 30, 47, 53, 58, 61); *ys* (10, 13, 14, 22, 32, 34, 36, 41, 59); *hys* (21, 33); *theyr* (17, 18, 30, 48); *sometymes* (22); *Lyfe* (26), *Galleryes* (55); *tyes* (56); *sayd* (59); *eyther* (60), *ly* (63)

C. Final *l* in words of romance language origin is invariably doubled, e.g. *generall* (3), *Materialls* (15), *Cloystrall,* (25), *spirituall* (28), *Severall* (34), *Circumstantiall* (35), *sensuall* (44)

D. Final *e* is invariably doubled in common monosyllables, e.g. *bee* (5, 7, 8, 61); *mee* (11); *wee* (20); *hee* (23); *shee* (39, 40, 41, 52)

E. Peculiar spellings, but not necessarily idiosyncratic: *Scisme* (2, 6), *Yett* (4), *growen* (14, 31), *Thay* (15), *Tastles* (19), *flatt* (19), *Doe* (20 for dough), *Harmelesnes* (20), *Flegme* (21), *Critiqs* (28), *scarse* (41), *frinds* (46), *Simpathy* (50), *extasye* (53), *beleevs* (63).

PUNCTUATION

The stopping of Donne is meticulous, to the point of superfluity, by modern standards, as well as by comparison with the pointing of the 1633 edition. He favours syntactic, more than breathing stops, to clarify the thinking. When a word of identical form, but different function, is repeated, a comma usually separates the first from the second, as in line 1 after *all*.

A. Syntactically superfluous commas, with elocutionary emphasis. The comma sometimes marks off a phrase, in which the normal order of words is inverted.

5   should my Humilitee/ To other Saint, then you, directed bee

11–13   I thought yt some Apostleship in mee,/ To speak things which by Fayth alone I see:/ That ys, of you

14   where no one ys growen, nor spent

29   Cholerique Critiqs, which in all/Religions, find faults . . . /Have, through thys Zeale, vertu, but in theyr Gall.

33   who knowes hys vertues Name, or Place, hath none.

43   Hence comes yt, that your Beauty wounds no harts

48   As to partake your vertues, and theyr might

     So lines 50, 51, 52 and 63

B. Donne employed twelve semicolons (an unusually high number for any writer at this date) in this poem; they are mainly time pauses, between co-ordinated statements of some weight. In a few instances these stops have a longer time value than at present, e.g. in 8, 14 and 59. Note the inconsistent capitalization, after semicolons, of succeeding words, as in lines 8, 31 and 59. This is known to occur elsewhere in Donne's poetry.

C. Colons are employed twice (at the end of lines 12 and 51), both syntactic, indicating resumptive function.

D. Except in line 62, full-stops are placed only at the end of tercets, on 14 occasions.

CAPITALS

A. Donne, like other Elizabethan and Jacobean authors, used capitals for status nouns (see pp 75–7 of my *Orthography in Shakespeare*; and p 230 of the index to *A Substantive Grammar of Shakespeare's Non-Dramatic Texts*. Examples are: *Saints* (1), *Scisme* (2), *Heresee* (6), *Convertite* (7), *Market* (9), *Fayth* (10), *Apostleship* (11), *Ornament* (15), *Humors* (18), *Seasons* (18), *Flegme* (21), *Blood* (22), *Sanguine* (24), *Melancholy* (27), *Critiqs* (28), *Gall* (30), *Gold* (31), *Soules* (32), *Complexione* (32), *Sister* (52), *Galleryes* (55), *Master* (56).

B. Personal whim, attributable perhaps to the style of penmanship, may account for the heavy capitalization of abstract nouns and adjectives; e.g. *Humilitee* (4), *Materialls* (15), *Substance* (17), *Doe-baked* (20), *Harmelesnes* (20), *Danger* (23), *Cloystrall* (25), *Men*

(25), *Contributions* (26), *Lyfe* (26), *Zeale* (30), *Name* (33), *Place* (33), *Anguish* (misspelt, 34), *Severall* (34), *Occasion* (35), *Circumstantiall* (35), *Dignitee* (37), *Beauty* (42), *Influence* (45), *Sight* (46), *Simpathy* (50), *Matter* (50), *Devotion* (62).

c. Donne may have exerted influence on the Augustan poets' habit of employing capitals with nouns (the German printers' tradition). He seems to have been prone to sporadic employment of capitals after semicolons in mid-line, and even after commas, as in line 55. Lines 7, 10, 22, 24, 28, 31–4, 39–41, 49–52 (about a quarter of the total) unaccountably begin with a letter in the lower case, even after a full-stop, as in line 10.

The prose works published during Donne's lifetime, bulk larger than the poetry; they are *Pseudo-Martyr* (1610), *Ignatius his Conclave* (1611), *Devotions upon Emergent Occasions* (1624), and desultory collections, such as *Five Sermons upon Special Occasions* (1626). *Ignatius his Conclave* was first planned and written in Latin; when translated into English, it sacrificed some syntactic and rhetorical vigour.

Biathanatos, composed as a syllogistic exercise on the theme of suicide between 1602 and 1609, was not published until after Donne's death. A manuscript copy, now in the Bodleian Library, with marginal notes in Donne's hand, was sent by the author to Sir Edward Herbert, under cover of an autograph letter, written about 1610. The transcript of this letter, reproduced below (E. Simpson, *A Study of the Prose Works,* p 146), is followed by the printed version in the first edition of the *Letters,* published 1651:

S^r

I make account that thys Booke hath inough perform'd y^t wch yt undertooke, both by Argument and Example. Itt shall therfore the lesse neede to bee yttselfe another Example of ye Doctrine. Itt shall not therefore kyll yttselfe; that ys, not bury itselfe. for if ytt should do so, those   5 reasons by wch that Act should bee defended or excusd, were also lost w^t ytt. Since ytt ys content to liue, ytt cannot chuse a wholsomer ayre then yor Library, where Autors of all complexions are preserud. If any of them grudge thys Booke a roome, and suspect ytt of new, or dangerous   10 Doctrine, yo^u, who know us all, can best Moderate. To those Reasons, wch I know yor Loue to mee wyll make in my fauor, and dischardge, yo^u may add thys, That though thys Doctrine hath not beene tought nor defended by writers, yet they, most of any sorte of Men in the world,   15 haue practisd ytt.

>   yor uery true and earnest frinde, and
>   Seruant and Louer
>   J: DONNE.

Apart from the scribal abbreviations of recurring monosyllables (e.g. in *Sir, that, which, the, with* and *your*), and spellings (not peculiar to Donne) such as *inough, chuse, Autors, dischardge, tought* and *frinde*, the observable features of Donne's orthography are:

A. Interchangeable employment of vocalic *y* and *i*, already noted in the poetry (e.g. in *this, it, is, will, kill*).

B. Unprincipled doubling of consonants, especially at the end of words as in *itt, ytt.*

C. Indiscriminate use of filler *-e* (e.g. in *Booke, lesse, neede, bee* (vb), *yttselfe, ayre, roome, mee, beene, sorte*).

D. Inconsistent representation of unsounded *e* in preterite and past participle endings of weak verbs, e.g. in *perform'd* (1), *preserud* (9), *practisd* (16).

E. Authorial idiosyncracy in the use of capitals (e.g. *Booke* (1), *Argument* (2), *Example* (2), *Doctrine* (4), *Act* (6), *Library* (8), *Moderate* (vb 11), *Reasons* (12), *Love* (12), *Men* (15). Capitals are not dependent on punctuation either. In line 5 lower case *f* is used after a full-stop, whereas in line 13 *That* occurs after a comma.

The printed text of 1651 shows rapid progress in orthography during the intervening years, though not in accidence, for *hath* was still preferred to *has*:

SIR,
    I make accompt that this book hath enough performed that which it undertook, both by argument and example. It shall therefore the lesse need to be it self another example of the Doctrine. It shall not therefore kill it self; that is, not bury it self; for if it should do so, those reasons, by which   5

that act should be defended or excused, were also lost with
it. Since it is content to live, it cannot chuse a wholesomer
aire then your Library, where Authors of all complexions
are presented (sic). If any of them grudge this book a room,
and suspect it of new or dangerous doctrine, you who know   10
us all, can best moderate. To those reasons which I know
your love to me will make in my favour and discharge, you
may adde this, that though this doctrine hath not been
taught nor defended by writers, yet they, most of any sort
of men in the world, have practised it.   15
Your very true and earnest friend and servant and lover
J. DONNE.
(ibid. pp 146–7)

Scribal abbreviations have naturally been removed and the spelling
modernized, with few exceptions, such as *accompt, lesse, chuse, aire*
and *adde*. Weak past-participle endings are spelt in full, whether *e*
is pronounced, as in *defended,* or silent, as in *practised*. Only three of
the capitals remain – *Doctrine* inconsistently (cf lines 4, 10 and 13).
Clay Hunt in *Donne's Poetry* says that the poet used a capital 'when
a word had a particular intellectual significance for him' (Preface,
p xiii). But this can hardly be relevant to the prose use of common
words like *Men,* and verbs such as *Moderate*. Donne was not in this
letter using capitalized words in special senses, to which he
intended to draw attention.

Orthography was a subject of some importance in Donne's lifetime, as is shown by the many published treatises designed to
rationalize English spelling. This ideal was never realized; but
during the Civil War printers moved diplomatically to achieve a
measure of standardization, involving compositorial editing of
most authors' manuscripts.

The spelling *accompt* was a pedantic refashioning in the fifteenth
century of a medieval French borrowing, with synonymous forms,
acunter and *accompter*. According to the OED, the senses of *account*
('statement', 'narration', 'description') were derived from the
original meaning ('reckoning', 'counting'), but did not appear
until Sir Walter Raleigh's *History of the World* (1614). Donne's
phrase *make account* suggests 'believe', 'consider'.

The prose of Donne contains as much formal variety as the poetry, though the earliest was schematic, rather than figurative. Its point-for-point language never attained the grandeur or complexity of the *Sermons,* which belong to the last sixteen years of Donne's life. None of Donne's prose lends itself readily to structural analysis; attempts to dissect and display rhythmical units, associated with metrical feet, are not convincing.

Prose writers were schooled in the classical rhetoric of Cicero and Quintilian, and taught the effect of rhythmical periods and modulated clauses, relying upon the varied incidence of stressed syllables. For the literary tyro, the epistolary style, of which Donne's is a good example, was ideal. It appealed mainly to the ear, its Latin name being *Ars Dictaminis,* known in England as 'formularie'. Donne chose topics appropriate to his desire for novelty, which seldom involved pretentious neologism.

Phrasing, syntax and vocabulary are the ingredients of a prose style, and function best when sentence stress is on the semantically significant words. The new learning stimulated Donne, partly through the novelty of its language, which was well adapted to the rhythm of his prose, and did not impair the logical coherence of his paragraphs. The rhetoric of climax and antithesis, which he chose, embodies the pitch of the voice, deliberate pause, syllable duration and disciplined control of phrase. These constituted Donne's dynamic contribution to the writing of Elizabethan and Jacobean prose.

CHAPTER II

The *Satyres, Metempsychosis (The Progresse of the Soule)*, and Verse Letters

🦑🦑🦑🦑🦑🦑

KNOWLEDGE of textual recension is requisite to the study of any group of Donne's poems. The edition prepared from various manuscript sources by John Donne, the younger, in 1633, contained five *Satyres* (which the poet is alleged to have revised in 1607, but had given no titles), *Metempsychosis,* and twenty-nine verse letters. The editing was careful, though eclectic; consequently there were choices that present knowledge of stemmata suggests had less than substantive value. The importance of such variant readings can be gauged from a 'Note on Text and Canon' in the second (one-volume) edition of H. J. C. Grierson's *Poems of John Donne* (O.U.P., 1933). The text used here is that of W. Milgate in the Oxford English Text, 1967. In essence, the copy-text of all reliable recensions is the first edition of 1633.

Milgate's text helps the reader in supplying paragraphs and inverted commas for passages of dialogue, quite frequent in the *Satyres.* He preserved the spelling and punctuation of the first edition, making variant readings from manuscript conform to the style of 1633 (see Textual Introduction, p lxxiii). At the end of speeches he replaced Donne's semicolons with full-stops or interrogation marks, where these were necessary. In the present study the title *Metempsychosis* is used for *The Progress of the Soule,* to distinguish the satire, in stanza form, from the commendatory *Second Anniversary (Of the Progres of the Soule)*, written some time later in couplets.

Donne began the *Satyres* about the time of the *Elegies*; but there seems some doubt whether the first was in circulation by 1593. Because of their language and versification, the *Satyres* are often regarded as the least satisfying of Donne's compositions; nevertheless, they were still read a century after Donne's death. To Dryden (*Discourse Concerning the Original and Progress of Satire,* 1693),

they were crude and undignified. In 1735 Pope published, alongside of the originals, re-modelled versions of *Satyres* 2 and 4; but
only the thematic materials were used, the expansive lines being of
his own invention. Such treatment was inevitable, because Pope's
talent was ill accommodated to Donne's irregular and prosaic
metre. The third *Satyre* was another to be 'versified', by Thomas
Parnell, Pope's protégé and Irish contemporary.

Gosse traces the rise of satire in the last decade of the sixteenth
century to Isaac Casaubon's lectures, in Geneva, on Persius, though
the commentary on this little-known Latin poet was not published
until 1605 (*Life and Letters,* vol. 1, p 30). Most Elizabethan practi-
tioners of satire (Joseph Hall, Thomas Lodge and John Marston)
preferred Horace, Juvenal and Ariosto. The classical distinction of
high, middle and low styles was undoubtedly influential in encour-
aging the harsh and scurrilous language of Elizabethan satire,
which obviously belonged to the last of Quintilian's conventions.
The crudity of Donne's technique, compactness of expression and
realistic detail, are ascribed to his closeness to Persius, who was one
inspiration of the cynical portraits.

Debunking unsavoury types in a disordered society, Donne's
inventive *Satyres* are pamphleteering 'humours', catalogues of
vices, conflicts and religious disagreements, penned from a Catholic
point of view. *Paradox* 3 observes that 'Discord is never so barren
that it affords no fruit.' Donne's fruit is the irony of the descriptive
adjective or metaphor; Aristotle, for instance, is 'Nature's
Secretary' (*Satyre* 1, 6). The vignettes exaggerate, distort the
rhyme, and revel in puns, all typical ingredients of Elizabethan
ridicule. The laughter has an undercurrent of grim seriousness, a
consistent aim being to undermine Petrarchan sentiment.

The sceptical, bewildered amusement in the *Satyres* reflects the
intellectual chaos of the time, the confusion that scholastically
trained minds experienced from the impact of revolutionary
science. Despair and doubt were not, however, the sources of
Donne's poetic individuality. He was fertile in analogy, and perceptive in paradox, but no philosopher. The crotchety logic was
not original, but derived from Donne's reading in Spanish authors,
especially of Góngora, Luis de Granada, Jorge de Montemayor,
and St John of the Cross. In March 1623 he confided to the
Marquess of Buckingham that he possessed more Spanish books
in his library than English ones.

The astringent *Satyres* often employ colloquial and metrical contractions, which the 1633 edition omitted to mark, causing some confusion in the scansion of lines. Donne was well acquainted with the metrical principles of his age. The types of prosodic elision current were not necessarily true contractions of speech, nor were they strictly observed in scribal orthography. Extra syllables at the medial pause, or at the end of a line, were widely employed; but in Donne's *Satyres* ten syllables were deemed mandatory for the pentameter, even though the line included a defective foot. The essence of Donne's metrical usage was spontaneity, not rule. Idiosyncratic shifts of stress, coupled with daring but inconsistent elision and tight control of syllables, were responsible for the crudity of his metre. The apparent irregularities are more obtrusive in decasyllabic couplets than in the freer measures of the *Songs and Sonets*. In the *Satyres* there are 167 theoretical elisions, but only 25 contractions of speech. *Satire* 1 contains some examples of Donne's metrical licences:

41 Háte vértŭe, | thoŭgh she bĕ nákĕd, aňd báre (10 syllables; 4 primary stresses)

46 Hĕe lóst thàt, | yĕt hĕe'wăs cloáth'd bŭt ĭn beásts skín (11 syllables and 4 primary stresses; theoretical elision not in Grierson or the 1633 edition)

58 Th'Ínfănt ŏf Lóndŏn, | Heíre tŏ'an Índià (10 syllables and 4 primary stresses; the first elision not in Grierson or 1633 edition)

77 Aňd ăs fídlĕrs stóp lów'st, | ăt híghĕst soúnd (10 syllables and 5 primary stresses; elision not in Grierson or 1633 edition)

78 Sò | tŏ the móst bráve, | stóops hĕe nígh'st the gróund (10 syllables and 5 primary stresses; elision follows Grierson and 1633 edition)

90 'T máy bĕ yŏu sméll hĭm nòt, | truélў Í dóe (11 syllables and 4 primary stresses; elision follows Grierson and 1633 edition)

It is fair to Milgate to note that the elisions (not in Grierson) introduced to preserve the syllable-count have the warrant of Donne's holograph of the *Letter to Lady Carey* (1612), also in pentameter couplets.

Most common in Donne's metric is the deliberate imposition of a prose rhythm upon the prosodic pattern; it is noticeably effective in the opening lines. The crabbed style, the halting, hesitant movement, is frequently emphasized by authorial punctuation. Donne seems to cultivate by design a short-winded syntactic development of the thought. The *Satyres* are most difficult when the expected metrical stresses are flouted by rhetorical ones. The impression of chaotic instability is dissolved only when the reader rediscovers the *Satyre* as a dramatic sketch or series of mimic dialogues.

The *Satyres* are not all of a piece; the passages below serve to illustrate different attitudes, themes and styles:

A. *Satyre 2*, lines 49–60, 77–80, 85–90, 97–102

The speaker of lines 49–57 is Coscus, a lawyer-poet, reminiscent of those at Lincoln's Inn. This *Satyre,* written about 1594, pillories incompetent poetry and the abuse of law, with which Elizabethans were familiar from Stubbes's *Anatomy of Abuses* (1583).

>   'I'have beene
> In love, ever since *tricesimo*'of the Queene,   50
> Continuall claimes I'have made, injunctions got
> To stay my rivals suit, that hee should not
> Proceed.' 'Spare mee.' 'In Hillary terme I went,
> You said, If I returne next size in Lent,
> I should be in remitter of your grace;   55
> In th'interim my letters should take place
> Of affidavits–': words, words, which would teare
> The tender labyrinth of a soft maids eare,
> More, more, then ten Sclavonians scolding, more
> Then when winds in our ruin'd Abbeyes rore.   60

>   *   *   *

> Shortly ('as the sea) hee'will compasse all our land;   77
> From Scots, to Wight; from Mount, to Dover strand.
> And spying heires melting with luxurie,
> Satan will not joy at their sinnes, as hee.   80

>   *   *   *

> Peecemeale he gets lands, and spends as much time   85
> Wringing each Acre, as men pulling prime.
> In parchments then, large as his field, hee drawes

Assurances, bigge, as gloss'd civill lawes,
So huge, that men (in our times forwardnesse)
Are Fathers of the Church for writing lesse.   90

* * *

But when he sells or changes land, he'impaires   97
His writings, and (unwatch'd) leaves out, *ses heires*,
As slily'as any Commenter goes by
Hard words, or sense; or in Divinity   100
As controverters, in vouch'd Texts, leave out
Shrewd words, which might against them cleare the doubt.

There are eight diplomatic elisions in the above, but only two –
th'interim (56) and *he'impaires* (97) – appear in the 1633 edition. By
this date the fetish of syllable number was moribund in syllabic
verse, the merging of contiguous open-vowels being left to interpretation by the reader or actor. For both monosyllabic *hee'was* and
'T may were impossible. The use of capitals in *Abbeyes, Acre,
Commenter* and *Texts* is characteristic of Donne's holograph remains, and accords with the printing of capitalized nouns by Continental presses, and later in neo-classical poetry.

Donne was better acquainted with foreign literatures than most
contemporary English poets, as appears in the borrowings *tricesimo*
(thirtieth year), *Sclavonians* (barbarous-tongued people, perhaps
the old inhabitants of Dalmatia) and *ses heires* (old legal French 'his
heirs'). From the fourteenth century the spelling *Sclave*, from
Greek *Sklabos*, was regular, until replaced by *Slav* in the nineteenth
century. Legal terms give rise to a few semantic obscurities in this
satire; but *pulling prime* (86) is not one; it recalls the courtiers'
gambling recreation of *primero,* a game that resembled modern
poker. In line 54 *size* (O. French *sise*) is an aphetic form of *assize*, in
common use from the fourteenth to the sixteenth century.

Few readers of Donne's *Satyres* appreciate the movement of his
verse within the line, or from one line to the next. Though the
rhyme-words here are mostly strong monosyllables, Donne does
not invoke monosyllabic lines to excess; he tends rather to halt the
rhythm by juxtaposing stressed syllables within the line, as in

85   Péeceméale he géts lánds, | and spénds as múch tíme
88   Assúrances, | bígge, as glóss'd cívill láwes

where the modulation was less harmonious to Renaissance tastes than in the fluid lines

58 The ténder lábyrinth of a sóft máids eáre
79 And spýing heíres mélting with lúxurìe

which contain the occasional metaphor.

The directness of language is surprizing. Little grammatical complexity endangers the sense; while inverted word order, except in line 51, is rare. Nor is the style of this satire garnished unduly with schemes of words, though Donne anticipates his later skill in lines 57–60:

> *words, words, w*hich *w*ould *t*eare
> The *t*ender *l*abyrinth of a *s*oft *m*aids eare,
> *More, more,* then *t*en *S*clavonians *s*colding, *more*
> Then *w*hen *w*inds in our *r*uin'd Abbeyes *r*ore.

The interplay of alliterative consonants, liquid, nasal, sibilant and trilled, blends merrily with the rhetorical use of *ploce*, in the repetition of *words* and *more*. The schemata are intended to emphasize Donne's exasperation at those who misapply legal language in their courtships.

B. *Satyre 3*, lines 89–110

Written about 1597, this *Satyre* suggests that Donne had already withdrawn his loyalty to the Catholic faith. During 1596–7 he had volunteered to join the naval expeditions, under the Earl of Essex, to Cadiz and the Azores, in which England took the initiative against Spanish power. The moralistic tone of the poem is directed against casual and irresponsible religious affiliations, and anticipates the kind of thinking that kindles the mature letters to friends and patrons.

> Keépe the trúth whĭch thoú'hast foúnd; | mén dŏ nŏt stánd
> Iň só'ill cáse hére, | thăt Gód hath wĭth hĭs hánd   90
> Sígn'd Kíngs blańck-chártĕrs tŏ kíll whŏm thĕy háte,
> Nór aře thĕy Vícařs, | bŭt hángmèn tŏ Fáte.
> Foóle ańd wrétch, | wĭlt thŏu lét thў Sóule bĕ tý'd
> Tŏ máns laẃes, | bў whĭch she shăll nót bĕ trý'd

A̽t the lást dáy? | Wĭll ĭt thèn bóot thèe   95
Tŏ́ sáy ẵ Phílĭp, | ŏr ẵ Grégŏ̀rỳ,
Ẵ Hárrỹ, | ŏr ẵ Mártĭn taúght thĕ̃e thís?
Iš nŏt thís ĕxcúse fŏr mĕre cóntrẵriès,
Équẵllỹ stróng? | cánnŏt bóth sídes sáy sò?
Thẵt thóu mẵy'st ríghtlỹ'obéy pówer, | hĕr boúnds knów; 100
Thóse pást, | hĕr nátŭre ănd náme's cháng'd; | tŏ́ bé
Thèn húmblĕ̃ tŏ́ hĕr ìs ĭdólẵtriè;
Ašͅ stréames ar̃e, | Pówer ìs; | thòse blést flówers thẵt dwéll
Aͅt thĕ̃ roúgh streámes cálme heád, | thríve ănd próve wèll,
Bŭt hàvĭñg léft thĕir róots, | ănd thĕmsélves gívĕn   105
Tŏ́ the stréames týrannŏus ráge, | ălás, ar̃e drívĕn
Thrŏugh mílls, | ănd róckes, | ănd wóods, | 'ănd'ăt lást, ălmòst
Cŏ̃nsúm'd iñ góiñg, | iñ the séa ar̃e lóst:
Sò́ périšh Soúles, | whĭch móre chúse méns ŭnjúst
Pówer frŏ̃m Gód claým'd, | thĕn Gód hĭmsélfe tͅo trúst. 110

This intricate passage can be satisfactorily scanned in the light of
sense and rhetorical emphasis. Primary stresses are seen to vary
from two to six, the heavily loaded lines being 89, 100, 104 and
110, because here the poet contrasts the power of God to man-
made law. For Donne it is quite feasible to have four adjacent
stressed syllables, as line 104 shows. Verses 100 and 103 are
especially weighted, by length, aphoristic content and clinching
verbs at the end of the line. They are preceded by prosaic rhetorical
questions, which are admirable preparation for the kind of hortatory argument that dominates the *Sermons*.

It is to be observed that eight of the eleven couplets are enjambed
syntactically, enhancing the vehemence and impetuosity of
Donne's convictions. In the *Satyres* he avoids sequences of closed
couplets, a factor that, taken with the alarmingly irregular disposition of stress, distinguishes Donne's practice from that of Ben
Jonson, and the Neo-classical poets who followed him. There
appear, too, to be more inversions of stress in Donne's poetry than
in any other poet of the sixteenth and seventeenth centuries. Like
others, however, he freely employed the licence of rhyming on
unstressed final syllables e.g. 95/6 *thee*/Grego*ry*, 101/2 to *be*/idola-
trie; and he is daring in invoking imperfect and off-beat rhymes, as
in 97/8 *this*/contra*ries*, and 107/8 al*most*/are *lost*.

The elisions in lines 89, 90, 93, 94, 100 and 107 are not in the 1633 edition, nor in Grierson's pioneering work of 1912, but were introduced by Milgate. It is unlikely that Donne would have approved any syllabically orientated text, such as this. His metric was a tacit plea for liberation, not for the straight-jacket, and Grierson's judgement in abiding by the copy-text was commendable. The scope of the rhythmical modulations, beginning with the trochaic down-beat of the opening feet of line 89, is clear evidence of Donne's desire for freedom. There are as many as twenty-three internal pauses in this passage, though three of the lines have no medial rest for the voice. Frequently a pause is found in the middle of a foot. What Donne sought, and through variations of stress and pause achieved, was control of pace and emphasis. The evident counterpoint of rhetorical and metrical patterns compelled rhythms to overflow the line. The design of Donne's prosodic momentum is unclassifiable, because he eschewed repetitive means of securing it.

In lines 93, 94, 100–102 the poet personifies *Soule* and *Power* (a word inconsistently capitalized) in the feminine gender. The long simile of lines 103–108 is the most effective figure of classical lineage. Note that it follows an authoritative epigram, *As streames are, Power is*, which is itself a simile, attracting attention by inversion of the normal order of words.

Though M. F. Moloney, in *John Donne, His Flight from Mediaevalism* (1965, p 141) describes the final lines of this *Satyre* as 'felicitously-phrased platitudes', the implications for the state of Donne's religious convictions at the time are significant. The passage shows that he had read Christopher Goodman's *How Superior Powers ought to be Obeyed* (1558), as well as Luther's *The Christian in Society,* from which he probably derived the metaphor *hangmen to Fate* (92). Donne accepted the Christian religion and the supreme power of God as axiomatic, but was confused and distressed by man's démarche from Christianity's essential ideals. In lines 96/7 the Defenders of the Faith recalled are Philip II of Spain, Pope Gregory XIII (or XIV), Henry VIII and Martin Luther, who represent the opposed Catholic and Protestant creeds. Donne argued from the position of a seeker after truth, amid bigots and schismatics, and his wavering solution was refuge in a *personal* faith.

Metempsychosis (the satire's original title) was written four months
before Donne's marriage, in the summer of 1601, while he was
Secretary to Sir Thomas Egerton, Lord Keeper of the Seal and
Master of the Rolls. In that year the poet was returned to Parlia-
ment, as member for Brackley, Northants. One book of the mock-
epic was completed in fifty-two stanzas, of ten lines each, the
metrical form and somewhat archaic style being adaptations of
Spenser. Note, for instance, the usage *'vouch* thou *safe* to looke' (36),
in which the elements of the compound (verb + adjective) are
separated by the second personal pronoun. This practice was common in the romances of the fourteenth and fifteenth centuries, but
the OED offers no example later than Golding's in *Ovid's Meta-
morphoses* in 1565. The opening seventy lines have dignity and a
more masculine vigour than what follows, an attack in the manner
of medieval bestiaries on men and women in the public eye.

Donne seems to have exhausted this experiment, which was not
intended for publication, when he ran out of parallels between
animals and heretics, among them Mahomet and Luther, people he
secretly admired for the intellectual freedom they invariably
achieved. The caustic attitude towards courtiers and the female sex
had no rational basis in the Pythagorean theory of transmigration,
on which Donne elaborated in the prefatory epistle. How the
sequence of reincarnated soul was intended to end is uncertain;
but, from the final wording of the preface, the recipient is more
likely to have been Calvin than Queen Elizabeth.

> I censure much and taxe; And this liberty costs mee more   5
>   than others,

*   *   *

> All which I will bid you remember, (for I would have no   20
> such Readers as I can teach) is, that the Pithagorian doctrine
> doth not onely carry one soule from man to man, nor man
> to beast, but indifferently to plants also: and therefore you
> must not grudge to finde the same soule in an Emperour, in
> a Post-horse, and in a Mucheron, since no unreadinesse in   25
> the soule, but an indisposition in the organs workes this.
> And therefore though this soule could not move when it
> was a Melon, yet it may remember, and now tell mee, at
> what lascivious banquet it was serv'd. And though it could
> not speake, when it was a spider, yet it can remember, and   30

44

now tell me, who used it for poyson to attaine dignitie.
How ever the bodies have dull'd her other faculties, her
memory hath ever been her owne, which makes me so
seriously deliver you by her relation all her passages from
her first making, when shee was that apple which Eve eate,   35
to this time when shee is hee, whose life you shall finde in
the end of this booke.

(*lines 5, 20–37*)

The pagan doctrine here expounded, Donne treated with characteristic scepticism. He doubted whether the neo-Platonic mystics,
who propagated the Pythagorean theory, could claim direct access
to God. *Mucheron* (25), from French *mousseron,* is a derivative of
mousse (moss) and entered the language in the fourteenth century;
according to the OED the spelling *mushroom* did not prevail until
two hundred years later. In lines 27–36 the personal pronoun
whose referent is *soule* (27) first appears as neuter (*it*), then as
feminine (*shee, her*). In line 35 Donne shows a preference for the
weak preterite *eate,* used alongside of *ate.*

The word *soul,* repeatedly employed by Donne, had many connotations. In Christian contexts the soul or spirit was regarded as
immaterial and indestructible. It survived the death of the body
into which it had been implanted, and by which it acquired sensory
experience. The soul could, however, transcend sensation by the
faculty of imagination. The interaction of body and soul was
axiomatic to theologians, who believed that living creatures were
each endowed with a new soul, whose spark of the divine made it
immortal. Christian Platonists, such as Pica della Mirandola,
visualized the soul in another dimension, its *form,* conferring
individual features and characteristics (cf Aristotle, *De Anima,* II
414a). Control of the animal passions was supposed by moralists to
be lodged in the keeping of man's reason.

A thirteenth-century *vade mecum,* entitled *De Proprietatibus
Rerum,* compiled by the Oxford scholar Bartholomaeus Anglicus,
and translated by Trevisa in the next century, was edited by
Stephen Bateman in 1582. In this work, commonly entitled
Batman uppon Bartholome, the soul is described as comprehending
three aspects, the vegetable, sensible and rational, dominant in the
lives of plants, animals and men respectively. The vegetable soul
was responsible for growth and reproduction; the sensible for

motion, appetite, passion and apprehension; the rational (peculiar to mankind) for reason, understanding, will and wit, the last with the connotation of common-sense. Wit was regarded, *inter alios*, by Donne, as a faculty that could be relied on to guide the soul. Platonists argued that the soul's responsibility included keeping the body sound, and that illness was a species of spiritual corruption. What Donne sportively revealed, through the running commentary of *Metempsychosis,* was the cumulative deterioration of the soul, beginning with biblical history.

The sources of Donne's knowledge of Pythagoras were undoubtedly Aulus Gellius's *Noctes Atticae,* Tertullian's *De Anima* and Plato's *Timaeus* and *Phaedo.* His parody of the Great Chain of Being abounds in grotesque conceits and comic irony, and some contemporaries, e.g. Ben Jonson, considered it blasphemous. The narrative skill and lively description of nature in its aberrent forms was discontinued, because, after his marriage, Donne the satirist *manqué* became a moralist. The unusual stanza form, rhyming a a b c c b b d d d, with the Spenserian Alexandrine in the last line, was also abandoned.

According to Milgate's textual note, the manuscript behind the 1633 edition of *Metempsychosis* was imperfect, and conjectural changes have had to be made by all editors; the largest proportion consisted of marks of elision and contractions. His version of stanzas II–IV and VII departs from Grierson's text only in lines 27, 30 and 37:

II

Thée, | éye of heáven, | this gréat Soúle eńvies nòt,
By thỳ mále fórce, is áll wee háve, | begót.
In the fírst Eást, | thou nòw begínst to shíne,
Súck'st eárly bálme, | and Íland spíces thére
And wílt anón in thy loóse-reín'd careére   15
At Tágus, | Pó, | Séne, | Thámes, | and Dánow díne,
And sée at níght thy Wésterne lánd of Mýne,
Yét hast thou nót mòre nátions seéne then shée,
Thát before thée, | óne dáy begánne to bée,
  And thỳ fraíle líght being quénch'd, | shall lóng, lóng
    oút lìve thée.   20

III

Nor, holy *Janus,* in whose soveraigne boate

The Church, and all the Monarchies did floate;
That swimming Colledge, and free Hospitall
Of all mankinde, that cage and vivarie
Of fowles, and beasts, in whose wombe, Destinie   25
Us, and our latest nephewes did install
(For thence are all deriv'd, that fill this All,)
Did'st thou in that great stewardship embarke
So diverse shapes into that floating parke,
    As have beene mov'd, and inform'd by this heavenly
    sparke.   30

IV

Great Destiny the Commissary of God,
That hast mark'd out a path and period
For every thing; who, where wee of-spring tooke,
Our wayes and ends seest at one instant; Thou
Knot of all causes, thou whose changelesse brow   35
Ne'r smiles nor frownes, O vouch thou safe to looke
And shew my story, 'in thy eternall booke;
That (if my prayer be fit) I may'understand
So much my selfe, as to know with what hand,
    How scant, or liberall this my lifes race is spand.   40

VII

For this great soule which here amongst us now   61
Doth dwell, and moves that hand, and tongue, and brow,
Which, as the Moone the sea, moves us; to heare
Whose story, with long patience you will long;
(For 'tis the crowne, and last straine of my song)   65
This soule to whom *Luther*, and *Mahomet* were
Prisons of flesh; this soule which oft did teare,
And mend the wracks of th'Empire, and late Rome,
And liv'd where every great change did come,
    Had first in paradise, a low, but fatall roome.   70

Saintsbury said of Donne's metrical scheme that 'it ruins itself from
the outset by starting with a couplet, the very worst preparation of
the ear for the distinctive rhyming which is to follow' (*History of
English Prosody*, II, 161–2). But the rhyming scheme is less distinctive than it appears, as there are four pentameter couplets in the
stanza of ten lines. The pattern chosen does not materially affect

Donne's accustomed modulation of the satirical rhythm by internal pauses and shifts of stress. The iambic base is preserved in line 17 of stanza II only. Syntactic inversion is more frequent, however, occurring ten times in forty lines (11, 12, 16, 18, 26, 27, 33, 34, 63 and 64). Moreover, twelve of the forty line-endings are syntactically enjambed, the run-on verses occurring chiefly in the quatrain of the third to sixth lines. The Spenserian partiality for the periphrastic auxiliary verb *do* in lines 22, 26, 28, 62, 67, 69, and the absolute participial construction in line 20, again suggest the probable model for Donne's *Metempsychosis*. The following lines are unmistakably in the Spenserian tradition of rhythmic ease and fluidity:

> For though through many streights, and lands I roame,
> I launch at paradise, and saile toward home;
>
> *(lines 56–7)*

> A young *Colossus* there hee stands upright,
> And as that ground by him were conquerèd
> A leafie garland weares he on his head
> Enchas'd with little fruits, so red and bright
> That for them you would call your Loves lips white;
>
> *(lines 135–7; see also Stanza XIV)*

Donne was twenty-nine when he wrote this poem, and the sketches of naturalistic love in the lawless age, before the Decalogue of Moses, were based on his reading of Genesis, Exodus, Leviticus and Job. Donne had pondered deeply on the exegetical commentaries written by Fathers of the Church. The *Westerne land of Myne* (17) suggests the West Indies or the Continent of America. In line 21 Noah is named *holy Janus,* on the authority of a Dominican friar Annius of Viterbo, whose historical digest, *Antiquitatum Variarum Volumina* XVIII (1498), stated that Noah found favour with the Lord (Genesis vi 8), and was the first priest to offer sacrifice. Noah was thought to have two faces, because his life spanned the antedeluvian world, as well as the era of survivors of the flood; the information came from Josephus, who cited the Chaldean historian, Berosus.

The *swimming Colledge, and free Hospitall* (or lodging place) was the Ark, which housed the founders both of the Church and of earthly kingdoms. *Vivarie* (24) is derived from Latin *vivarium,* an enclosure for housing birds, animals or fish, hence the *floating parke* of line 29; Donne's use of *vivarie* is the earliest recorded in the OED. Looser meanings of *nephewes* (26) are said to have been 'grandsons' or 'descendants'; the word was borrowed from O. French *neveu,* Lat. *nepos,* in the late thirteenth century. *Destiny, the Commissary of God,* is personified as Fate, 'which God made, but doth not controule' (line 2), and is likened to a deputy who exercizes the jurisdiction of a bishop in distant parts of the diocese.

The style of *Metempsychosis* is not low, in the classical sense required for satirical writing; it is less conversational than is customary with Donne. There are a few classical allusions, for instance to *Janus* (21), and *Colossus* (153), but these are a rarity in all his poetry; *the eye of heaven* (11) means the generative sun, not Apollo. However ambitious the conception, Donne would hardly have risked publication, while he was still actively trying to secure high office through influential patrons.

Donne's verse letters belong to the years 1597 to 1614; they seem to have been composed before he was ordained Dean of St Pauls, and were pre-eminently private exchanges of friendship or esteem, not intended for publication. The majority of the unconventional eulogies, addressed to court ladies and patrons, were written after 1608. As a person of humble birth, Donne had access to the intellectual circles of the upper classes, largely because of his talent for sophisticated verse, cynical wit and personal candour. It is worth noting that he used the familiar *thou* in addressing intimate friends, but deferential *you* in the epistles to patronesses. The fulsome compliment that circulated in manuscript among the upper ten undoubtedly had a snob value. The letters to aristocratic ladies, such as Lucy, Countess of Bedford, are said to be apologies for the indiscretion of publishing the *First and Second Anniversaries,* in memory of Elizabeth Drury, in 1612.

Donne did not see himself as a professional poet, looking for public approbation, in the manner of Lodge, Drayton, Daniel and Jonson. In relation to the time, the sincerity of his regard in the eulogies is not strictly a critical issue. The word *sincere,* when it entered the language from French and Latin in the second quarter of the sixteenth century, meant 'genuine, pure, uncorrupted', and was mainly employed to endorse the veracity of religious doctrine, justness of laws, or clarity of colours. Only in the late eighteenth century did the sense of *sincerity* come to be extended to 'an honest account of a writer's personal feelings'.

Donne's epistolary activity should be judged as an ingenious poetic exercise in moralizing, while simultaneously entertaining persons whose company and approval he sought. He had the humanist's genius for friendship, which suffered from few literary inhibitions. The religious introspection and dialectical skill of these poems reflect the depth of his doctrinal and scholastic studies; and the style bespeaks the integrity and faith of an artist. Apotheosis of feminine discretion and virtue, upon which much exegetic argument turns, should not be taken at its face value. Extravagant compliment is still a mark of courtesy in polite society, and hyperbole is part of the evidence that Donne's eulogies belong to the realm of fantasy.

There is a further reason why the verse letters should be examined closely; they place Donne among pre-Augustan emulators of classical verse, making a contribution as significant for seventeenth century poetry as that of Ben Jonson. Donne's place in the tradition of epigram, inherited by Dryden and Pope, is just as important as his eccentric versification proved to be for the prosody of Milton.

The original epigram of Greek melic poetry spoke to the audience in the poet's own voice, and conveyed with pithy dignity his fugitive emotions. The Latin poets Catullus, Horace, Ovid, Martial and Juvenal carried on the tradition and adapted the epigram to satirical, as well as epistolary verse. In England, the neatly phrased couplet became the accepted purveyor of classical succinctness, whether in praise or dispraise. The rhymed couplet could not, however, be so practised in epitaphs, eulogies, epistles and satires without careful syllabic control and modulation.

Donne's attitude to the classical tradition differed from Jonson's in its tincture of esoteric reading, especially of Lucretius, Tertullian, Aquinas, Dante and du Bartas. Through his indecorous freedom of expression, and lack of smoothness in verse, he moved further from the classical ideal than other of his contemporaries. The conceits in Donne are more complex and tenacious, and this gives to some of the verse letters that 'metaphysical' character, which the reader apprehends, however much the term may be disputed. The conceit is inadequately defined as extravagant comparison that surprises by its singularity of metaphor, simile, or hyperbole. With Donne the motive is the transposing of feelings into ideas, used as a means of arriving at truth by intuitive knowing. Though the metaphysical requires Rosemond Tuve's 'multiple logical bases' (see *Elizabethan and Metaphysical Imagery,* p 264), in Donne the dialectic has Christian and theological foundations.

The Storm, with which the verse letters begin, was an exercise in *descriptio,* known in rhetoric as *chronographia* – elaborate detail surrounding an event in time. Donne evaluates the experience, partly by religious associations, partly by dramatic monologue, in the manner of Ovid's *Heroical Epistles.* The poem was written in the summer of 1597, in the form of a letter to the poet's friend in Lincoln's Inn, Christopher Brooke. In that year the Azores expedition, in which Donne served under the Earl of Essex, set sail from Plymouth, only to be driven back after a few days by an unforeseen gale. Donne's account, though not in his characteristic style, has the immediacy of a participant, indulging in the 'colours' of rhetoric to make the writing lively.

> Then like two mighty Kings, which dwelling farre   25
> Asunder, meet against a third to warre,
> The South and West winds joyn'd, and, as they blew,
> Waves like a rowling trench before them threw.
> Sooner then you read this line, did the gale,
> Like shot, not fear'd till felt, our sailes assaile;   30
> And what at first was call'd a gust, the same
> Hath now a stormes, anon a tempest name.
> *Jonas,* I pitty thee, and curse those men,
> Who when the storm rag'd most, did wake thee then;
> Sleepe is paines easiest salve, and doth fullfill   35
> All offices of death, except to kill.
> But whén I wákt, | I sáw, that Ì sáw nót;
> Í, | and the Súnne, | which should téach mee'hád forgót
> Eást, | Wést, | Dáy, | Níght, | and I coúld but sáy,
> If the'wórld had lásted, | nów it hàd beene dáy.   40
> Thousands our noyses were, yet wee 'mongst all
> Could none by his right name, but thunder call:
> Lightning was all our light, and it rain'd more
> Then if the Sunne had drunke the sea before.
>   *(lines 25–44)*

The narrative is deceptively simple, owing to the dominance of monosyllabic words, mostly of Anglo-Saxon origin. The poem reveals little complexity in the syntax of subordination, except in lines 19–21, which illustrate Donne's liking for *catachresis*:

> Mildly it kist our sailes, and, fresh and sweet,
> As to a stomack sterv'd, whose insides *meete*,
> *Meate comes*, it *came*;

A protracted simile, the necessity of rhyme, and a penchant for punning combine to obscure, in this instance, the orderly unfolding of meaning. A Baconian explanation of the tempest would argue that Donne had been studying the new philosophy, and reading du Bartas's *La Semaine*, of which Sylvester made an English translation, entitled *Divine Weeks and Works,* published eight years later.

Three related similes enliven the first six lines. Variable winds are like warring kings in aggressive alliance. Waves resemble 'a rowling trench', and the gale's crack on the sails is likened to the sound of shot. *Sailes assaile* (30) is typical of Donne's temptation to resort to word play. A similar tendency appears in the paradoxes of lines 36 and 37. Schemes of word and thought are preferred to tropes; but the metonymic use of *salve* in line 35, and the hyperbolic effectiveness of lines 40 and 44 should not be overlooked.

Donne's impact on Dryden and Pope may be observed in the antithetical balance of line 32: 'Hath now a stormes, anon a tempest name.' *Ecphonesis* in the invocation to *Jonas* (33) recalls the Book of Jonah i, 5–6; while *I* (38) is a confusing Elizabethan orthography for the exclamation *ay.*

The narrative flow of the passage is the result of its simple word choice and enjambement on six occasions; but Ovidian ease is broken in lines 37–40, which confront the reader with problems of stress, dependent on syntax and elision.

The earliest eulogistic epistles of Donne, placed between 1597 and 1608, were short and Horatian in tone, although experimental in form. Both he and Jonson wrote encomiums to friends in fourteen lines, not in sonnet form, but in one of the following arrangements:

A. seven rhymed couplets

B. four triplets ending with a couplet

C. three quatrains and a couplet, rhyming a b b a a b b a c b b c d d

D. or with some similar scheme for the first twelve lines, such as quatrains with alternate rhyme.

There are nine such poems among Donne's earlier verse letters, four addressed to two brothers of the Woodward family, with whom Donne had agreed to correspond in verse. Consequently, there are casual, modest, and sometimes prosaic, references to the technicalities of the art, such as the following:

> these Rymes which never had
> Mother, want matter, and they only have
> A little forme, the which their Father gave;
> They are prophane, imperfect, oh, too bad
> To be counted Children of Poetry
>
> (*To Mr. B. B.,* II 9–13)

One expression of affection for Rowland Woodward comprises two fourteen-line efforts in couplets, with a four-line coda of rhyming pairs.

Several rhymes in these letters are daring, because they depend on the convention that sounds are adequate, even when they occur in unstressed elements of polysyllables, e.g. in a letter to Thomas Woodward, lines 4–6:

> Yet as a firme house, though the Carpent*er*
> Perish, doth stand: as an Embassad*our*
> Lyes safe, how e'r his king be in dang*er*

Donne never hesitates to employ off-beat rhyme, with none but a visual affinity, e.g. in matching sci*ence* with Quintess*ence* (*To Mr. B. B.,* lines 1–3).

One of the most revealing poems in this group is the 36-line epistle *To Mr. Rowland Woodward,* consisting of twelve triplets, from which the following are taken:

> There is no Vertue, but Religion:
> Wise, valiant, sober, just, are names, which none
> Want, which want not Vice-covering discretion.
>
> Seeke wee then our selves in our selves; for as
> Men force the Sunne with much more force to passe,   20
> By gathering his beames with a christall glasse;

So wee, if wee into our selves will turne,
Blowing our sparkes of vertue, may outburne
The straw, which doth about our hearts sojourne.

You know, Physitians, when they would infuse   25
Into any'oyle, the Soule of Simples, use
Places, where they may lie still warme, to chuse.

So workes retirednesse in us; To rome
Giddily, and bee every where, but at home,
Such freedome doth a banishment become.   30

Wee are but farmers of our selves, yet may,
If we can stocke our selves, and thrive, uplay
Much, much deare treasure for the great rent day.

Manure thy selfe then, to thy selfe be'approv'd,
And with vaine outward things be no more mov'd,   35
But to know, that I love thee'and would be lov'd.

(lines 16–36)

Rowland Woodward, who assembled an extant portfolio of
Donne's manuscript poems, was a fellow-member of Lincoln's
Inn, and Donne's junior by a year. About 1604, Woodward wrote
to the poet in retirement after his marriage, asking for some copies.
The reluctant Donne speaks of the 'chast fallownesse' of his muse,
and minimizes his efforts in the *Elegies* and *Satyres* as 'long-song
weeds' and 'thornes' (line 5). He eschews the vanity of men's
works, since, in the scales of God, they weigh as heavily as sins. In
stanzas 6–12, Donne describes his most recent state of mind.

The gist is that the cardinal virtues of Plato in the *Phaedo*
(prudence, justice, temperance and courage), though acknowledged by Aristotle and Aquinas, are unwanted abstractions, of
discretionary rather than positive value. They are subordinate to
the Christian virtues of faith, hope and charity. Recalling Augustine's *City of God* (XIX 25) and *De Vera Religione,* Donne argues that
self-knowledge is like a lens that concentrates the sun's beams on
the straw it wishes to consume. So men should apply themselves
to the dross of sins that surround the human heart (16–24).

Lines 25–30 seem to have been suggested by an experiment
described in the *Hermetic and Alchemical Writings* of Paracelsus (II
15). Oil was thought to be metal in a liquid form, and the alchemist

could infuse into it the *Soule of Simples* (26), namely the pure essence of basic elements, keeping the infusion at a constant heat by the use of horse dung. Donne's analogy is over-subtle. The advantage of the home-loving man's tranquillity (he says) is self-cultivation, mental stock-taking and the building of spiritual reserves; for, paradoxically, the sought-after freedom of the roamer is actually a banishment. *Retirednesse,* for Donne, resembles the tenant farmer's industry; it instils virtue into the soul, as the alchemist infuses elements into metals.

The injunction *Manure thy selfe* (34) continues the farming image, urging the cultivation of the soul as preferable to the pursuit of 'outward' things. He ends by assuring Woodward of their mutual love – a polite way of declining to provide the desired copies of new verses.

Donne's technique of dialectic is well illustrated here. The *sententiae* or brief moral precepts tend to be oracular. Enjambement extends the rhythm of run-over lines on seven occasions, and meticulous punctuation (seldom the editor's) ensures reading for the sense of the argument. Donne's partiality for parentheses does not appear at all in this letter.

The method of dialectic is important for the choice of Donne's images. Three extended tropes (groups of figures) help to enforce the argument. The long simile in lines 19–24 is internally illumined by three metaphors: *gathering his beames* (21), *Blowing our sparkes of vertue* (23), *straw,* which doth *about our hearts sojourne* (24), each independently incompatible with the others, and the trio irrelevant to the pursuit of Religion. In context, this comparison can be called a *conceit,* and one that, in its total effect, goes beyond the epigrammatic and punning *concetti* of the Italian poet Marino, with whom Donne is often compared, and even beyond some strained conceits of Spenser. Donne's ingenuity sustains the simile throughout its far-fetched turns of thought. No sixteenth century predecessor or contemporary equalled Donne in this taste or style. His kind of *conceit* does not, indeed, find a place in the OED scale of meanings, until after Donne's lifetime.

In the pseudo-trope of lines 25–30, the initial triplet does not take the form of simile, but simulates it to announce the analogy in the succeeding triplet. The poem concludes with a third figurative group, incorporating horticultural metaphors, the last flouting Puttenham's insistence on decorum: *farmers of our selves*

(31), *stocke our selves* (32) and *Manure thy selfe* (34). In Donne's ardous passage, many phrases, such as *much deare treasure* (33), acquire a metonymic significance that engrosses the mind through aptness and intellectual fecundity; Donne does not use conceits for decorative novelty.

In 1610 Donne wrote a letter *To Sir Edward Herbert, at Julyers*. Nineteen years later, this distinguished and philosophic gentleman, the brother of George Herbert, the poet, and son of Donne's bene-factor, Mrs Magdalen Herbert, became Lord Herbert of Cherbury. He was eleven years Donne's junior, and had written a satirical exercise on *The State Progress of Ill* (1608), which was indebted to Donne's satires; hence the references in the following passage to the Ark of Noah, and the man-beast relationship that comprised its world. Donne preserved the philosophic tone of Herbert's effort, and the thought is treated in undramatic rhythm, if one compares the handling of the couplet with that in the *Elegies*, when he wrote under the impact of plays by Kyd, Shakespeare and Chapman.

> Man is a lumpe, where all beasts kneaded bee,
> Wisdome makes him an Arke where all agree;
> The foole, in whom these beasts do live at jarre,
> Is sport to others, and a Theater;
> Nor scapes hee so, but is himselfe their prey: 5
> All which was man in him, is eate away,
> And now his beasts on one another feed,
> Yĕt cóuplĕ'ĭn ángĕr, | aňd néw mónstĕřs bréed.
> Hòw háppў'iš hée, | whĭch hăth dùe pláce ăssígn'd
> Tŏ'hĭs beásts, | aňd dìsăfórĕstĕd hĭs mínde!   10

>   *   *   *

> As Soules (they say) by our first touch, take in
> The poysonous tincture of Originall sinne,   20
> So, to the punishments which God doth fling,
> Our apprehension contributes the sting.

>   *   *   *

> We do infuse to what he meant for meat   25
> Cŏrrósĭvenešse, | ŏr iňteňse cóld ŏr héat.
> Fŏr, Gód nó sùch spĕcífiq̆ue póyson háth
> As kills we know not how; his fiercest wrath

Hath no antipathy, but may be good
At lest for physicke, if not for our food.   30

*   *   *

Since then our businesse is, to rectifie
Nature, to what she was, wee'are led awry
By them, who man to us in little show;   35
Greater then due, no forme we can bestow
Ŏň hím; | fŏr Mán iňtò hǐmsélfe căn dráw
Aĺl; Áll hǐs faíth căn swállŏw,'oř reásŏn cháw.
Aĺl thăt ǐs fíll'd, | aňd áll thàt whǐch dŏth fíll,
Aĺl the roúnd wórld, tŏ mán ǐs bŭt ǎ píll;   40
Iň áll ǐt wórkes nòt, | bŭt ǐt ís iň áll
Póysonŏus, | ŏr púrgătǐve, | ŏr córdǐall,
For, knowledge kindles Calentures in some,
Aňd ìs tŏ óthěrs ícy̆ *Ópìùm.*

(lines 1–10, 19–22, 25–30, 33–44)

In the opening lines, Donne recalls Plato's *Republic,* IX 588–90:
Is not the noble that which subjects the beast to the man, or
rather to the god in man; and the ignoble that which subjects the man to the beast? . . . The soul is perfected and
ennobled by the acquirement of justice and temperance and
wisdom, more than the body ever is by receiving gifts of
beauty, strength and health, in proportion as the soul is
more honourable than the body.

(Jowett's translation)

The monsters in line 8 of Donne's letter are mentioned in Plato's
dialogue. Man's kneading from a lump of clay is a commonplace of
Plato, Protagoras and the Bible. Augustine in his commentary on
Genesis (i 28) maintained that man's nature is compounded of that
of many beasts. Ambrose in *De Noe et Arca* regarded the Ark as a
symbol of harmony, and Noah as the type of wisdom. *Disaforested*
(10) is a legal term for *purlieu,* land made available for cultivation,
which had once been forest, and therefore a royal preserve exempt
from common law. *Our first touch* (19) refers to the belief that the
soul, like the body, is corrupted by contagion with sin. *Apprehension* (22) has the paradoxical meaning of 'misunderstanding', of
punishments inflicted by God at the Fall of Man.

The source of lines 26–7 is de Forest's *De Venenis* (1606), which Donne had cited in the Preface to *Pseudo-Martyr,* published in the same year as de Forest's treatise. Donne argues in lines 28–30 that the greatest anger of God has no antipathy (or malignancy), but serves as a physic for our good. Man is greater than the material world, his task being to rectify the animalistic tendencies of nature.

In medieval physiology, the *cordiall* (42) was used to stimulate *vital* spirits, residing in the heart and distributed by the arteries. *Calentures* (43) were diseases contracted by sailors in the tropics, the symptoms being delirium and a desire to leap overboard. When introduced by Nashe in *Christs Teares over Jerusalem* in 1593, this word seems, from its spelling *Calentura,* to have been adopted from Spanish. *Opium* (44), from Greek *opos* (vegetable juice), was known to the ancients as a sedative and narcotic, entering English in Trevisa's translation of Bartholomaeus's *De Proprietatibus Rerum.* Opium is *icy,* because it numbs, having the opposite effect of Calentura, which raises the temperature. Donne reasons that knowledge of books, such as Sir Edward possesses, can have the different effects upon the mind that poisons, purgatives and stimulants have upon the body.

Donne's theological learning is grounded in the rational philosophy that underlies Pope's *Essay on Man;* but his main desire was to understand the soul, and that divine solicitude which shields the soul from the laws of nature. According to Photius of Byzantium, the concept of man as a microcosm of the universe originated with Pythagoras. Donne rejects the theory in line 35. In the Great Chain of Being man was supposed to excel in the quality of reason, which he alone possessed; but compared with other creatures, the beasts and plants, he was said to be deficient in other faculties, as he was in reason to the Supreme Power. Regarded as an amalgam of the four humours (Earth, Air, Fire and Water) man was bound to have the characteristics of brutish creation, but ought to use reason to discipline natural appetites.

The language is in the epistolary tradition of classical writers, such as Horace, yet characteristically Jacobean. Archaic *bee* (1) is employed for *are* for the sake of rhyme, and *eate* (6) for *eaten* for the sake of metre. The elegant style retains *hath* and *doth* in the third person singular present indicative. Periphrastic auxiliary *do/did* is used four times (lines 3, 21, 25, 39), as was customary, for metrical reasons or from stylistic habit; the practice had abated by the eighteenth century. The phonologically unexplained form *chaw* (38), for *chew* (from O. English *cēōwan*), did not appear in the language until 1530.

Granted the licences of *aphaeresis* (*scape* in line 5) and elision in lines 8–10, 34 and 38, there is little prosodic difficulty for the reader, who realizes that *contributes* (22) and *intense* (26) are stressed on the first syllable. *Theater* (4), with three syllables, invites modern ears to accept a crude, off-beat rhyme with *jarre*; but a variety of pronunciations may have made this less incongruous to Elizabethans. *Hath/wrath* (27/28) is a near-rhyme, and all the rhymes in 41/44 are off-beat in character. The skill with which the couplets are varied in pause and stress is an attractive feature of the versification. Of the thirty-two lines quoted, only five are syntactically or rhythmically enjambed, and stress-shifts are less libertarian than in the *Satyres,* the primary stresses varying from three to six. Pope must have studied carefully the pentameter prosody of Donne's verse epistles.

A passage that elicited Donne's most characteristic rhetoric occurs in lines 37–42, where *all* (heavily stressed) is repeated seven times, six substantivally, meaning 'everything', and the other in '*all* that which' (39), as a pronominal adjective. This colourful scheme of *ploce* has an important bearing upon the modulation (stress, pause and emphasis), as the scansion shows.

The letters to men are moral and speculative; those to women are in the courtly convention, often regarded as sycophantic. Donne admires in women of superior status their integrity and intellectual capacity, particularly in fostering the arts. The age of the salon, presided over by a wealthy female savante, had unfortunately not arrived. Therefore the virtue Donne extols is Christian, and it thrives in practice within the domestic circle. Donne was aware that women of rank are flattered by witty compliments, and in notable cases he carried fanciful adulation to extravagant limits. Of abstract veneration at the shrine of friendship, Donne is still the best exemplar. The modern reader has to accept hyperbole as amusing social bravado, ironically heightened by Donne's assumption of humility. Honour (says Donne) in a letter *To the Countess of Bedford* (7–9) is something external; kings can direct it, but men of low birth alone can bestow it.

Lucy, Countess of Bedford, the recipient of this observation, was the nearest to being a literary patron; her favours were extended to Donne, Drayton, Jonson and several other poets. The undated epistle, in triplets, beginning 'Honour is so sublime perfection' is one of eight addressed to the lady whom Donne met at Mitcham about 1608. She was the eldest child of Sir John Harrington (later Baron Exton), herself wrote poetry, and was known as a person of steadfast religious convictions. Lines 22–38 are central to Donne's Thomistic conception of homage:

> You, for whose body God made better clay,   22
> Or tooke Soules stuffe such as shall late decay,
> Or such as needs small change at the last day.

> This, as an Amber drop enwraps a Bee,   25
> Covering discovers your quicke Soule; that we
> May in your through-shine front your hearts thoughts see.

> You teach (though wee learne not) a thing unknowne
> To our late times, the use of specular stone,
> Through which all things within without were shown.   30

> Of such were Temples; so, 'and of such you are;
> *Beeing* and *seeming* is your equall care,
> And *vertues* whole *summe* is but *know* and *dare*.

> But as our Soules of growth and Soules of sense
> Have birthright of our reasons Soule, yet hence   35
> They fly not from that, nor seeke presidence:

> Natures first lesson, so, discretion,
> Must not grudge zeale a place, nor yet keepe none

Donne says that the clay from which this lady is kneaded is of finer quality and more durable; that it was possibly made of *Soules stuffe* (23), that is, the attenuated spirit that knows no decay, because it is immortal. This metaphysical problem was discussed by Augustine in the commentary to Genesis vii 5. Donne believed that body and soul have an integral relationship that cannot be dissolved. A union like this would need little modification for the soul's final destination in heaven.

Donne then likens the lady's active soul, in its transparency of thought, to a bee encased in amber; hence the reference to her *through-shine front* or countenance (27). The notion of transparency is sustained in line 29 by the reference to *specular stone* (Pliny's *lapis specularis*), which enabled passers-by to see what transpired inside Nero's Temple of Fortune, described by Guido Panciroli (Donne's source). The Italian author's name is mentioned in *Ignatius his Conclave*.

This leads to a distinction between *being* and *seeming* (32), made by Aristotle in *De Anima,* and expanded by Aquinas in *Summa Theologica.* Lines 34–6 reason that the *Soule of growth* (vegetative) and the *Soule of sense* (sensitive) are the earlier inheritances, but that does not give them *precedence* (Donne's *presidence*) over the soul of Reason. Discretion is the sum of nature's teaching, and needs perseverance in religion. The gist of the poet's praise is that the Countess's visible integrity resides in her *being* what she *appears to be* [author's emphasis].

There is nothing unseemly in this line of thought; it lends colour to the aptness of the term 'metaphysical' in relation to Donne's use of theology and philosophy in poetry. There are several senses in which the word was used in Donne's lifetime. Gabriel Harvey in his *Letter-book* (1577) speaks of 'salutations Divine and *metaphysical*', implying 'that which transcends the physical or natural'. Greene in *Menaphon* (1589) talks of 'the excellence of such a *Metaphysicall* vertue' in fair Samela, whom he describes as 'a miracle of nature' (75). Marlowe in the second part of *Tamburlaine* IV ii 62–4 (1590) has 'Marble stone,/ Tempered by science *metaphysical*/ And Spels of magicke from the mouthes of spirits', where the word clearly signifies 'supernatural'. The principal rhetorical device in this tribute is speculative similitude; *so* (31), which is used later as a rhyme word, appears, in a variety of grammatical functions. Donne's taste in triple-rhyming stanzas for dialectical verse is skilful and resourceful; paradoxical schemes of words, such as '*Covering* discovers' (26, *ploce*) and *within without* (30, *polyptoton*) are never obtrusive.

Discussing Donne's letters to the Countess of Bedford and the Countess of Huntingdon, J. B. Leishman disparages the 'fundamentally unserious wit' of the 'metaphysically complimentary style', in which the poet 'pretends to assume that these noble friends and patronesses are divinities' (*The Monarch of Wit,* p 126). But Donne's study of theology, though deep and controversial, was, at this period, unprofessional; he felt at liberty to utilize his researches in a score of analogies, quite novel to the recipients of his praise. Deliberately, he gave an unfamiliar twist to the

Petrarchan tradition, as light-heartedly in the epistolary as in the lyrical verse. It would be a mistake to regard this as trivial in its impact upon religiously-minded people.

Donne apparently wrote the second verse letter to the Countess of Huntingdon, quoted below, between 1612 and 1614, his mind having for some years been pre-occupied with controversy against the recusants, while working with Thomas Morton, who was in the service of the Earl of Huntingdon. Donne was in the process of rejecting some of Aquinas's teachings, originating from the metaphysics of Aristotle, who regarded theology as the highest of the speculative sciences (*Metaphysics,* II i 3). Donne's analogies, grounded on doctrines he deemed dubious, were therefore treated with less than his usual seriousness. Leishman's criticism of the tribute to the Countess of Huntingdon is the same as Dr Johnson's objection to eulogies of women written by Dryden: they 'mingle earth and heaven, by praising human excellence in the language of religion' (*Lives of the Poets,* 'Dryden', p 41).

Elizabeth Stanley, Countess of Huntingdon, was known to Donne as the third daughter of Sir Thomas Egerton's second wife, the widowed Countess of Derby, whom the poet's employer married in 1600. Elizabeth herself was married three years later, but continued to live at York House (Sir Thomas's London residence) until 1604. She was many years Donne's junior, and must have been an attractive person, since Sir John Roe wrote flattering letters to her also. It has been suggested that the Countess, who was also a patron of letters, enabled Donne to meet his financial obligations, at a time when the Countess of Bedford was unable to help him (E. Hardy, *Donne, A Spirit in Conflict,* p 158).

The metrical form of the poem, the pentameter quatrain with alternate rhyme, is familiar to readers of Gray's *Elegy written in a Country Churchyard,* though the sense-rhythm is different from Gray's solemn progression.

> Madame,
> Man to Gods image, *Eve,* to mans was made,
>   Nor finde wee that God breath'd a soule in her,
> Canons will not Church functions you invade,
>   Nor lawes to civill office you preferre.
>
> Who vagrant transitory Comets sees,   5
>   Wonders, because they'are rare; But a new starre

Whose motion with the firmament agrees,
  Is miracle; for, there no new things are;

In woman so perchance milde innocence
  A seldome comet is, but active good   10
A miracle, which reason scapes, and sense;
  For, Art and Nature this in them withstood.

As such a starre, the *Magi* led to view
  The manger-cradled infant, God below:
By vertues beames by fame deriv'd from you   15
  May apt soules, and the worst may, vertue know.

If the worlds age, and death be argu'd well
  By the Sunnes fall, which now towards earth doth bend,
Then we might feare that vertue, since she fell
  So low as woman, should be neare her end.   20

But she's not stoop'd, but rais'd; exil'd by men
  She fled to heaven, that's heavenly things, that's you;
She was in all men, thinly scatter'd then,
  But now amass'd, contracted in a few.

She guilded us: But you are gold, and Shee;   25
  Us she inform'd, but transubstantiates you;
Soft dispositions which ductile bee,
  Elixarlike, she makes, not cleane, but new.

(*To the Countess of Huntingdon, lines 1–28*)

Line 1 is a misreading of Genesis i 27, introduced by St Ambrose's commentaries on the Epistles of St Paul, as stated in Donne's Sermon at St Paul's, Easter 1630 (IX viii 190). There was disagreement in theological circles on the question whether woman was created in the image of God or of man. Line 2 raised another contentious issue, the medieval belief that women were not endowed with souls; the heresy was ironically dismissed by Donne in *Problem 3*, and rejected by consensus of public opinion. *Canons will not Church functions you invade* (3) is difficult, partly because the syntactic order is inverted, and because *will* has the sense of 'wish'. The sentence means 'Church rules do not want you (as a woman) to encroach on the ecclesiastical duties of men'. *Civill office* (4) signifies 'office at the disposal of the state', from which women were debarred.

Comets were held to be *vagrant* and *transitory* (5) according to the new astronomy of Galileo and Tycho Brahe; the superstitious regarded them as portents of evil. Under the traditional astrological dispensation, the fixed stars (those above the moon), which numbered 1022, were arranged in the eighth firmament, and their relation to each other did not change. In this sphere a new star was universally accepted as a miracle (5–8). By analogy, *innocence* in a woman is a rarity, *active good* a wonder; they are exceptions to reason and experience, and contrary to both art and nature (9–12).

As the miraculous star led the Wise Men to the God-child in Bethlehem, so the light of virtue, shed by the lady's reputation, might inspire good souls, even the unfit ones, to emulate exemplary conduct (13–16).

Luther and Melanchthon both calculated the world's age as between five and six thousand years, and considered all life to be in decline. Melanchthon maintained that the sun was coming nearer to the earth, and that its declination (*Sunnes fall*) would spell death (17 and 18). Regarding this forecast, Donne expresses scepticism by witty analogy: if virtue has stooped to soulless womanhood, the world must assuredly be approaching its end! (19–20).

This proves the turning point in the argument; for according to Donne, woman has *not* declined. Because of the exclusiveness and condescension of men, she has been exalted to share in heaven's blessings. But virtue, first utilized as a veneer to gild the mass of mankind, is now concentrated on a few individuals (21–4).

The Countess is this gold, and the model of all womankind. By transmutation to unsullied virtue, she instructs others. For a virtuous woman, like the elixir of infused gold sought by the alchemists, improves the natures of amenable men without necessarily reforming them (25–8).

The scholastic argument is too closely reasoned and well-intentioned in its idealism to be sacrilegious. Leishman suggests that 'Donne is merely playing with scholastic concepts' and introduces them 'almost accidentally' (op. cit. p 132). But Donne discarded a good deal of Thomistic theology, while enjoying the analogical subtlety of its dialectic. He is unmistakably a churchman who treats un-seriously philosophical ideas that have lost their validity for his way of life. As a convert in the making, his wit in deliberation is well under control. His letters in prose to Goodyere show this to be the case.

A comparison of the poem with its prose explication will illustrate the economy of Donne's language, its skilful verse enjambement, and tight argument. This discipline is dependent to an appreciable extent on relation words, such as the indefinite relative *who* (5), and the connectives *so* and *as* in lines 9 and 13. Lines 21–2 demonstrate the conversational tone achieved by colloquial contractions, e.g. *she's* and *that's* (twice). In polite conversation *'s* for *is* was by then tolerated; but *'re* for *are* was apparently not. Ben Jonson used *they'r* in his humour plays, but for dramatic writing the usual combination employed by compositors was *th'are*. Donne's *they'are* (6) shows the modern form in the process of becoming.

It is not an accident that maximum employment of elision and contraction occurs in Donne's *Satyres*; his many devices are inseparable from the conversational technique and dramatic presentation. His purpose was, perhaps, to show that metrical regularity in verse of this kind was a fiction that could be circumvented by acknowledged licences. His most lucid passages, however, are often those in which he used elision least, and these establish him as a poet well within the syllabic tradition.

CHAPTER III

The *Songs and Sonets*

🌀🌀🌀🌀🌀🌀

DONNE'S reputation among modern critics rests principally on some fifty poems, called the *Songs and Sonets,* first grouped under this title in the second edition (1635). The majority were written for private circulation in the twenty-one years between 1593 and 1614, but most were composed in the first seven. Three appeared in print as songs, with musical settings, in Alphonso Ferrabosco's *Ayres* (1609), William Corkine's *Second Book of Ayres* (1612), and John Dowland's *A Pilgrim's Solace* (1612): they were respectively *The Expiration, Breake of Day* and *Love's Infiniteness* (the last re-written and entitled 'To ask for all thy love'). These lyrics belong to the earlier group of the *Songs and Sonets,* those written before 1600, contemporaneous with the *Elegies* and *Satyres.* The later group consists of poems composed after Donne's marriage to Ann More in 1601.

The *editio princeps,* by H. J. C. Grierson (1912), included fifty-five poems among the *Songs and Sonets,* but the authenticity of two has since been put in doubt. The student now has the benefit of other English editions with different aims: John Hayward's (None-such, 1929), Theodore Redpath's (Methuen, 1956) and Helen Gardner's (Clarendon, 1965), the last being the text quoted in this chapter.

Most poems have love as their theme, and Gardner divides the entire text into two groups, which may be related to Donne's life before and after 1600. The first comprises poems of cynical attitude, apparently due to frustration; the second, with as much finesse of wit and more tenderness, defends love achieved as perfect union. The poems selected here are from both groups, it being evident from the rhythm that a different animation and emphasis under-lie the language, whatever the metrical form chosen. The stanza forms vary a great deal, both in the number of lines, and the number of feet within the line. The only poem named as a sonnet is *The Token,* but it has eighteen lines.

The motivation and cynical wit of the first group have been prejudicially handled by John Buxton in *Elizabethan Taste*:

> Donne used verse to compliment, or amuse, or rival his friends . . . He was carefree and light-hearted in the use of an exceptional talent: . . . He supposed, rightly or wrongly, that his poetry would be understood only by those friends for whom he wrote it, and even when in 1614 he was thinking of publishing a collection of his poems this was to be 'not for much public view, but at my own cost, a few copies'. . . .
>
> Donne's poetry is the poetry of those who were the arbiters of taste in the 1590s and 1600s when they were talking together in private; when they found it entertaining not to concur with the opinion of the common reader. . . . Donne caught the tone of voice of the best company of his time in their hours of relaxation, in their private chambers: the ready learning and the instant wit, the generosity of praise and the cruelty of ridicule, the impudence and the flattery. . . . He was reluctant to allow the permanence of print to something that was by nature extemporary and fleeting.
>
> ('The Donne Fashion', *pp 320–7*)

Impressionism such as this, and selection of the more outrageous poems in anthologies, have provoked the mistaken idea that 'libertinism' was the more original, indeed the generative aspect of Donne's genius. Buxton's observations are truer of the spirit in the *Elegies* than of the most important poems of the *Songs and Sonets.*

The exciting effect of Donne's often-styled philosophic lyrics resides in realistic enlargement of a situation or idea, with turns of rhythm to ensure the sense in reading. He secures this by remaining within the *I–thou* relationship of logical argument, in which the second is merely a listener. This means that Donne's associations in imagery or technique are remarkably consistent, and on an intimate level resembling dialogue on the stage, which flags when it becomes abstract. Though he uses the method of scholastic dialectic, Donne differs substantially from the Thomistic view-point, especially in the interaction of body and soul. Grierson says appropriately that 'he will not accept the antithesis between soul and body . . . In the highest spiritual life, as in the fullest and most perfect love, body and soul are complementary' (*Poetical Works*, vol. II, p 161). Donne differs from Dante in not accepting the Thomist system of ideas as ultimate truth, but using it as a means of disciplining his mind.

In his use of speculative theology, Donne can be repetitive, and less original than the verse manner would lead us to believe. The Catholic poets of medieval Italy and sixteenth-century Spain had experimented on similar lines, without altogether abandoning the neo-Platonic tradition. When Donne asserted in his letter to Sir Henry Wotton (*c* 1600) that he was 'no great voyager in other mens works', and could recall, not their ideas, but merely the number of pages he had read, he probably had in mind creative writing. His theological, legal and scientific studies were those from which his memory recovered untold images.

The function of Marinism in Renaissance poetry was apparently to surprise through conceits, reflecting an unusual twist of the mind. The term is derived from the practice of the Neapolitan, Giambattista Marino (1569–1625) in his epic romance *L'Adone* (1623), which abounds in metaphors and subtleties of this type. Donne's themes, and rhythmic conception of them, were finely adapted to his scholastic method of introspection. The surface harshness is uncannily dovetailed to the rhetorical emphasis, compelling the re-reading of poems to catch the imaginary intonations of Donne's voice.

C. S. Lewis, endeavouring to differentiate two main streams of English Renaissance poetry, remarked that the 'surly defiances' of Wyatt's naturalistic poems are like Donne's, 'with most of the genius left out' ('Donne and Love Poetry in the Seventeenth Century', *Studies presented to Sir Herbert Grierson,* pp 64–84). Donne, he argues, merely perfected what modern critics regard as his special invention, poetry of 'the speaking voice', which may be no truer, in aesthetic terms, than the Platonic decorousness of Spenser. Both styles are sincere in different ways. To the question 'what constitutes the metaphysical?', Lewis answers that it is an amalgam of disparate elements, such as hyperbole, and tension and relaxation of the conceits. The imagery from law, science and philosophy deliberately avoids the poetical, and has a touch of 'pedantry and dandyism'. But the merit of imagery from whatever source remains 'its power of conveying a meaning more luminously'. Lewis's underrating of Donne's *Songs and Sonets*, for their excogitation and lack of inevitability, is as vulnerable as Buxton's; but it is tempered with the reservation that, 'any account of Donne which concentrates on his love poetry must be unfair to the poet, for it leaves out much of his best work.'

The strength of Donne is the innate vigour of his language, and insatiable curiosity to comprehend, without prejudice to his faith, the science of the universe that Copernicus and Galileo had opened to him. He drew upon this, and upon legal theory, in preference to images from nature, which Elizabethan poets usually saw through the eyes of Greek mythology. With Paracelsian passion for experiment, Donne sought original phrasing, elaborate distinctions and mannerist analogies, controlling thought by a flexible rhetorical discipline, which is a tribute to his humanism. The skill in dialectic was not planned as an antidote to neo-Platonic mysticism; and the tendentious logic should not be taken at its face value. Undue praise has been given to poems by critics who are insensitive to Donne's different voices, and cannot discriminate between flippancy and moral sincerity. Donne's indecorous philosophy of love in some of the *Songs and Sonets* was born of varied experience, and no doubt appealed to the male friends for whom he wrote. But not all women were admirers of his candour; they preferred the lute-song rhythms of the lyrics to the unflattering subtlety of the man of the world.

Donne was, above all, the inventor of the serio-comic dramatic monologue, to be distinguished from Browning's circumambulatory portraits by its directness of approach. Whether the tone was self-tormented, perverse or serene depended on mood and circumstance; for Donne's temperament was capable of depression as well as elation. Pen in hand, he used his rare gift of transmuting the mundane experience of a city-dweller into words of explosive power. Critics seldom fail to distinguish Jack Donne, the rake, from John Donne the prelate; but they are the same person. It was not adversity alone that turned him from rakishness. Donne used his imagination to create different roles, and a Protean personality is sufficient cause to reconcile deferential courtesy to some women with assertive masculinity to others.

Private circulation of the poems arose partly from the responsibility of Donne's position as Egerton's secretary, and partly from
his desire for freedom of expression. Besides analogy, the wit
bristles with iconography from emblem books, and phenomena
from Pliny's natural history. Donne's exhilaration often springs
from a challenging opening line, but rests upon the infinite variety
of wit and conceptual structure of the poems. A unique sense of
form and an unusual gift of rhythmical thinking accompany the
twists and turns of the argument, which tests to the full the gamut
of stress modulation. In the *Songs and Sonets* the pattern is so well
adapted to the dialectic that the stanza forms (predominantly
iambic) are seldom repeated. Some are very complex, and there is a
strong preference for rhymed couplet arrangements.

Students of Donne's imagery have tended to classify and
number examples, in determining referents and sources. Evalua-
tion of the responses that images produce in the minds of readers
would be more instructive. An observation of Doniphan Louthan
is here pertinent: 'Much of Donne is sensual in subject matter
without being notably sensuous in imagery. We might say that
Donne is at the opposite pole from Spenser' (*The Poetry of John
Donne,* p 59). Some able critiques of Donne scarcely mention
imagery at all. Indeed, paucity of simile is an explicable feature of
the *Songs and Sonets,* one reason being that the dominant tropes,
hyperbole and irony, are more energizing to the situations the
passion of love excites.

GARDNER, GROUP I

A relaxed tone and loquacious irony in the cynicism are the
principal sources of Donne's inimitable art in the song-like verses
written before 1600: considered here are *Communitie, The Indifferent*
and *Love's Deitie.* The latter two are the more subjective, but all
possess an element of frustration that terminates in promiscuity,
and finds reason in plenty to excuse it. The vitality of such poems
has little to do with the biographical background. Each embodies
a circumscribed theme resembling the art of the miniature; and
tidily fitting the reflections into the small compass affords its creator
the purest satisfaction. The gem that dazzles by its symmetry is in
itself a fascinating, but not a profound, accomplishment.

Communitie

Good wee must love, | and must hate ill,
For ill is ill, | and good good still,
   But there are things indifferent,
Which wee may neither hate, nor love,
But one, | and then another prove,   5
   As wee shall finde our fancy bent.

If then at first wise Nature had
Made women either good or bad,
   Then some wee might hate, | and some chuse,
But since shee did them so create,   10
That we may neither love, nor hate,
   Onely this rests, | All, | all may use.

If they were good | it would be seene,
Good is as visible as greene,
   And to all eyes it selfe betrayes: 15
If they were bad, | they could not last,
Bad doth it selfe, and others wast,
   So, | they deserve nor blame, nor praise.

But they are ours | as fruits are ours,
He that but tasts, | he that devours,   20
   And he which leaves all, | doth as well:
Chang'd loves are but chang'd sorts of meat,
And when hee hath the kernell eate,
   Who doth not fling away the shell?

The simplistic character of this six-line octosyllabic stanza, rhyming a a b c c b, is evident from its abundant use of monosyllables; there are only fourteen exceptions in twenty-four lines, never more than one in a line. Donne here reduced diction to its essential elements, making it as perspicuous as the syntax. The title of the poem was taken from the 1635 edition.

The lines, with the exception of 7, are end-stopped, and most rhymes are strong and true; the single terminal modulation is the off-beat rhyme indìfferènt/bént (3/6). H. C. Wyld in *Studies in English Rhymes from Surrey to Pope* explains the soundness, in Donne's time, of the rhymes *love/prove* (4/5) and *last/wast* (= waste, 16/17). Because the lines are metrically self-contained, only twelve internal pauses are necessary. Stress modulation presents difficulty in only one line: Thĕn sóme | wĕ mìght | háte, aňd | sòme chúse. Punctuation is designed to secure the desired emphasis in reading, for example in lines 4, 11, 12 and 17. The capitalization of *All* in line 12 helps to bring out this emphasis.

The first stanza, though a plea for old-fashioned Mosaic distinctions, argues for freedom of choice in matters to which the law is indifferent. The second stanza alleges, with mock seriousness, that women, like Eve, were created amoral (a fallacious premise); they are fancy-free in the eye of Nature. In the third stanza, the flippancy is sustained by confusion of the *sensitive soul* with the *rational* (*Good is as visible as greene*), and consequent subversion of moral values. Evil is held to destroy itself, and good to be self-evident. Because women are alleged to be morally neutral, and therefore *things,* they deserve neither blame nor praise. The conclusion is that they are made for man's use, like fruits of the earth, to be tasted, devoured or neglected, without public stigma. In every line of the final stanza the conceits (simile or metaphor) relate to the appetites. The paean to promiscuity ends with a triple crudity, supposed to be amusing to the male sex.

This is the simplest example of Donne's cynical chop-logic, to undermine the moral order that he initially pretended to maintain. He expects no serious-minded person to accept this argument for free love, much less for the uncivilized status of women it propagates. Rather the argument is an invitation to detect the fallacy elaborated in lines 13–18. The poem is a young student's *jeu d'esprit,* which regards no aspect of human relations with the sacred gravity of the law. Donne reacts playfully to the Petrarchan tradition, in which a lady pours scorn on the advances of her would-be lover.

Communitie should be read in conjunction with Donne's fourth *Paradox,* 'That good is more common than evill', from which it cannot be long separated in time. Here is an excerpt significant to the argument:

> *Evill* buries it selfe in night and darknesse, and is chastised and suppressed when *good* is cherished and rewarded. . . .
> *Evill manners* are *parents* of *good Lawes*; and in every *evill* there is an *excellency*, which (in common speech) we call *good*. For the fashions of *habits*, for our moving in *gestures*, for phrases

in our *speech*, we say they were *good* as long as they were used, that is, as long as they were *common*; and wee eate, wee walke, onely when it is, or seemes *good* to doe so. . . . Of *indifferent* things many things are become perfectly good by being *common*, as *customes* by use are made binding *Lawes*. But I remember nothing that is therefore *ill*, because it is *common*, but *Women*, of whom also; *They that are most common, are the best of that Occupation they professe.*
(*Selected Prose, ed. Simpson, Gardner and Healey, p.* 10)

The success of *Communitie* hinges partly on the sophisticated use of *ploce*, i.e. sporadic repetition of key words: *good* occurs 5 times, *ill* 3, *bad* 3, *love* 4, *hate* 4, *all* 4, *some* 2, *ours* 2, *chang'd* 2. There are subtle shades of antithetical balance too, in lines 1, 2 and 9 syntactic, in lines 19 and 20 syllabic and metrical. But the song-like rhythm remains uppermost in the mind.

An incentive for Donne's penning of sportive love-philosophy, at a time when he was writing *Paradoxes, Elegies* and *Satyres,* was the fashionable sway that Petrarch held over English poets during the 1590s. Donne was as deeply affected by the Italian poet as Sidney and Spenser, but too much a man of the world not to laugh at the clichés and absurd convention of the lovelorn male wooer. Like Sidney, he debunked the tradition, which he also respected for its self-effacing courtliness. The truth seems to be that Donne felt himself more alienated than his contemporaries from stock conventions of style. Among the miscellaneous prose pieces of his youth, written for the recreation of Sir Henry Wotton and his friends, was Donne's 'Essay of Valour', printed in Sir Thomas Overbury's *A wife now the widdow of Sir T. Overbury,* 1614. As the following extracts show, it acccounts for Donne's forwardness, and familiar attitude to women:

A man of armes is alwaies void of ceremonie, which is the wall that stands betwixt *Piramus* and *Thisbe,* that is, Man and Woman, for there is no pride in women but that which rebounds from our owne basenesse . . . so that onely by our pale asking, we teach them to deny. And by our shame-fac'tnesse, wee put them in minde to bee modest: whereas indeed it is cunning Rhetoricke to perswade the hearers that they are that already, which he would have them to be. . . .

73

No woman takes advice of any in her loving; but of her
own eies, and her wayting womans: Nay which is worse,
wit is not to be felt, and so no good Bed fellow: Wit applied
to a woman makes her dissolve her sympering, and discover
her teeth with laughter, and this is surely a purge for love;
for the beginning of love is a kind of foolish melancholly....

No man so soone surpriseth a womans affections, as he
that is the subject of all whispering, and hath alwaies twenty
stories of his owne deedes depending upon him.
(*Complete Poetry and Selected Prose,* ed. J. Hayward, Nonesuch
1942, pp 418–20)

The Indifferent

A more appropriate example of the Elizabethan intellectual's dis-
sent from romance would be hard to find than the following, a
social monody dramatized in Donne's inimitable manner:

I can love both faire and browne,
Her whom abundance melts, and her whom want betraies
Her who loves lonenesse best, and her who maskes and
     plaies,
    Her whom the country form'd, and whom the town,
     Her who beleeves, and her who tries,   5
     Her who still weepes with spungie eyes,
  And her who is dry corke, and never cries;
I can love her, and her, and you and you,
I can love any, so she bee not true.

     Will no other vice content you?   10
Will it not serve your turn to do, as did your mothers?
Have you old vices spent, and now would finde out others?
    Or doth a feare, that men are true, torment you?
     Oh we are not, be not you so,
     Let mee and doe you, twenty know.   15
  Rob mee, but binde me not, and let me goe.
Must I, who came to travaile thorow you,
Grow your fixt subject, because you are true?

     Venus heard me sigh this song,
And by Loves sweetest Part, Variety, she swore,   20

74

She heard not this till now; and't should be so no more,
  She went, examin'd, and return'd ere long,
    And said, alas, Some two or three
    Poore Heretiques in love there bee,
  Which thinke to stablish dangerous constancie.   25
  But I have told them, since you will be true,
  You shall be true to them, who'are false to you.

The catalogue of types in stanza one was suggested by Ovid's
Amores, II iv; but the *song* the poet is said to *sigh* (19) hints at
Petrarchan parody, especially in the first two stanzas. The last
stanza consists of Donne's comments, adjudging constancy to be a
vice and free love a virtue. Ironically, Donne makes Venus, who
has overheard the sensualist's plaint, support sexual variety against
true love, decreeing that inconstant men shall be assigned to constant women. Implied in the idea that Petrarchan devotion is
heresy, is the conviction that the Italian poet elevated love to a
religion. Donne never abandoned his penchant for snide comment
at the expense of theology. Burlesque of the schools of logic was
considered witty in intellectual circles.

In Donne's first *Paradox,* 'A Defence of Womens Inconstancy'
he advances a similar argument, this time to men, but with less
sophistry:

> That Women are *Inconstant,* I with any man confesse, but
> that *Inconstancy* is a bad quality, I against any man will
> maintaine: For every thing as it is one better than another,
> so is it fuller of *change;* . . . Women changing more than
> Men, have also more *Reason.* They cannot be immutable
> like stockes, like stones, like the Earths dull Center; . . .
> Why should that which is the perfection of other things, be
> imputed to Women as greatest imperfection? Because
> thereby they deceive men. Are not your wits pleased with
> those jests, which coozen your expectation? . . . *Inconstancy*
> is a most commendable and cleanely quality, and Women in
> this quality are farre more absolute than the Heavens, than
> the Starres, Moone, or any thing beneath it; for long
> observation hath pickt certainety out of their mutability.
> . . . They are borne to take downe the pride of wit, and
> ambition of wisedome, making *fooles* wise in the adventur-
> ing to winne them, *wisemen* fooles in conceit of losing their

labours; . . . This name of *Inconstancy,* which hath so much
beene poysoned with slaunders, ought to bee changed into
variety, for the which the world is so delightfull, *and a
Woman for that the most delightfull thing in this world.*
(*Selected Prose,* ed. Simpson, Gardner and Healey, pp 5–7)

The language and form of *The Indifferent* are more complex than in
Communitie, but there is a similar preference for monosyllables.
The stanzas have nine lines, rhyming a b b a c c c d d, the syllables
in the line varying from seven to thirteen. A metrical innovation is
the trochaic opening line in each of the stanzas, followed by two
alexandrines in iambs. Lines 5 and 6 have regularly eight syllables;
and all the remaining lines are iambic pentameters. Donne's modulation permits frequent trochaic inversion of stress in the first foot,
eight times in stanza one, seven times in stanza two, but only once
in the last stanza; the variations are accommodated to changes of
direction in each division of the poem.

The play Donne makes with personal and relative pronouns
throughout the poem is typical of his method; so is the assonance
of vowels, indulged in stanza two, which contributes to the song-
like quality of its expression. Switching the pronoun from *her* to
you in line 8, and to *any* in line 9, has semantic importance, since
the interest moves from the general to the particular woman, and
finally to the sex as a whole. At a first reading it is not clear that
Donne intended *you* in the second half of line 26 and at the end of
the ensuing line, to indicate direct speech; a second glance shows
this to be essential to correct interpretation.

Donne often used the verb *tries* (5) in the sense of 'tests', and the
adverb *still* (6) in the sense of 'always'. *Do* in line 11 and *know* (15)
have strong sexual overtones. In lines 11 and 12 Donne enquires
whether the women of his time were any better than their mothers,
or whether they preferred novelty in their pleasures. *Travaile* (17)
was a direct borrowing from O. French, meaning 'trouble' 'painful
labour'; from the twelfth to the fifteenth century the same spelling
served for *travel,* noun or verb.

Rhetorical patterning is subtly employed in the first and second
stanzas. In line 2 *abundance melts* and *want betraies* are antithetical
metaphors, which contrast the luxury-pampered miss and the
impoverished trull, compelled to trade her favours. Throughout
the catalogue of beauties, tropes are matched to underline the

realism, as *spungie eyes* (6) and *dry corke* (7), both Donnian and anti-Petrarchan metaphors.

Constancy as unreason, the theme of stanza two, in lines 10–13 and 17–18, asks five rhetorical questions; the classical schools, derived from Greek, classed this as *erotema,* a device for securing greater vehemence of expression. Donne used it to strengthen the view that both sexes have the same apprehension in regard to permanent attachments; and this he saw as a situation that every sensible person would approve. Vehemence in style is force, emphasis is iteration, which Donne generally signalled by elocutionary stopping. Repetition may take several forms; in Donne it invariably invokes similar sounds or thematic words, to keep the mind attentive to the argument.

Love's Deitie

I long to talke with some old lovers ghost,
  Who dyed before the god of Love was borne:
I cannot thinke that hee, | who then lov'd most,
  Súnke só lów, | as to lóve òne which did scórne.
But since this god produc'd a destinie,   5
And that vice-nature, | custome, | lets it be;
    Ì múst lóve hér, that lóves not mée.

Súre, | they which máde him gód, | meánt nòt so múch:
  Nor he, | in his young godhead practis'd it.
But when an even flame two hearts did touch,   10
  His office was indulgently to fit
Áctives to pássives: | Córrespóndencìe
Only his subject was. I cannot bee
    Lóve, | till I lóve hér, that lóves mée.

But every moderne god will now extend   15
  His vást prerógative, as fár as Jóve.
To rage, | to lust, | to write to, | to commend,
  All is the purlewe of the God of Love.
Oh were wee wak'ned by this Tyrannie
To'ungod this child againe, | it could not bee   20
    That Í should lóve, who lóves nòt mée.

Rebell and Atheist too, | why murmure I,
  As though I felt the worst that love could doe?

Lóve might make mé leàve lóving, | or might tríe
A deeper plague, | to make her love mee too,   25
Which, | since she loves before, | I'am loth to see;
Falshood is worse then hate; | and that must bee,
    If shée whom Í lóve, should lóve mée.

This is a Petrarchan complaint, with a difference. The seven-lined
stanza rhyming a b a b c c c, consists of a quatrain of alternately
rhymed iambic pentameters, followed by a triplet, the last line
being a neatly varied octosyllabic refrain. The peculiarity of this
refrain is that stressed syllables (usually five) outnumber the unstressed ones, largely because of sense emphasis on repeated *love*
(*ploce*) and the personal pronouns.

The meditative urbane tone of the first three lines has its ease
abruptly broken by the fourth, which has a prosaic rhythm beginning with three stressed syllables. This accords with Donne's
technical practice of subverting the iambic pattern, whenever the
sequence moves too smoothly, about once in every four lines. In
most stanzas, the modulation is aided by enjambement, occurring
in lines 11, 12, 13, 15, 20 and 24; or by the occasional introduction
of Latin polysyllables, as in line 12.

Donne suggests that the Romano-Hellenic *God of Love* (Cupid)
was not only of minor importance, but a misfit in the order of
nature, whose influence on the relationship of sexes was arbitrary
and mischievous. Cupid, he argues, *produc'd a destinie* (5) by
introducing fatalism into love. Custom (or 'second nature') endorsed this impishness; hence the prevalence of the unrequited love
of the refrain. *Vice-nature* (6) is slightly ironical, since the poet
suggests an element of 'viciousness'. Donne alleges (10–14) that
young Cupid irresponsibly misused the mandate originally intended to match hearts inflamed with the same passion. Love cannot truly exist (says the refrain), until attachment is reciprocated
(14).

Upstart gods soon usurp the power of Jove; thus Cupid's
usurpation incites anger, lust, epistolary extravagance and ex-
orbitant adulation (15–18). If the god were deprived of his
tyranny, unrequited love would end. Characteristically for Donne
the complaint does not end on this note. He confesses to a taste for
rebellion and religious contumely. Cupid's motive may well have
been to inhibit love, or to aggravate the situation by *a deeper*

plague (25), making the pursuer the pursued. Since the lady has already been in love, reciprocated affection would be a falsehood, and a destiny *worse then hate* (27).

The preterite *sunke* (4), for *sank* (a Western form), was derived from the past participle, and in common use among sixteenth and seventeenth-century writers, including Jonson. The adverbial use of *Sure* (8), meaning 'certainly' (an American colloquialism for 'of course'), did not appear in literature until the mid sixteenth century, but is found sporadically in Elizabethan drama. *Purlewe* (18) is said by the OED to be an erroneous fifteenth-century spelling for *purley* from Anglo-French *purale*, later gallicized to *purlieu* (see note on *disaforested,* in the letter *To Sir Edward Herbert,* p. 57).

In lines 12/13 *Actives to passives: Correspondencie/ Only his subject was* (again prosaic modulation), *Actives* symbolizes the male sex, *passives* the female, the trope employed being metonymy. *Correspondencie* signifies 'sympathetic response' rather than 'congruity', the word being current in the last decade of the sixteenth century. The poetical order of *Only his subject was* is among the few examples of syntactic inversion (*hyperbaton*) in this poem.

Wit as artifice; argument that is teasing; ingenious manipulation of ideas to the stanza form and rhyme scheme – these are the keynotes of the earlier *Songs and Sonets*. They were not intended to carry much conviction, nor yet to plumb any depths of imagination. Those that celebrate promiscuity were simple, informal mosaics, invented to amuse Donne's sophisticated male friends; yet they came to be appreciated by Coleridge for their 'pure and genuine mother English' (*Biographia Literaria,* 1817, ed. J. Shawcross, p 14).

GARDNER, GROUP II

Donne's mature secular poems have endured by reason of their detachment and intellectual concentration, qualities that are omnipresent, even when conceits and other images are absent. Concluding stanzas, in which the poet surprizes, controverts or denies conventions with irony, are often as telling as Donne's challenging openings. He was especially conscious of poetry's need for verbal economy. Thinking of the Psalms, he said: 'where all words are numbered, and measured, and weighed, the whole work is less subject to falsification' (*Sermons,* II, p 50).

The mistaken impression somehow gained ground that Donne lacked decorum, and used difficult language. In reality, classical simplicity, whether of syntax or vocabulary, is seldom obliterated, even with the occasional flow of majestic Latin polysyllables. Explication of poems became the rule because of the scholastic presentation of ideas, through dialectic, which was Donne's most characteristic medium. The ideas, the technical handling of them in verse, were important to a poet, who was determined to be uniquely himself.

The Anniversarie

All Kings, and all their favorites,
　　All glory'of honors, | beauties, | wits,
The Sun it selfe, | which makes times, as they passe,
Is elder by a yeare, now, | then it was
When thou and I first one another saw:　　　　　5
All other things, to their destruction draw,
　　Only our love hath no decay;
This, no tomorrow hath, | nor yesterday,
Running | it never runs from us away,
But truly keepes his first, | last, | everlasting day.　　　10

　　Two graves must hide thine and my coarse,
　　If one might, | death were no divorce.
Alas, | as well as other Princes, | wee,
(Who Prince enough in one another bee,)
Must leave at last in death, | these eyes, and eares,　　　15
Oft fed with true oathes, | and with sweet salt teares;
　　But soules where nothing dwells but love
(All other thoughts being inmates) | then shall prove
This, | or a love increaséd there above,
When bodies to their graves, | soules from their graves
　　remove.　　　20

　　And then wee shall be throughly blest,
　　But wee no more, then all the rest.
Here upon earth, we'are Kings, | and none but wee
Can be such Kings, | nor of such subjects bee;
Who is so safe as wee? | where none can doe　　　25
Treason to us, | except one of us two.

True and false feares let us refraine,
Let us love nobly, | 'and live, | and adde againe
Yeares and yeares unto yeares, | till we attaine
To write threescore: | this is the second of our raigne.   30

This poem, by its reference to *Kings,* seems to have been written after James I's accession in 1603. It attains an eloquence and seriousness present in few of the poems of the earlier group. Courtesy and decorum of expression Donne obviously reserved for more exalted relationships (marked by *thou* in line 5), and for persons of rank. The note of fidelity associated with noble rank (*Kings, favorites* and *Princes*), and with pagan worship, inhibits the mutuality of the lovers from being merely romantic. *The Anniversarie* may be regarded as a transitional poem, not completely liberated from the artifice of the promiscuity group.

In the ten-line iambic stanza, rhyming a a b b c c d d d d, couplet monotony is avoided by variation of the syllable measure. Lines 1, 2 and 7 are octosyllables, and line 10 an Alexandrine, possibly suggested by that of the Spenserian stanza; the remaining six verses are pentameters. No other poet would have attempted such an unpromising form; yet Donne handles it admirably, by flexible disposition of pauses to suit the nuances of the speaking voice.

The parentheses in lines 14 and 17 are typical of Donne's halting of rhythm by prosaic interpolation. In the impassioned last stanza, on the other hand, enjambement helps to speed the rhythm of lines 23, 25, 28 and 29. But only one run-on line (18) was permitted in the two earlier stanzas, because they are more sententious. Instances of syntactic inversion in lines 6, 8, 24 and 27 are all on metrical grounds, chiefly for the sake of rhyme.

The stanzas are linked by repetition of significant words (*ploce*) e.g. *All* (1 twice, 2, 6, 18, 22). This monosyllable, heavily stressed, occurs four times at the beginning of lines, causing trochaic inversion of the first foot. Other instances of *ploce* are: *Kings* (1, 23, 24); *first* (5, 10); *one another* (5, 14); *other* (6, 13, 18); *our* (7, 30); *hath* (7, 8); *no* (7, 8, 12, 22); *day* (8, 10); *Run* (9 twice); *us* (9, 26 twice, 27, 28); *last* (10 twice, 15); *wee/we* (13, 21, 22, 23, 25, 29); *Prince* (13, 14); *bee* (14, 24); *soules* (17, 20); *love* (7, 17, 19, 28); *their* (20 twice); *none* (23, 25); *graves* (20 twice); *yeare* (4, 29 three times). This means that 21 words (the less significant omitted) were repeated 63 times in 30 lines. *Ploce*, alliteration and assonance are common devices throughout Donne's lyrics, but the first is a prime unifying force.

The tropes in *The Anniversarie* are Donnian in the highest degree. There is a somewhat ambiguous personal metaphor, involving the *Sun,* in line 3; but more effective instances are the verbs *hide* and *dwell* of lines 11 and 17. Sometimes a clause or phrase is metaphorical e.g. *death were no divorce* (12), and *All other thoughts being inmates* (18). Donne used hyperbole in different functions – some extravagant, others passionate. Generally, there is credible or creditable reason for this figure, as in lines 23 and 24, where love is equated with mundane political power; the hyperbole is resuscitated at the end of line 30.

There is in *The Anniversarie* a certain underrating of the honours of the Court, from which Donne was at this time excluded. To counterbalance this, Donne asserts the sovereignty of dedicated love and, with less assurance, its immortality. In the second stanza, the promise of eternity is undermined by consciousness of the impermanence of things physical. The severance to which death condemns illicit lovers is denial of a common grave. There is but one consolation, that their souls will be re-united in heaven.

In the final stanza Donne states the scholastic view of the life hereafter, that the departed are blessed, not according to their deserts, but in such a way that spirits in salvation feel content with their dispensation. This belief was allied to another, that during life the soul had been in bondage to the body. As sovereigns enjoy divine right, so genuine lovers have to make the most of their mutual trust; for the ennobling fact of self-perpetuating love lies in its immunity to unfaithfulness.

Time's evanescence is important in Donne's humanist pleading, and he uses the pagan Sun as a kind of measuring rod. Every egocentric love relationship, haunted by a fear of evanescence, inevitably builds upon a belief in its own transcendence. It resembles the state of kings, whose security depends on the reciprocal loyalty of ruler and subject. But all the art and eloquence of Donne's logic is needed to make plausible this tenuous Laurentian doctrine.

Aire and Angels

Twíce or thríce had Í lóv'd thée,
Befóre I knéw thy fáce or náme;

Só in a voíce, | só in a shápelesse fláme,
Aṅgells afféct us óft, | and wórship'd bée;
    Stíll when, | to whére thou wért, | I cáme,   5
Some lóvely glórious nóthing Í did sée.
    But sínce my soúle, | whose chíld lóve ís,
Tàkes límmes of flésh, | and élse could nóthing dóe,
        Mòre súbtile then the párent ís,
Lóve mùst nòt bé, | but táke a bódy toó,   10
    And thérefore whát thou wért, | and whó,
        Ì bíd Lóve áske, | and nów
That it assúme thỳ bódy, | Í allów,
And fíxe it sélfe in thỳ líp, | eỳe, and brów.

    Whilst thús to bállast lóve, I thoúght,   15
    And sò mòre stéddily to have góne,
With wáres which woùld sínke àdmirátiòn,
I sáw, I hàd lóves pínnace óverfraúght,
    Év'ry thy haíre for lóve to wórke upón
Is múch tòo múch, | some fítter múst be soúght;   20
    For, | nòr in nóthing, | nòr in thíngs
Extréme, | and scátt'ring bríght, | can lóve inhére;
        Thén | as an Aṅgell, | fáce, and wíngs
Of aíre, | not púre as ìt, | yet púre doth weáre,
    So thỳ lóve may be mý lóves speháre;   25
        Jùst súch dispáritìe
As ìs twixt Aíre and Aṅgells púritìe,
'Twixt wómens lóve, and méns will éver bée.

The prosodic craftsmanship here displayed is remarkable, but not
Donne at his most capricious; he writes well within the tradition
that English poetry had adopted from the Italian. The dominant
measure is iambic, but lines 2, 6, 11, 15 and 28 alone are conventional. The opening line is trochaic truncated, with seven syllables;
and it should be observed that trochaic substitution modulates at
least five other lines, notably in the first foot. Stress depends pre-
eminently on vocal emphasis, with the result that there is some
ambiguity in the metrical weight of certain syllables; therefore
scansion calls for individual interpretation. It would be unjustified,
because of the indeterminate stress in lines 8–10 and 12, to regard
Donne as a writer of free verse.
    The fourteen-line stanza of *Aire and Angels* resembles sonnet

structure only in the bi-partite division (here reversed) of octave and sestet, which appears to be deliberate in both stanzas. In the sestet, rhymed a b^8 b a^{10} b^8 a^{10} (where the figures represent the number of syllables in the model), the situation is explained; in the octave, rhymed c^8 d^{10} c^8 d^{10} d^8 e^6 e e^{10}, the poet reasons about this situation. The stanza is seen to depart from the sonnet form in the anomalous syllables of the lines, and consequent rhythmical variation. No less than seven of the verses fall short of the pentameter norm. Donne's ingenious matching of syllable count and rhyme-scheme in the pair of stanzas permits only two concessions: line 1 has only seven syllables in the first stanza, eight in the second; line 5 has eight syllables in the first stanza, ten in the second. The supernumerary syllable in the second line of stanza 2, *And so more steddily to have gone*, leaves the metrical reader with two options: (a) the practical, to elide the *i* of *steddily*, (b) the theoretical, to invoke the convention of combined contraction (*synaloepha*) *t'have*, thereby achieving a monosyllable.

The poem uses 208 words, only 34 of which have more than one syllable, five of the latter being repetitions (*Angells, nothing, body*). Eight of the lines consist of monosyllables only. In the first stanza Donne rhymes throughout on words of one syllable, seven of them verbs; in stanza two, eight rhyme-words are monosyllabic, including five verbs. These habits are significant for Donne's method: the more complex the stanza form, the simpler the vocabulary; and to make the schematics feasible, the longer the stanza, the less he is encouraged to repeat it in the same poem. Principally for rhyme or special emphasis, Donne indulges in syntactic inversion. *Aire and Angels* is fond of inverting the order of adverbial phrases, and noun or adverbial clauses. The position of the adverbial adjective in '*Ev'ry* thy haire' was an Elizabethan poetic convention.

It is clear that pronouns and verbs loom large in Donne's technical equipment, especially as rhyming counters, where their prominence is magnified. The pronoun of address *thou/thee* dominates this poem, and possessive *thy* chimes, like an echo, with the first personal pronoun *I/my*, e.g. in lines 13 and 25. It would be interesting to discover how many times Donne rhymes *thee/bee* (= are) in the *Songs and Sonets*. Twice *wert* appears in the second person singular of the preterite indicative (5, 11), as used by Shakespeare and Jonson, alongside of *wast*. By the sixteenth century both forms had replaced M. English *were* in the indicative; and in the seventeenth century *wert* was commonly extended to the second person singular of the past subjunctive (see instances in Ben Jonson's *Grammar*).

There are various assessments of Donne's meaning in this detached meditation, some comparing it with an earlier poem, *The Extasie*. J. Stampfer in *John Donne and the Metaphysical Gesture* regards the poem as 'a vision of radical innocence' in which 'the world of ideas and the natural world overlap' (p 136–8). *Some lovely glorious nothing* (6) symbolizes the general feeling of romantic love. But Donne paid his inamorata a compliment that he would not have appear jejune or effusive. The woman, idealized from experience with other women, has been met, and the new love is therefore claimed as a recognition, sparked off by her voice or the fleshly desire her beauty engenders. Donne wants to give substance to the still nebulous, and recalls Thomas Aquinas's neo-Platonic doctrine in *Summa Theologica* (1 li 2) in which angels, though spirits and therefore ethereal, appear to men in perceptible shape, to communicate some important message.

The first octave is more difficult. Donne expounds the idea, expressed in other poems, that the soul takes on *limmes of flesh* (8). Love, conceived as the bodiless child of the soul, should not (he says) be more subtle than the parent, and so should not exist as spirit only. Indeed, the spirit of love should itself assume a body, and the form he naturally envisages is the body of his mistress.

Having given love a physical similitude, Donne likens it to a ship, ballasted with praise, a moderate load of which would make the ship move steadily. But admiration overdone brings the pinnace (a light craft) to the verge of sinking. The suggestion in the second sestet is that dotage upon physical features is futile in the progress of love. The octave argues that true love is a middle way, between the extremes of negation (the denial of the self), and fruitless adoration.

In the Ptolemaic system of the universe, popular until the seventeenth century, each of the nine concentric spheres revolving round the earth was supposed to have an angelic intelligence watching over it. To this belief Donne refers in *So thy love may be my loves spheare* (25). His mistress's return of love is visualized as the sphere to which his own passion is the controlling angel. The concluding lines (26–8) maintain that man's love bears the same relationship to woman's, as the angel does to air; in short, it is the pure form impressed upon the element of which it is composed.

To arrive at this implausible interpretation, certain assumptions are necessary: the ambiguous pronoun *it* in line 24 must refer to *Angell* (23); and the reader has to accept that Donne's angels, as incorporeal beings, are without sex; for the view of Aquinas was that angels were of the male sex. Donne shared the Elizabethan conviction that a man's love was 'purer' (i.e. of greater fidelity) than a woman's.

The germinal conceits of lines 7 and 15–18, the many generative analogies, and the ironic wit of the conclusion, all make *Aire and Angels* a 'metaphysical' composition. The intricate scholastic theology is by no means transparent; but the difficulties are largely academic: the impalpability of Thomist angels, and the degrees of purity which different densities of air may attain.

A Nocturnall upon S. Lucies Day, being the shortest day

'Tís the yeáres mídníght, | and it ìs the dáyes,
Lucies, | who scarce seaven houres herself unmaskes,
 The Sunne is spent, and now his flasks
 Send forth light squibs, | no constant rayes;
  The world's whole sap is sunke: 5
The generall balme th'hydroptique earth hath drunk,
Whither, | as to the beds-feet, | life is shrunke,
Dead and enterr'd; | yet all these seeme to laugh,
Compar'd with mee, | who am their Epitaph.

Study me then, | you who shall lovers bee   10
At the next world, | that is, | at the next Spring:
 For I am every dead thing,
 In whom love wrought new Alchimie.
  For his art did expresse
A quíntessénce éven from nóthingnèsse,   15
From dull privations, | and leane emptinesse:
He ruin'd mee, | and I am re-begot
Of absence, | darknesse, | death; | things which are not.

All others, | from all things, | draw all that's good,
Life, | soule, | forme, | spirit, | whence they beeing have; 20
 I, | by loves limbecke, | am the grave

Of all, that's nothing. | Oft a flood
  Have wee two wept, | and so
Drownd the whole world, | us two; | oft did we grow
To be two Chaosses, | when we did show   25
Care to ought else; | and often absences
Withdrew our soules, | and made us carcasses.

But I am by her death, | (which word wrongs her)
Of the first nothing, the Elixer grown;
  Were I a man, | that I were one,   30
  I needs must know; | I should preferre,
    If I were any beast,
Some ends, | some means; | Yea plants, | yea stones detest,
And love; | All, | all some properties invest;
If I an ordinary nothing were,   35
As shádow, | 'a líght, and bódy múst be hére.

But I am None; | nor will my Sunne renew.
You lovers, | for whose sake, the lesser Sunne
  At this time to the Goat is runne
  To fetch new lust, | and give it you,   40
    Enjoy your summer all;
Since shee enjoyes her long nights festivall,
Let mee prepare towards her, | and let mee call
This houre her Vigill, | and her Eve, | since this
Both the yeares, | and the dayes deep midnight is.   45

The nine-line stanza, rhyming a b[10] b a[8] c[6] c c d d[10], has octo-syllabic third and fourth lines, and a trimeter as the fifth. The six remaining lines are iambic pentameters, the last four in couplets. Donne's metrical skill is shown in the pause manipulation and enjambement, the latter occurring ten times. The word *every* (12) is trisyllabic. In line 36 the 1633 edition has no mark of elision after *shadow,* where a metrical pause makes the coalescence of vowels awkward. The manuscript from which the poem was printed un-fortunately omitted stops at the end of lines, thereby increasing the difficulty of interpretation.

The lady celebrated in this seasonal poem is generally con-sidered to be the Countess of Bedford, whose Christian name was Lucy. According to the old Julian calendar, St Lucy's festival fell on December 13, regarded as the shortest day of the year, when the sun entered the zodiac sign of Capricorn. In line 28 there is evidence of Donne's affectionate feelings for a lady who is dead. Lady Bedford had a serious illness in 1612, but recovered.

Some two dozen images, unromantic but sympathetic, communicate the poet's ambiguous mood of despair, the dominant note being one of melancholy extinction. Few poems convey the pervading sense of depression and silence more movingly. In his second Prebend Sermon at St Paul's, 29 January 1625, Donne wrote:

> God hath accompanied, and complicated almost all our bodily diseases of these times, with an extraordinary sadnesse, a predominant melancholy, a faintnesse of heart, a chearlesnesse, a joyelesnesse of spirit.
>
> (*Sermons* VII 1 68–9)

To approach this poem through its figurative language is to deepen one's understanding of the role of metaphysical conceit, particularly through the co-operation of tropes with schemes of thought, those which distinguish and compare. Peter Ramus's logic had given an impetus to this Renaissance development; while Aristotle long before had recommended the efficacy of originality and surprise in metaphor. Donne's art was to extend metaphor to its limits by invoking paradox, analogy and other distinctions. The metaphors used in *A Nocturnall* are especially elaborate in their logic; it seems that the Great Chain of Being and the theory of correspondences fascinated Donne, and that his judgement was constantly exercised to restrain the excesses of wit and fancy.

The poet pictures himself as a microcosm of the world, both natural and divine. The planetary and terrestrial influences upon the 'humours' of man were among the principal reasons for philosophical instruction in astrology and natural history. Donne's avocation was to find some order in the universe, under God, and to enquire into the role of memory in man's imaginative and spiritual life.

The poem begins in a mood of emotional and mental inertia. At the winter solstice the day *unmaskes* itself for scarcely 'seaven houres' (line 2); the choice of verb strikes an immediate dramatic note. *The Sunne* (3), source of life's vitality, has been weak; now at midnight his *flasks* ('powder-horns'), i.e. the stars, emit but a feeble light. The word *squibs* (4) recalls the innocuous charges used in the training of recruits. *The world's whole sap is sunke* (5) implies that its energy is at a low ebb, the image being that of a tree dormant in 'a drear-nighted' December. *Th'hydroptique earth* (6) is a powerful image for aridity; the epithet means 'one suffering from an insatiable thirst'. Donne erroneously coined this adjective, from Greek *hudropikos*; an unaspirated form *ydropike* (mod. *hydropic*) had been in English use since the fourteenth century, and was employed by Caxton and Lydgate. The metaphor *balme* (O. French *basme*, Lat. *balsamum*) in the same line symbolizes the resin or aromatic sap of the tree that the dry earth absorbed. Mixed with oil this resin formed an ointment used medicinally by the ancients, who also valued it in embalming. Paracelsus believed that a balm preserved the 'vital essence'. Donne, with a touch of ironic actuality, protracts the image. A mummy-like corpse is depicted upon a bed, shrunk to macabre proportions (7–8). Though sun, earth and life are exhausted, there is yet room for hyperbolic laughter (8); the poet sees himself as the ultimate nothingness, an *Epitaph* (9) of the person that has passed away.

In the second stanza *Spring* (11), as another world for lovers, is a conventional image (10–11). Grierson interprets *every dead thing* (12) as 'the quintessence of all negations' (*Poems,* II, p 37). Donne, in the next line, has the masculine image of *love* as *new Alchimie,* whose miracle is to *express* (i.e. 'extract') from him the quintessence of less than nothingness. *Quintessence* (15) was originally the fifth element, *aether,* from which heavenly bodies were made. The alchemist's task was to distil this essence, supposedly latent in all matter. Donne used *elixir* and *quintessence* in the same sense, and stressed the latter word on the first and last syllables, as was usual in his time. There is a nice distinction between *dull privations* and *leane emptinesse* in line 16. *Absence, darknesse, death* (18) are subsumed in the verb *ruin'd* (17), a state preliminary to re-birth. With the logic of an Erasmus, Donne introduces paradox into the second stanza, as he associates alchemy with theology.

Stanza three opens characteristically with the schematic use of *ploce*; the metrically resonant adjective of totality *All* (19) recurs four other times in *A Nocturnall*. Donne uses alchemy to make significant distinctions and comparisons. Everyone but himself enjoys good from the universe; unfortunately love's *limbecke* (a shortened form of *alembic,* 'retort') made him the cemetery of all that is non-existent. In lines 22–7 retrospective glances are cast at the Petrarchan love of earlier days, with its hackneyed *flood* of tears that hyperbolically *Drownd the whole world* (24); when lovers took thought of things other than themselves, their state resembled *chaos* (the raw material of the universe, before God imprinted form upon it). Absence meant loss of soul, and therefore virtual death (25–7). The imagery here is drawn from the Book of Genesis.

The supernatural imagery continues in stanza four, with line 29, *Of the first nothing, the Elixer grown*. *Elixer* has here the figurative meaning of 'quintessence', 'soul', 'secret principle'. The OED has no example of the word with this significance before Chillingworth's, in *The Religion of Protestants* (1638). This Arabic term came to English from medieval Latin, through Roger Bacon in the thirteenth century, signifying an essence that could prolong life indefinitely. But the original meaning was the hypothetical substance that could convert other metals to gold. The sense of the 'philosopher's stone' first appears in Chaucer's *Canterbury Tales* (The Canon's Yeoman's Prologue and Tale, line 310).

Through the death of the woman he loves, the poet has become the quintessence of the *first nothing* (chaos) from which God created the world. The scholastic doctrine of the soul, borrowed from Aristotle, lies behind lines 31–4: as explained in Chapter II (*Metempsychosis*), this maintained that man has a rational soul, the beasts a perceptive one, enabling them to adjust means to ends; plants and stones have the power only to choose what they need, and reject what they dislike. In the *vita nuova*, Donne would choose the lot of an animal, which knows what it wants and enjoys the means of securing it. *Invest* (34) means 'inherit'; whatever his destiny, Donne says, every created thing has properties; even a shadow, the extreme form of nothingness, implies light and a body, which he now lacks.

This image leads into the final stanza, the threnody ending on the same note as its beginning. *My Sunne* (37) is the lady, whose spirit outshines (though no longer for Donne) the sun of nature. *Her long nights festivall* (42) may be interpreted as the lady's 'long sleep of death'. *Let mee prepare towards her* (43) is the poet's express desire to participate in his saint's feast, and the blessing of her resurrection. In *her Vigill* (44), *her* is not possessive, but a dative of advantage, because Donne proposes to watch on the eve of her festival. There is more than a suggestion that Donne had been reading St Paul, 1 Corinthians, xv 13, *et seq*.

Such a reading would explain the enigmatic parenthesis (*which word wrongs her*) in line 28, after the word *death*. In style and content *A Nocturnall* belongs to the period of Donne's poetic maturity. Nothing would, therefore, be more unlikely than Doniphan Louthan's contention that the word *death* is allegorical; thatDonne had been in love with Lucy Harrington; and that the poem is an expression of grief, written in 1594, on the eve of her marriage to Edward Russell, Earl of Bedford (*The Poetry of John Donne,* pp 144–8).

To appreciate a poem as subjective as *A Nocturnall,* one has to sense the dual intention of Donne's language. The midnight of the year he celebrates is a turning-point in the poet's life; he looks back to the past and forward to the future, two worlds in ironic contrast, linked by memory. The past images organic growth in a world of primitive physical love; the future envisages spiritual fulfilment through self-abnegation. The experience of organic love (Donne holds) any man can try for himself in the springtime of life; inevitably, it enlarges the ego, only to end in deflation. To the secular world, re-birth seems as grotesque as the alchemical dream of distilling the elixir of life; but the soul is capable of the higher plane of love, the one that Dante contemplates in the *Paradiso.* Catholic theologians, of a mystical turn of mind, believed that the extinction of personality was a necessary preliminary to spiritual resurrection; they shared the unhappy Mary Stuart's credo: '*En ma fin est mon commencement.*'

Two other questions call for explanation: 'In what way is the irony of Donne made manifest?' and 'In what sense is the poem baroque or grotesque?' There is *selbst Ironie* in the contrast of initial apathy and altered feeling, that the poet must have arrived at before he wrote the poem. Obscurely, he conveys the impression that he was an advocate of both worlds. Grotesqueness is suggested in his metaphorical leaps from one world to another, from one science to another, and from one condition of humanity to another, and in his fusion of successive states of feeling with logical explanation. The cosmic scope of analogies in *A Nocturnall* is in stark antithesis to the detailed observation of mundane nature and its laws. Out of a medley of discrete reflections, Donne achieves an artistic unity that outweighs the poem's occasional contradictions.

Sportive or solemn, Donne is an ironist whose querulous intelligence is as often misunderstood as Shakespeare's in that obscure obsequy, *The Phoenix and the Turtle*. The *Sonnets* of Shakespeare reveal an artist sceptical of his ability to evaluate his own emotions. Metaphysical poetry may, indeed, be the secretion of a sensitive intellectual, usually of Catholic upbringing, who cultivates an intuitive doubt of the reasoning to which, as a humanist, he is committed. Donne's tortured mind found some balance in witty self-castigation, which was not unrelated to his taste for paradox and conceits.

Variety of stanza form, and skill in modulation, are prosodic evidence of Donne's virtuosity in the *Songs and Sonets,* though not the principal reason for their acceptance among discriminating readers. Pierre Legouis in *Donne the Craftsman* (1962) supposes that 'Donne tried to revert to a freedom . . . English poetry had lost for less than twenty years' (p. 12); and he points to such precedents as Spenser's *August* in *The Shepheardes Calender* (1579) and Donnes's own *Satyres*.

    There is little evidence in the *Songs and Sonets* of conscious re-action to a metrical tradition; nevertheless, Donne was an experimenter. In the 49 stanzaic poems, he employs 46 different stanza forms, 44 of them unique, in the sense that they occur once only. So far as is known, a mere four of the stanza forms had been attempted before Donne used them (see Legouis, p 23). Non-stanzaic poems are only four in number: *The Token, The Apparition, Womans Constancy* and *The Dissolution*. The stanzaic poems have limits of from four to fourteen lines, but the five-line stanza was not attempted until the *Hymne to God my God, in my sicknesse*. Although the prevailing measure is the iambic pentameter, syllables in the line vary from two to fourteen, which is an exceptional range for any Elizabethan or Jacobean poet. Donne's individuality is shown by the unwillingness of later poets to use more than three of his stanza forms.

    The full extent of Donne's originality can only be appreciated when the rhyme-schemes are examined. Though he is adept at the couplet, he rhymes consecutively for three or four lines in such poems as *The Anniversarie*. In the quatrain, both the crossed and enclosed system of rhyming (a b a b) and (a b b a) are favoured. The ear has never long to wait for the return of sound; but Donne seldom practises internal rhyme, being content with effects of assonance.

Mostly in the rhyme-schemes does Donne depart from the Renaissance tradition of Puttenham in *The Arte of English Poesie* (1589). He prefers collocations of rhyme that can be readily manipulated to the thought in the opening stanza, though occasionally the model is established in a second or third line-grouping. No matter how long the stanza, the pattern is minutely repeated on more than forty occasions. He adopts few stanzas that are organic wholes, like Spenser's, a notable exception being the pentameter quatrain, with alternate rhymes, used by Gray in the *Elegy written in a Country Churchyard.* This habit contributes to the rugged segmentation of Donne's verse sentences. Between the medial pauses, he seems to employ fewer syllables than most poets, a possible explanation being that his thinking is analytic rather than synthetic.

Legouis is probably alone in regarding Donne's non-stanzaic poems in the *Songs and Sonets* as his most original contributions to English prosody; he quotes *The Apparition,* a poem of seventeen lines, as strong in the economy of its words. *The Dissolution* (24 lines) he describes as 'perhaps the most characteristic specimen of English free verse in a very short compass (pp 28-9). Here is Helen Gardner's text of the poem:

<pre>
Shee 'is dead; | And all which die
To their first Elements resolve;
And wee were mutuall Elements to us
      And made of one another.
My body then doth hers involve,   5
And those things | whereof I consist, | hereby
In me abundant grow, | and burdenous,
      And nourish not, | but smother.
My fire of Passion, | sighes of ayre,
Water of teares, | and earthly sad despaire,   10
      Which my materialls bee,
But neere worne out by loves securitie,
Shee, | to my losse, | doth by her death repaire,
      And I might live long wretched so
But that my fire doth with my fuell grow.   15
      Now as those Active Kings
Whose foraine conquest treasure brings,
Receive more, | and spend more, | and soonest breake:
This | (which I am amaz'd that I can speake)
</pre>

This death, | hath with my store   20
  My use encreas'd.
And so my soule more earnestly releas'd,
Will outstrip hers; | As bullets flown before
A latter bullet may o'rtake, | the pouder being more.

The criteria of free verse are (a) that it eschews regularity of stress for natural speech with a fluid rhythm, linking line to line without the bondage of rhyme; and (b) that it avoids conformable line length, or metred pattern which scans in repetitive feet. *The Dissolution* (or any other of Donne's non-stanzaic poems) does not qualify as free verse, merely because of variation in length of line (4 to 14 syllables). The pattern of the poem is: a^6 b^8 c^{10} d^7 b^8 ac^{10} d^7 e^8 e^{10} f^6 fe^{10} g^8 g^{10} h^6 h^8 ii^{10} j^6 k^4 kj^{10} j^{14}. The iambic measure is modulated by conventional trochaic inversion. Though eleven of the rhymes are at the fourth and fifth distance (which is unusual for Donne), this, too, does not make the verse free. So self-contained are the lines that only three (1, 6 and 20) are syntactically enjambed. The rhythm is melodious, with such graceful use of internal pause that *The Dissolution* can be safely classed as a traditional lyric.

Donne's individuality has deeper roots than the metrical. Rhythms invariably take the mould of the thought, and the ideas are the offspring of the passions that occasion them. The initial outburst of feeling is arresting, and provides an impetus to the dialectics. Donne's only break with the tradition was the decision to banish poetical ornament, and to enlarge the idea by figurative analogy. Petrarch, the poet against whose plaints he reacted, taught him the use of hyperbole to heighten an emotion. The appeal of Donne's wit is simultaneously to mind and heart. The rhetoric tends to be conservative. Donne's originality was in structuring the verse to the matter in hand, and emulating the tones of a speaking voice. Impact is made upon the reader before the sense is grasped.

The scholastic ingenuity of *The Extasie* has too often been regarded as a test of Donne's disingenuousness in the kind of dramatic monologue he invented. This poem of 76 lines (too long to quote here) Donne himself described in line 74 as 'a dialogue of one'; it is a stylized narrative in crossed rhyme, the scene being set in the first twelve lines. *The Extasie* has been mistakenly discussed

as an expression of Donne's views on sexual morality, as a plea for
seduction, and as a piece of specious rationalizing. Helen Gardner
answered such misapprehensions in an article 'The Argument
about "The Ecstasy"' in *Elizabethan and Jacobean Studies Presented
to F.P. Wilson,* pp 279–306.

Donne's aim was to debate the interdependence of body and
soul in mutual love, a theme that was aired in three dialogues by
the Italian writer, Leone Ebreo, entitled *Dialoghi d'Amore,* published in 1535. Donne seems, from borrowed phrases and thoughts,
to have seized the opportunity simultaneously of answering Lord
Bembo's Platonic casuistry in the last twenty pages of Castiglione's
The Courtier, translated by Sir Thomas Hoby in 1561; for example in
lines 23, 41–4, 59 and 63–4 of *The Extasie.* In this poem Donne
refers to the mystical state of trance. In neo-Platonic philosophy,
ecstasy is a state of mind in which the soul escapes from the body
and communicates directly with God. Plotinus in the sixth *Ennead*
described the state as 'an abandonment of self, a perfect quietude'.
This condition, the source of the Greek word *enthusiasm,* provides
man's spirit with new insights. Spirit, which is expressed from the
blood and heart, is the instrument by which the soul influences
man's actions. In Donne's thinking, the main function of the soul
is perception; that of the body, sense; and the souls of two persons
can be united only through their bodily senses. When the soul
leaves the body, the latter is temporarily dead to all sensation,
until the soul returns from contemplation.

On a secular plane there are several ways the state of oversoul
may be achieved. Leone Ebreo, Bembo and Donne hold that, for
lovers of single mind, the soul is liberated from the body by the
faculty of sight; hence the extravagant conceit of lines 7/8: 'Our
eye-beames *twisted* (i.e. intertwined), and did thred/ Our eyes, upon
one double string.' Love refined into a perfect essence is even
accommodated with 'soules language' (22), by which ecstatic
spirits communicate. Bembo and Donne maintained that union of
souls could be achieved through physical contacts, such as a kiss;
cf the first line of Donne's letter *To Sir Henry Wotton*: 'Sir, more
than kisses, letters mingle Soules.'

Lines 13–17 explain the oversoul as souls knit together, hence
single, but hanging over the 'sepulchral' bodies of the lovers like
uncertain victory. 'Because both meant, and spake the same' (25)
expresses the lovers' singleness of purpose. Ecstasy *unperplexes*

(i.e. unravels) the strands that bind body and soul (29). Donne tells us that, though the lovers were groping towards some unrealized union, sex was not the motive of their love: 'we saw not what did *move*' (32). Every individual soul contains a mixture of qualities, but lacks self-knowledge, until initiated. 'That abler soule' (43), which rectifies loneliness, is the product of transplanting or cross-pollenization; *interinanimate* is the appropriate verb (42).

'Why do we put up with our bodies?' Donne asks in line 50, a turning point in the poem. Rational souls (*intelligences*) are the guardian angels; bodies are merely the spheres in which they operate. We should be grateful for bodies, because they give us information about ourselves. The soul, indeed, perceives through the bodily faculties and senses; thus the body is a necessary *alloy* (56, Donne's word is *allay*) of the soul, which is our immortal part. Heaven's imprint on the *aether* (air beneath the moon), of which man is made, enables one soul to mingle with another; but visible man takes the form of a particular body (57–60).

'Our blood labours to beget/ Spirits, as like soules as it can' (61–2). Donne here means that the 'humors' (the elements mixed in man) rise upward by throwing off their material dross. 'That *subtile knot* which makes us man' (64) is a mingling of physical and spiritual things. Love must descend to the meeting-point of body and soul (the lower and the higher self), otherwise the soul cannot use its faculties (68): 'Else a great Prince in prison lies.' In lovers' relationships, Donne concludes, the angelic state cannot be forever maintained; true lovers, whose souls are spiritually united, in fact show little change when they descend to the physical plane.

Donne seems to have been the first writer to use the word *sex* (31) in a sense close to 'carnal knowledge' or 'intercourse'; cf a similar significance in *The Primrose* (16), which is the first instance recorded in the OED. *The Extasie* is intriguing to modern readers, who read Empsonian ambiguities into key words and phrases. With the Italian dialogues at hand, few statements are capable of equivocal interpretation; nevertheless, neither Leone Ebreo's work nor *The Courtier* has the same kind of subtlety.

It must not be supposed that Donne used philosophical or theological terms with consistency in his poetry, or that he was always of the same mind. From the *Sermons,* it is hard to determine what Donne's religious convictions actually were, and one should not expect in the *Songs and Sonets* an inflexible attitude to love. There was in Donne a strange mingling of passionate idealism and physical passion; and the latter should not be regarded as the dross in the alloy. What is constant is a certain whimsical unworldliness; perhaps the earlier cynical wit was a private courtier bravado.

CHAPTER IV

Anniversaries, Epicedes, Obsequies and Epithalamia

🔲🔲🔲🔲🔲🔲

DONNE, the courtier, has not received the attention requisite to a proper understanding of his literary personality. On 28 July 1614, he wrote to his brother-in-law, Sir Robert More:

> I must confess my weakness in this behalf; no man attends court fortunes with more impatience than I do. . . . I will not contribute so much to mine own ill-fortune, nor join with her in a treason against myself, so much as to be absent now, when my absence may give perchance occasion, perchance excuse to others of slackness in my business; therefore I have neglected my pleasure, and the little circumstance of my health (for in good faith, my life itself is no great circumstance to me), which I intended by going into the country. (Gosse, *Life and Letters,* II, p 46–7)

In his forty-second year, Donne was still hoping for preferment at the court of James I. The King, as a writer himself, expected unusual deference from poets whom he favoured, though Donne was not yet one. Among the aristocrats from whom Donne expected the promotion of his career were Sir Robert Drury, a wealthy Suffolk land-owner, and Robert Carr, Earl of Somerset. The poet, in straitened circumstances, had been under obligation to Drury for the hospitality of his London house, part of which Donne rented from 1610, the year in which he dedicated *Pseudo-Martyr* to the King, having previously taken the oath of allegiance.

For both Drury and Somerset, Donne wrote occasional poems, celebrating important events, such as a death or a wedding. It was customary for distinguished courtiers to command or request such compositions; and Donne, as a suitor for Court preferment, was constrained to respond in poems of suitable tone and language, for which there was a Tudor convention of figurative speech, as well as of assumed humility.

The *Anniversaries* of 1611 and 1612 were written, at Sir Robert Drury's instigation, to commemorate his daughter Elizabeth; they were the only poems of Donne published with his consent during his life-time, and there were four editions. For generations they were esteemed his most dignified, if not most popular, work; they were quoted by Webster and emulated by Drummond of Hawthornden and Dryden. An extraordinary circumstance was that Donne had never met Elizabeth Drury, when she died in December 1610, two months before her fifteenth birthday. Donne's confession, upon the censure of his book, is significant: 'It became me to say, not what I was sure was just truth, but the best that I could conceive' (Letter *To Sir G.F.*, from Paris, April 1612; Gosse, 1, p 306). At the time of this letter Donne was travelling with the Drurys on the Continent (November 1611–September 1612), which shows that he was more than a tenant of an annexe in Drury Lane. R. C. Bald discovered that Donne's sister, Anne, lived in the Drury household from 1598 to 1603; and it seems likely that Donne was first commissioned by Sir Robert to publish *To the Praise of the Dead, An Anatomie of the World* and *A Funerall Elegie* in 1611. *Of the Progres of the Soule* was begun at Amiens on Drury's French tour, and published in 1612, along with the earlier tributes, under the comprehensive title *The First and Second Anniversaries*. In the Catholic Church an 'anniversary' was the annual commemoration of the death of a saint.

The 1611 edition of *An Anatomie of the World* and its satellites was not entered in the Stationers' Register; it contains only 26 pages, of which *An Anatomie* occupies 19. In the 1612 edition (49 pages) the *Second Anniversarie* has a separate title page, and a prefatory poem of 42 lines, entitled *The Harbinger to the Progres* (which Ben Jonson attributed to Joseph Hall). Further editions of the *Anniversaries* were published in 1621 and 1625, the latter omitting the marginal notes. Grierson used the edition of 1633 (based on that of 1625) as the substantive text; it has the dubious merit of up-to-date spelling and punctuation; but F. Manley, for his text of the *Anniversaries* (Johns Hopkins Press, 1963) chose the first edition of each poem. There are no surviving manuscripts, except in the case of the *Funerall Elegie* (Bodleian Library), which is a copy of the 1621 edition. The *Funerall Elegie* was almost certainly the first poem to be written in the series, although it appears last in the edition of 1611, which was printed for Samuel Macham by an unspecified printer. Manley's edition is quoted in the pages that follow, because Grierson's is obviously a derived text.

The *Anniversaries* remain the most elusive of Donne's compositions; a common theme is the loss of the World-Soul. Stoicism and scepticism are at war in *An Anatomie of the World,* and the Phoenix of line 217 is introduced for the morally serious purpose of denouncing man's conceit in his superiority, and his neglect of human relationships.

The source of this disturbing homily is Montaigne's *Apologie for Raymond Sebund,* and there was a discursive precedent, of different mood, in Sir John Davies's *Nosce Teipsum.* Donne's paradoxes in the first of the *Anniversaries* are alarums of social disorder, not unlike those of St Augustine and the biblical prophets. Unless these poems are studied within the convention to which they belong, the images appear overdrawn, and the praise unnatural. The poems are not elegies or domestic hagiographies, but planned contemplations of ideal womanhood, not unlike Petrarch's *To Laura in Death.* They belong to the same period and temper as the *Essayes in Divinity.*

For Donne was now dedicated to the cause of religion, and deep in Ignatian spiritual exercises, to test his own worthiness for election to the ministry. The *Anniversaries* may be regarded as spiritual links between the religious reflections of the verse letters and the *Divine Poems*; and they are patterned on Ignatius Loyola's weekly meditations, as Louis Martz has shown in *The Poetry of Meditation* (pp 219–48). The Dominican order propounded five mysteries of the rosary, which suggest an analogy between Elizabeth Drury and the Virgin Mary. Martz believes that the *Anniversaries* 'represent Donne's most elaborate examples of the art of sacred parody and his most extensive efforts in the art of poetical meditation' (p 220).

Secular criticism of poetry in which there is a recurring sequence of religious meditation, eulogy and moralizing, is seldom pertinent to Donne's didactic aim; for such criticism concentrates on the incongruity of the images, and the irrelevance of some ideas to the general theme of man's degradation. If *An Anatomie of the World* (a poem of 474 lines) falls between the stools of incredible praise and prosaic moralizing, *Of the Progres of the Soule* (528 lines) is organic and less addicted to Petrarchan extravagance. Donne brought the poems together to demonstrate symbolically a dualism he consistently maintained – that the death of the body is a blessing, since it implies a release of the soul. But his talent for concentrated dramatic argument was not viable for expansive discourses, especially in rhymed couplets.

The critical problem in epideictic verse is the attitude of the poet to his subject. Classical theorists, such as Aristotle and Quintilian, made sincerity of praise a rhetorical issue, calling for judgement and evidence as qualifications in the praiser. Donne is not properly in this classical tradition; he flouts the decorum of oratory in a way of which he was fully conscious. In a similar sense he is outside the tradition of pastoral elegy, typified by Milton in *Lycidas,* which calls for typological tropes and conceits, indicating that grief-stricken loss and cosmic disturbance are conventions to be assumed. Donne had no genuine sorrow to lament in *An Anatomie,* but required the reader to accept the death of an immature girl as the source of moribund virtue in mankind.

The sacrifice of bliss, perpetuated in Eden, is an analogue of the body's decay; the ascent of the virtuous spirit, through grace, is the consolation in heaven of *The Progres of the Soule.* Elizabeth Drury's death is not simply a springboard for the *contemptus mundi* that was axiomatic to a Christian Platonist. When Donne addressed compliments to women, he invariably invoked theological learning to represent them as mystical or supernatural symbols. Hence the observation of William Empson on the *First Anniversarie*: 'The only way to make the poem sensible is to accept Elizabeth Drury as the Logos' (*Some Versions of Pastoral,* p 73). In this view Empson is not mistaken. Elizabeth Drury is a young virgin, symbolized as perfect, because created in the image of God. As the Epicedes and Obsequies show, by 1610 Donne was in a frame of mind to regard the death of any woman of immaculate reputation as a call for the regeneration of his own soul. All the poetry of praise of this intro-spective period is in pentameter couplets, used by Donne con-sistently for meditations. Despite their unusual conceits, the *Anniversaries* contain some of the poet's most moving and com-passionate writing.

An Anatomie of the World

And now the Springs and Sommers which we see,   203
Like sonnes of women after fifty bee.

And new Philosophy cals all in doubt,   205
The Element of fire is quite put out;
The Sunne is lost, and th'earth, and no mans wit
Can well direct him, where to looke for it.
And freely men confesse, that this world's spent,
When in the Planets, and the Firmament   210
They seeke so many new; they see that this
Is crumbled out againe to his Atomis.
'Tis all in pieces, all cohaerence gone;
All iust supply, and all Relation:
Prince, Subiect, Father, Sonne, are things forgot,   215
For every man alone thinkes he hath got
To be a Phoenix, and that there can bee
None of that Kinde, of which he is, but hee.

                         *   *   *

Shee by whose lines proportion should bee
Examin'd, measure of all Symmetree,   310
Whom had that Ancient seen, who thought soules made
Of Harmony, he would at next have said
That Harmony was shee, and thence infer,
That soules were but Resultances from her,
And did from her into our bodies go,   315
As to our eyes, the formes from obiects flow:

                         *   *   *

Shee, after whom, what forme soe're we see,   323
Is discord, and rude incongruitee,
Shee, shee is dead, she's dead; when thou knowst this,   325
Thou knowst how ugly a monster this world is:
And learnst thus much by our Anatomee,
That here is nothing to enamor thee:

                         *   *   *

Perchance the world might have recovered,
If she whom we lament had not beene dead: 360
But shee, in whom all white, and redde, and blue
(Beauties ingredients) voluntary grew,
As in an unvext Paradise; from whom
Did all things verdure, and their lustre come,
Whose composition was miraculous,   365

Being all color, all Diaphanous,
(For Ayre, and Fire but thicke grosse bodies were,
And liveliest stones but drowsie, and pale to her,)
Shee, shee is dead; shee's dead: when thou knowst this,
Thou knowst how wan a Ghost this our world is: 370

* * *

Vouchsafe to call to minde, that God did make   461
A last, and lastingst peece, a song. He spake
To *Moses*, to deliver unto all,
That song: because he knew they would let fall,
The Law, the Prophets, and the History,   465
But keepe the song still in their memory.
Such an opinion (in due measure) made
Me this great Office boldly to invade.
Nor could incomprehensiblenesse deterre
Me, from thus trying to emprison her.   470
    (*lines 203–18, 309–16, 323–8, 359–70, 461–70*)

In the larger part of the *Anniversaries*, Donne's mind is pre-occupied with the 'idea' of perfection, in a neo-Platonic context; in this respect his treatment resembles that of Spenser in the *Four Hymns* and of Shakespeare in Hamlet's prose speech, 'What a piece of work is man' (ɪɪ ii). The idealizations of Ficino and Pico della Mirandola are similarly realized in Botticelli's *Primavera* and Donatello's *David*. Donne's poems invariably have an admixture of realism; in *An Anatomie* the secular humanism of the universal man is contrasted with its Christian counterpart, embodied in the song of praise to Elizabeth Drury. Donne's lack of personal acquaintance with his subject was no aesthetic handicap. He met his wife at about the same age as Elizabeth, and she had blessed him with a selfless devotion close to martyrdom. He therefore understood, and the Bible confirmed, the regenerative influence of a pious woman in a muddled world. The 'ponderous redundancy' that Mario Praz finds in *An Anatomie of the World* (see *The Flaming Heart,* p 201) is symptomatic of an antipathy to this kind of poetry.

Donne's exordium to *An Anatomie* (1–6) harbours a thought from St Augustine's *De Trinitate* – that no man *knows* he has a soul, until it prompts him to pursue virtue, and praise it through his works. This was a favourite text among Christian Platonists, among whom a happy soul was the symbol of God's grace to man, to compensate for the loss of Paradise. To this Eden man seeks to return, through dedication to the *Logos* (divine principle, or 'Angelic Mind' of Pico and Ficino). Contemplation of the divine liberates the soul from its corporeal frame, and illumination through the *Logos* endows man with supreme wisdom.

In the Ignatian scheme of Louis L. Martz (*The Poetry of Meditation*, pp 222–3) lines 203–18 are in the form of a dissection or meditation, which satirizes the aberrations of the rational soul, e.g. in Astronomy, the *new Philosophy* of line 205. There is a relevant observation in Donne's Sermon at the burial of Sir William Cokayne, 12 December 1626:

> Young men mend not their sight by using old men's spectacles; and yet we look upon nature but with Aristotle's spectacles, and upon the body of man, but with Galen's, and upon the frame of the world, but with Ptolemy's spectacles. Almost all knowledge is rather like a child that is embalmed to make mummy, than that is nursed to make a man . . . If there be any addition to knowledge it is rather a new knowledge, than a greater knowledge; rather a singularity in a desire of proposing something that was not known at all before, than an improving, an advancing, a multiplying of former inceptions; and by that means, no knowledge comes to be perfect. (VII x 260)

Donne is disillusioned, not by the Copernican cosmology, but by pride in scientific knowledge, which the poet mocks in its own jargon. The structure of the universe, as explained by Galileo, is of such hubristic complexity that it defeats natural wisdom, which is God's gift to man. Bounds must be set to the arrogance of human reason, and the poet questions the world's progress, as advanced by the power of man's mind alone. While avid of new knowledge to improve the mind, Donne's conservatism clings steadfastly to a theocentric universe. The world is manifestly in ruinous disorder, and he is just as sceptical of progress in medical science:

> There is no health; Physitians say that we   91
> At best, enioy, but a neutralitee.
> And can there be worse sickenesse, then to know
> That we are never well, nor can be so?
> We are borne ruinous: poore mothers crie,   95

That children come not right, nor orderly,
Except they headlong come, and fall upon
An ominous precipitation.
How witty's ruine? how importunate
Upon mankinde? It labour'd to frustrate   100
Even Gods purpose; and made woman, sent
For mans reliefe, cause of his languishment.

(An Anatomie of the World, lines 91–102)

This is characteristic Renaissance pessimism, prompted by Psalm
38, 1–3. The belief was general that childbirth is ominous, when
the infant is not delivered head first. The last two lines revert to
the lyrical theme of eulogy. Woman is not simply man's helpmeet,
but the exemplar of Augustinian piety and love. The *shee,* with
doubled vowel, specially emphasized, is not *any* woman of comparable virtue, but God's idea of a perfect soul (Genesis i 26), with
untold capacity for influencing others.

The symbolic intention of references to Elizabeth Drury as a
'rich soule' in the eulogistic sections of *An Anatomie* lies in the
thought, rather than the expression, the aim being to supply a
suitable example, whereby the reader may arrive at a just interpretation of the effect of grace upon individuals. In Donne's
treatment the reader needs, however, to be acquainted with the
theological background, as well as the difference between Protestant and Catholic points of view. Symbolism and allegory
(which Donne's work is not) are more important for some parts of
the Bible than others, for instance Genesis, St Paul's Epistles and
Revelation – scriptures which Protestant thinkers took more
literally than Catholics. In such books figurative language contributes much to spiritual significance, and their impact on Donne's
style, not only in the *Devotions* and *Sermons,* was persuasive.

Protestantism held that the language of scripture possessed dual
significance: one literal and historical, which was paramount; the
other emblematic, requiring no privileged hermeneutist, but only
a pastor to explicate it for laymen. St Thomas Aquinas, on the
other hand, propounded a threefold significance of spiritual
exegesis: the allegorical (i.e. fictional), the moral and the anagogi-
cal (i.e. mystical, in a secondary spiritual sense). The last originated
with the Judaic Cabala, a body of rabbinical experts empowered to
interpret the divine mysteries of the Old Testament.

The literal sense of a text (which is also the grammatical) had priority with Protestants, even though it involved the use of figurative language. For Aquinas, metaphor, though valid, was a 'drawing aside' of the rational faculties. In his nineteenth *Devotion* ('Expostulation') Donne addressed the Deity as 'a *literall* God . . . that wouldest be understood *literally*, and according to the plaine sense of all that thou saiest. . . . Thou art a figurative, metaphoricall God too.' This passage confirms Protestant leanings at the time of the poem's composition (1611); for Donne, all personal history, including that of Elizabeth Drury, was as providential as the life of the patriarchs of the Old Testament.

Donne's *Anatomie* teems with elliptical allusions, which it is the task of annotation to gloss:

204 'Like sonnes of women *after fifty* bee.' An astute *meiosis*; for women of that age are normally past child-bearing. Offspring of a mother's late maturity were generally expected to be of small stature.

206 'The Element of fire is quite *put out*.' Fire was known to be the only element of the four that produced no life. Tycho and Kepler, by discrediting the Ptolemaic theory, exploded the doctrine of concentric elements, that fire surrounded the air, air surrounded the water, and water the earth. Donne anticipates by a decade Burton's *Anatomy of Melancholy* (1621), which reads:

> . . . there is no such element of fire at all. . . . those monstrous orbs of eccentrics . . . are absurd and ridiculous. For who is so mad to think that there should be so many circles, like subordinate wheels in a clock, all impenetrable and hard, as they feign, add and substract at their pleasure.
>
> (*The Anatomy of Melancholy*, II ii Mem. 3)

209–11 'And freely men confesse, that this world's spent,/ When in the Planets and the Firmament/ They seeke so many new.' Donne speaks of the 'plurality of worlds', which the writings of Copernicus, Kepler and Galileo propounded. Burton's account discloses contemporary interest in their discoveries:

> If the earth move, it is a planet, and shines to them in the moon, and to the other planetary inhabitants, as the moon and they do to us upon the earth: but shine she doth, as

Galileo, Kepler, and others prove, and then, *per consequens,*
the rest of the planets are inhabited, as well as the moon . . .
and those several planets have their several moons about
them, as the earth hath hers, as Galileo hath already evinced
by his glasses . . . Kepler, the emperor's mathematician,
confirms out of his experience that he saw as much by the
same help, and more about Mars, Venus; and the rest they
hope to find out, peradventure even amongst the fixed
stars . . . Then (I say) the earth and they be planets alike,
inhabited alike, moved about the sun, the common centre
of the world alike . . . If our world be small in respect, why
may we not suppose a plurality of worlds, those infinite
stars visible in the firmament to be so many suns, with
particular fixed centres; to have likewise their subordinate
planets, as the sun hath his dancing still round him? . . .
Why should not an infinite cause (as God is) produce
infinite effects? . . . But who shall dwell in these vast bodies,
earths, worlds, 'if they be inhabited? rational creatures?' as
Kepler demands, 'or have they souls to be saved? or do
they inhabit a better part of the world than we do?' . . .
Many new things are daily invented, to the public good; so
kingdoms, men, and knowledge ebb and flow, are hid and
revealed, and when you have all done, as the Preacher concluded, *Nihil est sub sole novum.* (ibid.)

217–18 To be a Phoenix, and that *there* can bee/ None of that
kinde, of which he is, but hee.' (The early editions have *then,*
Grierson's reading, but the errata slip prepared by Donne jus-
tifies *there.*) The long-lived Phoenix, a unique bird of Arabia,
was a popular emblem of the Renaissance; its nest of aromatic
herbs was fabled to be ignited by the sun. The young Phoenix
was supposed to be engendered by a worm that rose from the
ashes. Donne's metonymy suggests that, in a deteriorating
world, man has individualist pretensions, believing that he is
different from his fellows.

310–12 'measure of all Symmetree,/ Whom had that Ancient seen,
who thought soules made/ *Of Harmony.*' More than one Greek
philosopher taught that the soul was made of harmony, but the
likeliest sources were Pythagoras and Plato (*Phaedo* and
Timaeus).

314 'soules were but *Resultances* from her.' According to the OED
the word *resultance* was introduced by Capgrave in the fifteenth
century, and was obsolete by the end of the seventeenth. Donne
employed the word in different senses in three contexts, two of
them in *Pseudo-Martyr* (1610). Here the word means 'emana-
tions', Elizabeth Drury being the essence of that harmony
which enabled creatures of Noah's Ark to live in peace together.

361–4 'Shee, in whom all *white, and redde, and blue*/ (*Beauties ingredients*) *voluntary* grew,/ As in an *unvext Paradise*; from whom/
Did all things *verdure*, and their lustre come,/ Whose composition was *miraculous*,/ Being all color, all *Diaphanous*.' White, red,
blue and green were liturgical colours in Dante's *Purgatorio* xxx
(cf T. S. Eliot's *Ash Wednesday*, III). Ideal beauty resided in the
complexion of the face (mingling of white and red) and eyes of
blue. The verdant green of Paradise was a symbol of hope in
Cesare Ripa's *Iconologia* (1593). White light, the symbol of
eternity, was said to be a combination of all colours, giving the
air transparency and therefore associated with the miraculous.
Personification, at its finest, occurs in lines 367/8.

461–3 'God did make/ A last, and lastingest peece, *a song. He
spake*/ *To Moses*.' The reference is to the spirited exhortation of
Moses in Deuteronomy xxxii 1–43. The Israelite leader, in the
Promised Land, becomes a prophet, who recalls God's blessings
to a people once nomadic, but now settlers and tillers of the soil.
He warns against evils, such as loss of faith, attendant on their
relaxed existence, and the punishment that follows. The role of
Moses admirably suits Donne's lamentation in *An Anatomie of
the World*.

Although *An Anatomie* is a complaint with an ethical purpose, it
lacks the typological characters and fictional interest of literary
allegory, a kind often confused with its rhetorical forebear.
Originally, allegory implied no more than a continued metaphor
throughout a speech, poem or prose passage. In the sixteenth
century, however, the sense was extended to include picaresque
tales, philosophical discourses, and political satires with a utopian
line. Donne's *Anatomie* belongs to the second category; its unity is
emotional, rather than formal, while the imaginative analysis tends
to inhibit the organic wholeness of a literary form.

In the meditative parts, the symbol of an anatomist dissecting the sick world, limb by limb, has a deliberate satirical intention. It enables Donne to make biting comments on the disintegration of society, of which the religious conflict was a reflection. Death as a pollution and putrefaction of the carcass is a realistic symbol of the poet in the role of an anatomist, rather than a physician. Donne does not present a gratuitous survey of social diseases; the satire is secondary, but necessary to the regeneration of the world's soul, of which Elizabeth Drury is the prototype. Donne believed there was a link between secular and spiritual love. But philosophies, other than the metaphysics of religion, he associated with knowledge that drifts into pedantry.

The Second Anniversarie

According to the title-page, this poem celebrates 'the Religious death of Mistris Elizabeth Drury, the *incommodities* of the Soule in this life, and her [the soul's] exaltation in the next.' *Incommodities* are 'hurts' or 'annoyances'; the word was a French borrowing of the fifteenth century, obsolete by the middle of the nineteenth. *Of the Progres of the Soule* was a hymn of praise, begun in 1611, on the *first* anniversary of Elizabeth Drury's death; it purports to raise the soul from earthly bondage, *Our prisons prison* (249), and to assert the glory of eternal life.

The seven divisions of the *Progres* are more coherent than those of *An Anatomie*, each having a similar sequence of meditation, eulogy and moral. Donne is concerned with the vicissitudes and salvation of his own soul, as much as with Miss Drury's. The *Progres* has a richer imaginative unity, though not the powerful emotive impact of *An Anatomie*. Using the twelfth-century manual of St Bernard of Clairvaux, *Twelve Degrees of Humility and Pride*, Donne assails man's pre-occupation with the physical understanding. When he does raise the emotional tone, in the spirit of the Psalms, his apostrophe is to the symbolic Elizabeth Drury (e.g. lines 33–6) or to his own soul, as in lines 45–6. The hymn-like quality is a formal source of the poem's cohesion.

Arnold Stein, in an illuminating appendix on 'Donne's Religious Thought', remarks on the poet's spontaneity in religious expression, which he relates to a 'cultivation of extremes' (*John Donne's Lyrics,* p 221). The extremes in both *Anniversaries* are a Faustian ambition for learning, on the one hand, and a Christian penitent's nullification of the self, on the other. Some relevant qualities are illustrated in the following extracts.

Of the Progres of the Soule

This to thy soule allow,   183
Thinke thy sheell broke, thinke thy Soule hatch'd but now.
And thinke this slow-pac'd soule, which late did cleave,   185
To'a body, and went but by the bodies leave,
Twenty, perchance, or thirty mile a day,
Dispatches in a minute all the way,
Twixt Heaven, and Earth: shee staies not in the Ayre,
To looke what Meteors there themselves prepare;   190
Shee carries no desire to know, nor sense,
Whether th'Ayrs middle Region be intense,
For th'Element of fire, shee doth not know,
Whether shee past by such a place or no;
Shee baits not at the Moone, nor cares to trie,   195
Whether in that new world, men live, and die.

*   *   *

Shee, shee, thus richly, and largely hous'd, is gone: 247
And chides us slow-pac'd snailes, who crawle upon
Our prisons prison, earth, nor thinke us well
Longer, then whil'st we beare our brittle shell.   250
But t'were but little to have chang'd our roome,
If, as we were in this our living Tombe
Oppress'd with ignorance, we still were so.
Poore soule in this thy flesh what do'st thou know.
Thou know'st thy selfe so little, as thou know'st not,
How thou did'st die, nor how thou wast begot.

*   *   *

We see in Authors, too stiffe to recant,   281
A hundred controversies of an Ant.
And yet one watches, starves, freeses, and sweats,
To know but Catechismes and Alphabets
Of unconcerning things, matters of fact;   285
How others on our stage their parts did Act;
What Caesar did, yea, and what Cicero said.
Why grasse is greene, or why our blood is red,

Are mysteries which none have reach'd unto.
In this low forme, poore soule what wilt thou doe?   290
When wilt thou shake off this Pedantery,
Of being taught by sense, and Fantasy?

* * *

Shee, shee, not satisfied with all this waite,   315
(For so much knowledge, as would over-fraite
Another, did but Ballast her) is gone,
As well t'enioy, as get perfectione.
And cals us after her, in that shee tooke,
(Taking herselfe) our best, and worthiest booke.   320
Returne not, my soule, from this extasee,
And meditation of what thou shalt bee,
To earthly thoughts, till it to thee appeare
With whom thy conversation must be there.

(lines 183–96, 247–56, 281–92, 315–24)

Lines 183–96 are devoted to an imaginative account of the soul's
escape by death from its fleshly cell, and its instantaneous flight to
heaven through ascending hierarchies of air, fire, moon, sun,
planets and firmament (Tycho Brahe's planetary sequence).
Meteors were regarded as exhalations from Earth, which became
luminous when they reached the cold regions of the upper air.
Th'Ayrs middle Region (192) was deemed to be the domain of fire.
Baits (195) is a realistic metaphor; the now obsolete verb was
common parlance among travellers for 'halting at an inn for re-
freshment'. The point Donne emphasizes in lines 188–96 is the
swiftness of the soul in its ascent to heaven, compared with its
snail-like pace during tenancy of the body.

Lines 247–56 are part of the eulogy beginning at line 220.
Donne describes the brief habitation of the soul in the body of
Elizabeth Drury, sanctified through death to be an assigner of
duties to *Tutelar Angels* (236). The conception is far-fetched, but no
more fanciful than the speculations of Dante in the *Divina Commedia* or of Milton in *Paradise Lost*. Donne contrasts earthly and
celestial states with a profound awareness of man's vulnerability,
whereas Dante's idealistic Thomism visualizes these states as
coeval and coterminous.

Lines 281–92 are a satirical meditation on man's universal

ignorance, stubborn consistency and futile quest for factual knowledge, based on the readings of the senses. Donne sees the latter as the principal causes of pedantry, and he even questions the validity of science. This leads, at the end of the fourth eulogy (315–20) to his assessment of true knowledge as the pursuit of virtue through the Christian religion, in the spirit of St Bernard. For God is the enduring source of such knowledge as enables us to scale the ladder of perfection. Elizabeth Drury demonstrated her wisdom in preferring the Bible (320), a choice with which the poet associates himself. In lines 321–5 his hymn abjures 'earthly thoughts', and foresees the nature of the contemplation that the soul will enjoy in heaven.

In *John Donne's Poetry* (p 135) Wilbur Sanders casts doubts upon Donne's reasoning in the *Anniversaries*:

> Donne erects upon this foundation of human folly a wholly unwarrantable structure of divine wisdom, which has no more cogency than that it is the exact reverse of everything unsatisfactory in human knowledge. . . . 'Sense', the eternal scapegoat, gets the blame for everything the wit of man has, over the centuries, done amiss: . . . The very metaphor Donne uses to establish his heavenly knowledge, portrays it as equally probably a fallacy: . . . Heaven, on this showing, is a region where the laws of natural perspective no longer obtain – which is what sceptics throughout history have only too shrewdly suspected.

Donne was a thinker of strong emotions and moody temperament, who seems to have been intellectually moved by the doctrinal studies in which he was involved soon after his marriage. His spiritual and domestic future (in a real and not a metaphorical sense) depended on his making wise decisions, as will appear from the prose works on which he was then engaged, the *Essayes in Divinity* and *Devotions upon Emergent Occasions*. The structure of the latter (Meditation, Expostulation and Prayer) resembles the ordering of the discourses in the *Anniversaries*. Walton, in his *Life*, says that Donne, three years before his conversion to Anglicanism, devoted most of his time to the study of 'Textual Divinity' and the acquisition of Greek and Hebrew; there is plentiful recollection of such studies in the passages just considered. The immediate and noteworthy effects of Donne's entering the ministry in 1615 were his increased sensitivity to the vanities of life, and a steadfast determination to detach himself from the material world, especially after his wife's early death (1617).

Donne in the *Anniversaries* saw himself as Ecclesiastes, a preacher aspiring *inter alia* to be a satirist. With an acute sense of the ironic, as well as the moralistic, his negative rejection of the society in which he was an integral personality was due to causes within himself. The discord he discovers in a world without saints implies no lack of feeling for rational ethics. But like most converts, he clung to a new concept in dogmatics as to a rock in a sea of theological uncertainty. Donne's belief is in the soul as an axiomatic source of divine wisdom, and as an instrument of reunion with God. The language in which he writes is pellucid enough and vigorous; yet the *Anniversaries* remain a neglected corner of Donne's work, because they require the services of a hermeneut to explicate their symbolic secondary meaning.

EPICEDES AND OBSEQUIES

In its Greek original an *Epicede* was a funeral ode of praise, intended to be recited at the graveside. Donne himself did not use this term in the titles of his laments, but called them *Elegies*. Most of these contain hyperbolic eulogy, the earliest being that on Lady Marckham, who died on 4 May 1609. The text of the elegies quoted in this chapter is Grierson's.

Elegie upon the untimely death of the incomparable Prince Henry

Looke to mee faith, and looke to my faith, God;
For both my centers feele this period.
Of waight one center, one of greatnesse is;
And Reason is that center, Faith is this;
For into'our reason flow, and there do end   5
All, that this naturall world doth comprehend:
Quotidian things, and equidistant hence,
Shut in, for man, in one circumference.
But for th'enormous greatnesses, which are
So disproportion'd, and so angulare,   10
As is Gods essence, place and providence,
Where, how, when what soules do, departed hence,

113

These things (eccentrique else) on faith do strike;
Yet neither all, nor upon all, alike.
For reason, put to'her best extension,   15
Almost meetes faith, and makes both centers one.
And nothing ever came so neare to this,
As contemplation of that Prince, wee misse.
For all that faith might credit mankinde could,
Reason still seconded, that this prince would.   20

(*lines 1–20*)

Henry, eldest son of James I, died of typhoid fever on 6 November 1612, at the age of eighteen; only two years earlier he had been created Prince of Wales. Donne's tribute was one of many collected by Joshua Sylvester in *Lachrymae Lachrymarum*, printed by Humphrey Lownes, 1613. The Prince was an athlete, a patron of letters, and people's favourite, his politics being more flexible and less anti-Puritan than his father's. Among the contributors to *Lachrymae* was Donne's friend, Sir Edward Herbert, a poet noted for the turbidity of his style; and Drummond in his *Conversations* with Ben Jonson records Donne's confidence that he made his *Elegy* obscure in competition with that of Herbert. This is an unlikely piece of bravado; for Donne's poem is culpable of theological subtlety, rather than cloudiness.

Extravagance begins with Donne's initial assertion that his faith has been shaken and his reason perturbed, by the untimely loss of the prince, whom he apostrophizes as an instrument of salvation. Man, says Donne, has two centres, of reason and faith, the one for weighing, the other for evaluating. Reason enables man to understand the natural world; but his understanding is circumscribed (1–8). Donne compares reason, in relation to faith, with interpenetrating spheres. The larger sphere (faith's) contains objects of such proportion and shape that they are beyond comprehension; for instance, God's essence, place and providence, and the destiny of the soul after death. These impinge on faith differently, with different individuals (9–14). Reason, invoked to the uttermost, 'almost *meetes* faith' (16). Donne apparently means 'overlaps', by the merging of the two centres. Such a potentiality might have been realized in the person of the Prince; mankind will certainly believe what faith makes credible, provided it is seconded by reason. Prince Henry had all the attributes of a saviour (15–20).

This is the gist of Donne's argument in the cited passage; it is recorded that conservative Protestants regarded such praise as bordering on the blasphemous. But the death of a promising nobleman was of theological significance to Donne, who believed in the biblical hierarchies and the 'divinity that doth hedge a king' (*Hamlet* IV v 123) as firmly as Shakespeare. Prince Henry he pictured as the symbol of man endowed with divine intelligence, and worthy of the faith which loyal subjects accorded. Donne did not consider adulation of the 'chosen' as an extravagance of poetic compliment; to his Augustinian mind pious praise was a step to the love of God, and comparable to reverence for the Christ figure.

Donne's poetry of theological praise undoubtedly arose from his study of Tertullian and St Augustine, proponents of biblical rhetoric, as they discovered it in the Latin Vulgate. The Epistles of St Paul were accepted as perfect examples of the *anima naturaliter Christiana*. Early interpreters were convinced that the Bible's symbolic language embodied great spiritual and moral truths; and good Christians sensed the wisdom of such symbols spontaneously, through the *Logos* of the fourth gospel. The intellect was man's sensory guide; but he was destined for nobler ends, by imbibing the spirit that acknowledges the transcendency of God.

Augustine had himself been a professor of rhetoric, who considered dialectic indispensable to eloquent prose, and figurative language the natural ally of persuasion. He was, like Donne, an astute psychologist in combining devotion with discussion, and employing in sermons such schemes of words as would stir the imagination. But both Augustine and Donne, aware of the paradox in the man–God relation, could becloud the light of reason by super-subtleties, as in the following from the *City of God*:

For we both *are*, and *know* that we are, and *take delight* in our being and knowing. Moreover, in these three things no true-seeming illusion disturbs us; for we do not come into contact with these by some bodily sense, as we perceive the things outside us ... Without any delusive representation of images or phantasms, I am most certain that I am, that I know, and that I delight in this. On none of these points do I fear the arguments of the skeptics of the Academy who say: what if you are deceived? For if I am deceived, I am. For he who does not exist cannot be deceived; and if I am deceived, by this same token I am. . . . Neither am I deceived in knowing that I know. For, as I know that I am, so I know this also, that I know. And when I love these two [being and knowing], I add to them a third, that is, my love, which is of equal importance. For neither am I deceived in this, that I love, since in those things which I love I am not deceived; even if these were false, it would still be true that I loved false things. For how could I justly be blamed and prohibited from loving false things, if it were false that I loved them? Since these facts are true and real, who doubts that, when these things are loved, the love of them is itself true and real?

(XI 26, translated by M. Dods, revised by V. J. Bourke)

Donne shared the view of Augustine that a regenerate believer, through grace, acquired a new faculty of reason, surpassing that of natural man.

Obsequies to the Lord Harrington

John Harrington, second Baron of Exton, and brother of Lucy, Countess of Bedford, died of smallpox at her Twickenham home in February 1614, at the age of twenty-two, having inherited the title from his father the previous year. (Donne apparently spelt the name with double *r*.) He was a close friend of Prince Henry, a good-looking and religious man, and a classical scholar of some attainment. The *Obsequies*, longest of all the theological elegies save the *Anniversaries*, was written at least a year after the Baron's death, to restore Donne's waning friendship with the Countess, who a short time before had been seriously ill. Her gratitude is said to have been expressed by paying some of the poet's mounting debts. The tribute ends with Donne's avowed determination to abandon the writing of poetry:

> Doe not, faire soule, this sacrifice refuse,
> That in thy grave I doe interre my Muse,
> Who, by my griefe, great as thy worth, being cast
> Behind hand, yet hath spoke, and spoke her last.

Praising harmony and virtue in the soul of Lord Harrington, Donne's end was to hymn the goodness of God, as in previous elegiac meditations. Harmony was thought to be the source of order and proportion in the planetary system, even in the writings of the astronomer Kepler. The poem is devised as a meditation at midnight, when the world is at rest. Donne's imaginative thinking is admirably expressed in the following passages:

Faire soule, which wast, not onely, as all soules bee,
Then when thou wast infused, harmony,
But did'st continue so; and now dost beare
A part in Gods great organ, this whole Spheare:
If looking up to God; or downe to us,   5
Thou finde that any way is pervious,
Twixt heav'n and earth, and that mans actions doe
Come to your knowledge, and affections too,
See, and with joy, mee to that good degree
Of goodnesse growne, that I can studie thee,   10
And, by these meditations refin'd,
Can unapparell and enlarge my minde,
And so can make by this soft extasie,
This place a map of heav'n, my selfe of thee.

* * *

Thou at this midnight seest mee, and as soone   25
As that Sunne rises to mee, midnight's noone,
All the world growes transparent, and I see
Through all, both Church and State, in seeing thee;
And I discerne by favour of this light,
My selfe, the hardest object of the fight.   30
God is the glasse; as thou when thou dost see
Him who sees all, seest all concerning thee,
So, yet unglorified, I comprehend
All, in these mirrors of thy wayes, and end.
Though God be our true glasse, through which we see   35
All, since the beeing of all things is hee,
Yet are the trunkes which doe to us derive
Things, in proportion fit, by perspective,
Deeds of good men; for by their living here,
Vertues, indeed remote, seeme to be neare.   40

* * *

Now I grow sure, that if a man would have   165
Good companie, his entry is a grave.

Mee thinkes all Cities, now, but Anthills bee,
Where, when the severall labourers I see,
For children, house, Provision, taking paine,
They'are all but Ants, carrying eggs, straw, and grain;   170
And Church-yards are our cities, unto which
The most repaire, that are in goodnesse rich.
There is the best concourse, and confluence,
There are the holy suburbs, and from thence
Begins Gods City, New Jerusalem,   175
Which doth extend her utmost gates to them.

(lines 1–14, 25–40, 165–76)

In the complex syntax of lines 1–4 Donne purports to say that harmony *infused* into soul at birth does not necessarily last, as it did in the case of this youthful nobleman; ascended to heaven, his soul is now a part of God's universal scheme.

In the *Summa Theologica*, Thomas Aquinas distinguished between the 'acquired virtue' of natural man, and the '*infused* Virtue' bestowed by God upon Adam and his descendants. By the original sin of the Fall, human nature was not entirely corrupted; but man needs divine help (grace) to preserve integrity and to do the spiritual good that has merit in the eyes of his Maker (1 109 2). The Fall of Man, and its consequences in Donne's theology, are thoroughly Catholic. It is probable that he derived some ideas from medieval Latin treatises that are now overlooked, because Pollard and Redgrave's *Short-Title Catalogue of Books* (printed 1475–1640) does not include titles (other than Service-books) printed outside England, in Latin.

According to the OED, Donne was the first writer to employ the Latin word *pervious* (6), which he had already used in *Biathanatos* (98) with the sense of 'accessible to influence and argument'. The figurative word *unapparell* (12), meaning 'disrobe', is symbolic of intellectual nakedness.

Lines 25–40 are concerned with 'illumination', or 'spiritual enlightenment'. Harrington is symbolized as the *Sunne* (26), miraculously radiant at midnight, rendering all that was dark transparent, including the poet's inner self. About lines 35–40, Dr Johnson asked: 'Who but Donne would have thought that a good man is a telescope?' ('Cowley', *Lives of the Poets*, vol. 1, London, 1783, p 39). This question implies a rather cursory reading of the poem, in order to group the metaphysical poets as writers 'singular in their thoughts' and careless in their diction.

It is uncertain whether Donne in line 30, or William Browne in *Britannia's Pastorals,* first employed *glasse* with the meaning of 'an optical instrument for distant vision'. The word *telescope* did not come into the language until the latter half of the seventeenth century, though *telescopium* was borrowed from Latin in 1619, and *telescopio* (Galileo's word) a little later. The latter was adopted by the Italian from September 1611, his earlier instrument being termed a *perspicillum* (1610–11).

Donne was interested in optics as well as astronomy, partly because, among the medieval Augustinian-Platonists such as Grosseteste, some advance was made upon Euclid and Ptolemy – for instance, in the properties of the spherical lens or magnifying glass, used by the Arabs from the eleventh century. Donne was influenced in this passage by Kepler's *Mysterium Cosmographicum* (1596), which made much of Tycho Brahe's principle of abstract harmony. But more important for the time this poem was written, was the Jesuits' attempted humiliation of Galileo. This academic is said to have hated pedantry and refused to write in Latin; his book, *Sidereus Nuntius* (The Messenger of the Stars), was published in 1610, only a year after the Dutch invention of the telescope.

Donne does not at all say that 'man is a telescope'; what he asks for in line 29 is a clearer insight into his own person. Lines 30–40 declare that all-seeing God is man's instrument of vision; thus when the soul of Harrington sees Him, it looks deeply into itself. Donne does not, as yet, share this glory, but says he comprehends all, by the reflected merit of his friend's life and death (30–4). God, the Creator of all things, is at the same time our means of sight; we understand everything through Him; but the actions of virtuous men are instruments of perspective (*trunkes*), by means of which we perceive things in due proportion. The virtues of a good man, during his sojourn on earth, however remote, are brought closer to his friends' understanding (35–40).

The *perspective trunke* (37/8) was a hollow tube, with a convex glass at one end, a *camera obscura* rather than a telescope. Ben Jonson described one in *A New World in the Moon* (1620) as 'a thing no bigger than a flute-case'. By *perspective* Donne meant 'the relations of the parts of the whole organism', as observed by the mind.

When the word was introduced into English by Wyclif and contemporary writers, it meant 'the science of optics'; but Chaucer, Skelton and Shakespeare employed it in the derived, popular sense of an instrument such as a spy-glass, which was of many kinds. Not until the turn of the sixteenth century does one find *perspective* employed in the modern significance of 'relative magnitude according to distance', as the eye sees an object on a plane surface. The study of perspective was stimulated by the paintings of Ambrogio Lorenzetti of Siena in the fourteenth century.

Lines 165–76 meditate on the soul's spiritual elevation, which death makes possible – a virtual obsession in the Epicedes and *Sermons*. Cities and anthills are compared in their industry and wordly activity, ants being twice referred to in the Book of Proverbs. The churchyard is likened to a city, with holy precincts, to which the good return – the 'New Jerusalem' (Revelation xxi 2), though Donne was probably thinking of St Augustine's *City of God,* where the just are called by divine election.

Donne's dialectic is Augustinian and medieval while, paradoxically, much of the imagery is from the 'new Philosophy' that the poet treats with respectful scepticism. 'The strong lines', with fragmented phrasal syntax, offer fewer problems of interpretation than the stance that Donne adopts in religion, owing partly to a wavering attitude to Protestant reform, after his training in the Jesuit tradition. St Augustine held the rational soul to be a self-motivating spiritual force; but Donne regarded the soul in different, and sometimes loose, senses. Virgil K. Whitaker in *The Religious Basis of Spenser's Thought* (pp 30 and 35) explains some of the difficulties of a modern scholar:

> Our own indifference to theology results not so much from disbelief in God as from disbelief in metaphysics. We have little or no confidence in the processes of logic as compared with the observations of science. But the Elizabethan certainly believed in God, and he certainly believed in dialectic. We forget, furthermore, how fundamental a revolution in human thought was started by Bacon's distrust of the final cause. We ignore it, but to the Renaissance it was perhaps the most important of the four causes. Now the glory of God was the final cause of man's existence. 'What is man's chief end?' the Shorter Catechism begins,

and it answers: 'Man's chief end is to glorify God and to enjoy him forever' . . .

All parties agreed that before the fall Adam was endowed with perfect holiness and righteousness; since his soul was in complete harmony, his will was in complete control of his appetites, was turned toward God, and was completely free; he was subject neither to sin nor to death. The fall of man brought sin and, as a just consequence, God's condemnation to death and, except for the saved, to eternal damnation. In bringing sin, it corrupted man's nature so that his will was turned from God and no longer had control of his appetites.

Donne would have studied the theological reasoning and rhetoric of Tertullian and Augustine (both strong personalities) in Latin, and this has a bearing on the syntax and style of his language. He thought in symbols, and acquired from Renaissance Italy a sense of aesthetic form. But his pre-occupation was with the logic of distinctions, whose foundations were laid in Aristotle's *Organon*. Donne's intellectual acceptance of the new sciences was abstract, since he heeded Aristotle's warning that 'the rhetorician must not go too far in his use of special or technical knowledge' (*Rhetoric* I 2). He was thus left in a divided state of mind, his logic being merged with rhetoric, because sixteenth century rhetoric had no solid theoretical basis. Widely read in patristic Latin, he missed the classical discipline of Horace's control of words, or the orderly humanism of Cicero's style. Archetypal analogies between the physical world and the spiritual, were Donne's link with patristic theology. The 'scholastical quiddities', of which William Drummond wrote in a letter to Arthur Johnston (1637), were Donne's debt to St Thomas Aquinas.

EPITHALAMIA

Epithalamion was the Greek name for a 'nuptial song', which the Renaissance introduced to England in several spellings, late in the sixteenth century. The first recorded by the OED is Puttenham's anglicized form, *epithalamie*, 1589 (*Arte of English Poesie*, I xxvi), where is it described as a song sung 'very sweetly by Musitians at the chamber dore of the Bridegroome and Bride'. Spenser entitled his song *Epithalamion* (1595), preserving the Greek; while Marston in *What You Will* (1607) II i, used the anglicized plural of the latinism *Epythalamiums*.

Donne's versions are influenced by Spenser and the neo-Platonic tradition, especially in the first, the *Epithalamion made at Lincolnes Inne*, which appeared last in the 1633 edition of the *Poems*. Often quoted is the *Marriage Song on the Lady Elizabeth and Count Palatine*, celebrating nuptials on 14 February 1613. The passage below is from a poem dated December 26 of the same year, entitled *Ecclogue*, a dialogue concerning the notorious wedding of the King's favourite, Robert Carr, Earl of Somerset, to Frances Howard, one-time wife of the Earl of Essex. The conversation is between *Idios* ('a non-courtier') and *Allophanes* ('a person who resembles someone else'). The persons represented are, respectively, Donne himself and Sir Robert Ker, Earl of Ancrum, whose surname was identical in pronunciation to that of Somerset (*Carr*). In the Argument at the head of *Ecclogue*, Ker chides Donne for his absence from Court on the occasion of the wedding; the poet gives his reasons for retiring to the country.

Ecclogue

ALLOPHANES

Here [at Court] zeale and love growne one, all clouds
    disgest,   37
    And make our Court an everlasting East.
And can'st thou be from thence?

IDIOS
                  No, I am there.
As heaven, to men dispos'd, is every where,   40
So are those Courts, whose Princes animate,
    Not onely all their house, but all their State.
Let no man thinke, because he is full, he hath all,
    Kings (as their patterne, God) are liberall
Not onely in fulnesse, but capacitie,   45
    Enlarging narrow men, to feele and see,
And comprehend the blessings they bestow.
    So, reclus'd hermits often times do know
More of heavens glory, then a worldling can.
    As man is of the world, the heart of man,   50

Is an epitome of Gods great booke
  Of creatures, and man need no farther looke;
So is the Country of Courts, where sweet peace doth,
  As their one common soule, give life to both,
I am not then from Court.

ALLOPHANES

                    Dreamer, thou art.   55
Think'st thou fantastique that thou hast a part
In the East-Indian fleet, because thou hast
  A little spice, or Amber in thy taste?
Because thou art not frozen, art thou warme?
  Seest thou all good because thou seest no harme?   60
The earth doth in her inward bowels hold
  Stuffe well dispos'd, and which would faine be gold,
But never shall, except it chance to lye,
  So upward, that heaven gild it with his eye;
As, for divine things, faith comes from above,   65
  So, for best civill use, all tinctures move
From higher powers; From God religion springs,
  Wisdome, and honour from the use of Kings.
Then unbeguile thy selfe, and know with mee,
  That Angels, though on earth employd they bee,   70
Are still in heav'n, so is hee still at home
  That doth, abroad, to honest actions come.
Chide thy selfe then, O foole, which yesterday
  Might'st have read more then all thy books bewray;
Hast thou a history, which doth present   75
  A Court, where all affections do assent
Unto the Kings, and that, that Kings are just?
  And where it is no levity to trust?
Where there is no ambition, but to'obey,
  Where men need whisper nothing, and yet may;   80
Where the Kings favours are so plac'd, that all
  Finde that the King therein is liberall
To them, in him, because his favours bend
  To vertue, to the which they all pretend?
Thou hast no such; yet here was this, and more,   85
  An earnest lover, wife then, and before.
Our little Cupid hath sued Livery,

123

And is no more in his minority,
Hee is admitted now into that brest
  Where the Kings Counsells and his secrets rest.   95
What hast thou lost, O ignorant man?

(lines 37–96)

In the Argument prefaced to *The Shepheardes Calender*, Spenser un-
ashamedly characterizes *eclogues* as 'extraordinary discourses of un-
necessary matter'. Celebrating the twelve months of the year, each
poem ends with an appropriate pictorial emblem or a classical
motto. But the dialogue of Donne's *Ecclogue* has more substance;
it emulates the language of current Court masques, while retaining
Spenser's blend of Platonism and Christian belief.

    Disgest (37), with the opposite sense to *congest*, does not appear
in the OED. *Full* (43) signifies 'abundantly supplied with means'.
Donne says that kings are the vicarious pattern of God; it behoves
them to be generous, of their means and their capacity to make the
narrow-minded more liberal, especially in feeling and comprehension. Kings, ideally, are religious hermits, who often know
more of heaven's glory than wordlings (40–9).

    Lines 50–4 speak of *Gods great booke/ Of creatures*, a phrase of the
Fathers for the allegory of Creation, looking back to Plato's
Timaeus and to the works of Philo Judaeus, the Platonist of Alexandria. The idea of a 'book' may also have arisen from the notion
that God kept a register of good- and evil-doers. Plato was the
designer of the Great Chain of Being; Philo of allegorical explanations concerning names and places in the Hebrew Bible; and
Origen argued that finite creatures belong to the world of sense.
Donne's phrase was current among theologians (of which he was
not yet one) for the scriptural interpretations offered by commentators on Genesis and the Song of Songs. Their intention was
to find the emblematic significance of the Old Testament for parts
of the New.

    Emblems may have originated in Egyptian hieroglyphics, and
the fabulous beasts of the ancient world were used, not merely as
armorial symbols, but as visual images for turning the human
heart to truths of religion, as well as philosophy. Symbolic creatures
from the Old Testament had a place in the cosmology of Thomas
Aquinas, and Bonaventura said dogmatically that 'every creature is
a *vestigium* of the wisdom of God' (*Illuminationes in Hexäemeron*,

Sermon 12). Donne pretends that the country resembles the Court, because both are animated by the soul of peace.

The poet is a dreamer full of fantastic thoughts, says Allophanes, and his reply, which opens with three rhetorical questions, has suggestions from the Emblem books of the period, and from Marcelline's *Triumphs of King James the First* (1610). The *Ecclogue* is not, in truth, a debate, but consonant poetry of praise, in which both speakers extravagantly extol divine right, for the benefits a king bestows upon his subjects. An example is the conceit in line 64, which says that the origin of gold is sunlight, a symbol of kingly beneficence.

Amber (58) is a word derived, through Italian or Provençal, from M. Latin *ambar*, the ultimate source being Arabic *anbar*, meaning 'ambergris' ('grey amber'), a product of the sperm whale. In about 1400, fossil resin from the shores of the Baltic came to be known as 'yellow amber', perhaps erroneously. Which of the substances was employed for flavouring or cooking is uncertain.

As gold is produced in the bowels of the earth by the sun's rays, so divine things are argued to be tinctures of faith from higher powers, and so kings are the source of wisdom and honour (65–8). The word *tinctures* (66) carries overtones in Donne's analogy, for in alchemy tinctures were enigmatic principles that might be infused into material things, giving them a 'spirit' or soul. Lines 70–1 tell about the spiritual embodiment of Angels (God's messengers or intelligences); they were at once on earth and in heaven. Their function in the world was to guard the souls of men. In the scale of being there were nine orders of angels, derived from the fifth-century neo-Platonist, Dionysius the Areopagite (*On the Heavenly Hierarchy*), and from Dante's *Divina Commedia*.

Lines 75–84 contain three more rhetorical questions. Donne by-passed a ceremony that, according to Ker, had great symbolic significance. The Court of kings, he explains, has a history of un-rivalled loyalty and unanimity on the concept of royal justice. This is so, because *there is no ambition, but to'obey* (79); scandal is therefore a supererogation. Allophanes argues partially in lines 82–4, and specifically about the Court of James I, defending the King's bestowal of favours, with Robert Carr in mind. The glorification of *vertue* (84) and the wisdom of an *earnest lover* (86) are specious, and this constitutes a defect in Donne's poetry of praise. Lines 87–90 are unsavoury flattery of the King and his favourite.

Poetry of praise has inescapable disadvantages, in that some is invariably insincere, when addressed to patrons, on whose favour the poet is dependent. Donne seeks to avoid this difficulty by making his subject of tribute a symbolic figure, and his eulogy a form of Christian reverence. To the modern reader, this is not satisfying. For Donne is a poet of ideas and paradoxes; when the hermeneut does not convince, the *raison d'être* of his meditation falls away, except where saved by the poet's verbal skill. Donne is so able a craftsman that he does evoke some sympathy for Petrarchan admiration, and he does so more consistently than the Provençal and Italian originators of the hyperbolic cult of women.

CHAPTER V

The *Divine Poems*

🔳🔳🔳🔳🔳🔳

SINCE the first edition of Donne's *Poems* in 1633, the 'Divine Poems' (a title not used by the author) have had several additions from later collections. Excluding the two presentation sonnets to patrons, they number thirty-eight, one Latin poem *To Mr. George Herbert* being accompanied by an English version. Thanks to the important researches of Helen Gardner published in her Oxford English Text of 1952, it is now known that twenty-three sonnets and *A Litanie* were probably written before the *Anniversaries*, between 1607 and 1611. Only three sonnets, from the Westmoreland MS, the three *Hymns* and occasional poems appear to have been composed after Donne's ordination in 1615. Contrary to the opinion of earlier biographers, the majority of the *Divine Poems* were therefore the product of Donne's middle period, years of uncertainty and ill-health, when his pride and ambition for Court place had been humbled. The Divine Poems were closely related to his *Essayes in Divinity* and *Devotions upon Emergent Occasions*, many taking the form of Ignatian meditations, which he apparently did not consider inconsistent with Protestantism.

After much strenuous moral effort, Donne found fresh religious conviction during the composition of his polemical work *Pseudo-Martyr*. The language of these poems has a biblical simplicity and strength of will reflecting the struggle; the poet relies less on the efficacy of theological argument, more on the need for obedience to divine law, in its Hebraic conception. For Donne a true religion certainly existed, and every moral person was obliged to find it through prayer and spiritual exercises. Richard Hooker, Lancelot Andrewes and Donne played an enduring part in defining the new spirit of Anglicanism.

The first Divine Poems, composed about 1607, were the seven *La Corona* sonnets, representing spoken prayers of liturgical praise; the rhyme-schemes resemble patterns in Sidney's *Astrophil and*

Stella. This series was followed by a more ambitious composite
work styled *A Litanie*, written about 1608, during a long spell of
illness at Mitcham. There are twenty-eight nine-line stanzas in *A
Litanie*, each in the language of mental prayer, the object being
self-examination of the state of piety in a time of despairing
personal conflict.

Most of Donne's *Holy Sonnets* (nineteen in number, excluding
La Corona) were written before his wife's death in 1617. Helen
Gardner, in the Introduction to her edition of 1952 (pp xlix–l),
placed all twelve of the homogeneous group that appeared in the
1633 edition between the years 1609 and 1611; also the four
additional sonnets included in the second edition of Donne's
Poems (1635). Sir Edmund Gosse discovered a further three sonnets, when he purchased the Westmoreland MS in 1892; one
of these concerns the death of Ann Donne, this trio being of later
date. Gardner was the first to number each of the three sonnet
groups separately, the texts cited being from her edition.

Holy Sonnets 3 and 4

3

Thís is my pláyes lást scéne, | here heávens appoínt
My pílgrimàges lást míle; | and my ráce
Ídly, | yet quíckly rúnne, | hath thís lást páce,
My spáns lást íñch, | my mínutes lást poínt,
And glúttonous deáth, will íñstantly unjóynt   5
My bódy, and sóule, | and Í shall sléepe a spáce,
But my'éver-wáking párt shall sée that fáce,
Whose feáre alréady shákes my évery jóynt:
Thén, | as my soúle, to'heáven | her fírst séate, | tákes
    flíght,
And eáfth-bórne bódy, in the eárth shall dwéll,   10
Só, | fáll my sínnes, | that áll may hàve their ríght,
To whére they'are bréd, | and woùld présse me, to héll.
Impúte me ríghteous, | thus púrg'd of évill,
For thús I leáve the wórld, | the flésh, and dévill.

4

At the roúnd eárths imágin'd córners, blów
Your trúmpets, | Áṅgells, | and aríse, | aríse
From deáth, | you númberlesse infínitìes
Of soúles, | and to your scáttred bódies góe,
Áll whom the flóod díd | and fíre sháll o'erthrów,   5
Áll whom wárre, | deárth, | áge, | águes, | týrannìes,
Despáire, | láw, | chánce, | hath slaíne, | and yóu whose eýes,
Sháll behóld Gód, | and néver tást deáths wóe.
But lèt them sléepe, | Lórd, | and mée moúrne a spáce,
For, if abóve àll thése, my sínnes aboúnd   10
'Tis láte to aśke abúndance of thỳ gráce,
When wée are thére; | hére on this lówly gróund,
Teách mèe how to repént; | for thát's as góod
As if thóu'hadst seál'd my párdon, with thỳ blóod.

These sonnets are numbered vi and vii in Grierson's edition of
1912. The editor admitted that he could not find 'a definite
significance in any order', but considered each sonnet 'a separate
meditation or ejaculation'. This difficulty is now overcome, as
Gardner has demonstrated in her revealing Introduction and Commentary. A reliable account of the circumstances under which
these *Holy Sonnets* were written is given by R. C. Bald in *John
Donne, A Life* (pp 232–6):

Donne's emotions as well as his thinking, and indeed his
whole way of life, were insensibly becoming involved in
the solution of . . . theological problems. This the letters to
Goodyer show. His religious sense was steadily deepening.
. . . The essential cause was his lack of conviction of his
own salvation, without which no man was qualified to
preach the gospel of Christ. . . . Despair, it should be recalled, was in the seventeenth century sin as well as suffering, for it implied distrust in God and His mercy; and
Donne was afflicted by this distrust. . . . Here are all the
classic symptoms of what William James calls 'the sick
soul' . . .
Thus the years 1607–10 were probably the most disturbed and anxious years of Donne's life. He passed
through a spiritual crisis which was in large measure con-
cealed from those closest to him. . . . That Donne was able

to diagnose his own complaint is not surprising, for he was
doubtless well read in the literature of penitence and conversion from the *Confessions* of St. Augustine down to his
own time. . . . The frequent outcome of such crises is conversion, either sudden or gradual, but Donne still had some
years to wait before he was secure in the conviction of
God's ever-present mercy. . . . When the true date of most
of the 'Holy Sonnets' is recognized, however, a host of
difficulties vanishes. One is no longer startled by the utter
absence of inward peace, nor puzzled by the lack of any
sense of priestly vocation.

The dignity, fluency and persuasiveness of Donne's language resemble that of St François de Sales, whose *Introduction to the
Devout Life* (1609), in French, Donne had been reading. Chapter
XII (on Melancholy) advised: 'When you pray, make use of aspira-
tions and words, whether interior or exterior, which tend to confidence in God' (translation of Alan Ross, 1943, p 235). The *Holy
Sonnets* were probably interior meditations directed to this end.
The personal note of a Christian concerned about the fate of his
soul gives to Sonnets 3 and 4 their intense feeling, which has a
more powerful effect upon the reader than the liturgical themes of
La Corona. The vehement exclamations, insistent repetitions,
Ignatian self-abasement without a complaining tone, are characteristic of Donne's zeal to match the tenseness of his emotions with
the incandescent verbal resource of a preacher. Such ability convinced James I that Donne's true place was in the Anglican
ministry.

The form of the sonnet that Donne adopted is important to the
nature of the impact he intended. The rhyme scheme a b b a a b b
a c d c d e e was used by both Wyatt and Sidney; but the aesthetic
likeness does not go further than the employment of two rhymes
in the octave, and three in the sestet. For Donne's irregular rhythms
are not comparable to his predecessors' well-known prosodic de-
fects. He deliberately flouted the Petrarchan tradition of smoothness, as he did in his use of a final couplet, a form not favoured by
Italian poets, who divided the sestet into two tercets. Ironically,
Donne was a pedantic syllabist, practising a boldly libertarian
stress modulation, acceptable in verse dramatists, but not usually
among conventional lyricists.

Donne's commonest freedom was, in fact, theoretical elision, some viable, some impracticable; for instance, A: *synaloepha*, the obscuring of the first of two coincident vowels at the junction of words, as permitted in Italian prosody, e.g. in lines 3.7 (not feasible elocutionally) and 3.12; or B: the reduction of weak vowels, where unstressed syllables of single words end in the liquid consonants *l, m, n,* or *r,* e.g. in *heavens* (3.1), *gluttonous* (3.5) and *every* (3.8). The first of these licences was permissible also before aspirated syllables, probably through French influence, as in *heaven* (3.9). The custom of *metaplasm* made it, furthermore, feasible for some polysyllables to encourage ambivalent pronunciation, as in *righteous,* which has three syllables *ad hoc* in line 3.13. It may be assumed that such devices were visual, no reader being expected to observe the metrical niceties in pronunciation.

The advantage of Donne's metrical procedure was a subtler variety of rhythm (including prose rhythms) than would otherwise have been attainable. A disadvantage of the seemingly arbitrary changes of stress is to disappoint the melodic ear of some readers, for whose taste the rhythms are needlessly rugged. One such reader of Sonnet 4 in I. A. Richards's *Practical Criticism* (p 48) complained that, 'the feet are frequently not iambic, and there are sometimes four, and even six accented syllables to the verse.' In Donne's poetry, one has to accept that natural speech stress often runs counter to metrical expectation.

Donne's speech in the *Holy Sonnets* has not the scholastic ingenuity of his better-known lyrics; plain and idiomatic, it is spirited enough to be adaptable to his moods. The pauses and stress inversions are admirably suited to the passionate language, abounding in powerful monosyllables and positive predications. Line 3.9, with three internal pauses (after *Then, heaven* and *seate*), is instructive to the metrist, because its twelve syllables are theoretically scanned as ten, *to'heaven* being visualized as a monosyllable, among the many others in that line. There are seven primary stresses in the line, the final four monosyllables yielding two spondees. Timing, pace and semantic weight are important in reading Donne, for instance in Sonnet 4, in which numerous primary stresses have to be sensitively distinguished from the secondary ones. *Thou/thy* and *me/my,* have considerable antithetical significance.

It should be noted that the punctuation of the sonnets, derived from scribal copies, does not necessarily imply metrical pause. There are occasions, vice versa, when such a pause is obvious, despite the text's neglect of a stop. The rhythm of line 3.2 is difficult to capture, because both stress inversion and internal pause occur in the fourth foot. Line 3.4 is metrically defective, but editorially authenticated, the temptation being to substitute *latest* for *last* before *point*.

The contextual situation in these poems is worthy of study because they illustrate Donne's mannerist tendencies. Sonnet 3 has a less explosive opening than is usual with Donne; instead, its spatial imagery visualizes life as a graphic *pilgrimage* (3.2). The delayed impact is made by *gluttonous* and *unjoynt* in line 3.5, and the metaphorical allusion to the soul as *my'ever-waking part* (3.7). The meditation gathers characteristic momentum in the sestet, however, after the traumatic experience of the separation of soul from body. Its flight to heaven was a journey in which Donne confidently believed. Tongue in cheek, the poet entertains the hope that, if only his sins could be shed upon earth, where generated, he would, through grace, be *purg'd of evill* (3.13), and made worthy to enter God's Kingdom. Donne realizes at the end of the next sonnet that this consolation is vain, which makes it desirable that Sonnets 3 and 4 should be read together.

The opening lines of Sonnet 4 are dramatic and arresting; the rousing tone of the initial quatrain matches the desperate situation of the Day of Judgement, and this note is sustained with majestic detail of the causes of death in the second stage of the octave. Every reader is impressed by the trumpet-notes accompanying the apocalyptic vision, taken from Revelation vii 1, and by Donne's wit-conceit of a *round* earth, having four corners, each guarded by an Angel. The crescendo reached in the octave calls for the calm resignation of the sestet. Readers unfamiliar with the biblical analogues feel deflated, not because they miss the contrast, but fail to appreciate its aesthetic grace. In a sense, Donne contrasts the sonorous, prophetic language of the Old Testament with the peace of the Pauline doctrine of redemption. The puzzling words 'when we are *there*' (4.12) refer to 'God's great judgement seat', around which are gathered the 'numberlesse infinities/ Of soules' (4.3). From the 'lowly ground' of his imagined death-bed, Donne pictures his plight, as a sinner, and recognises the need for repentance, a Christian prerequisite for redemption.

Sonnet 4 is a poem of private experience and public appeal; verb tenses, repetitions such as *arise, arise* (4.2), adverbs of place (*there/here*), and changes of personal pronoun are pointers that enable the reader to re-create the situation of the poet concerned about the fate of his soul. Wilbur Sanders, in *John Donne's Poetry* (pp 131–2) compares the poem to Verdi's *Requiem*:

> The cast of both the apocalyptic terror and the penitential grief is operatic; and the transition from one to the other gives itself away precisely because it is so *effective.* . . . One feels the reflecting mind turning away from all the huge and momentous drama, seeking inwardly for collectedness and composure. . . . The terror and the penitence fuse together into a new third thing – a religiousness that grows spontaneously out of the natural man.

Sonnet 2 (added in 1635)

I am a little world made cunningly
Of Elements, and an Angelike spright,
But black sinne hath betraid to endlesse night
My worlds both parts, and (oh) both parts must die.
You which beyond that heaven which was most high   5
Have found new sphears, and of new lands can write,
Powre new seas in mine eyes, that so I might
Drowne my world with my weeping earnestly,
Or wash it, if it must be drown'd no more:
But oh it must be burnt; alas the fire   10
Of lust and envie have burnt it heretofore,
And made it fouler; Let their flames retire,
And burne me o Lord, with a fiery zeale
Of thee and thy house, which doth in eating heale.

This sonnet is numbered v in Grierson's edition of 1912, and III in the second edition of Donne's *Poems* (1635); Gardner dates it 'between the latter half of 1609 and the first half of 1611' (see *Divine Poems*, p 75). In line 11, the 1635 edition has the preterite *burnt*, and the O'Flaherty MS the perfect singular *hath burnt*. But if *the fire/ Of lust and envie* (10/11) are to be regarded as separate subjects, grammar requires the words *have burnt* (perfect plural) of the

Westmoreland MS. On this Grierson and Gardner are agreed, the point being settled by the plural *their flames* in line 12.

The sonnet, though observing the Donnian rhyme-scheme, is unusually structured, because the plaint about sin overflows the limits of the octave by a line, leaving only five for the meditator's petition to God. This petition reminds Louis L. Martz of a passage (1 88) in the Jesuit Luis de la Puente's *Meditations upon the Mysteries of our Holie Faith, with the Practise of Mental Prayer*, which Donne may have been reading. Puente's book was published in 1605, but an English translation did not appear until 1619 (see *The Poetry of Meditation*, p 53).

The first quatrain is concerned with man as a microcosm. Donne's 'little world' was the accepted epitome of man's life on earth. The journey of the body back to earth was of minor significance; that of the soul to heaven the important complement. The most explicit expression of this symbolic progress is found in the *Second Anniversarie* and the *Devotions upon Emergent Occasions*, writings that constantly remind one of Donne's Jesuit sensibilities and endless introspection. These leanings explain the passionate outburst of the sonnet's final couplet.

The *Elements* (2) of which man is physically composed were believed to be Fire, Air, Earth and Water; these were mutable, but incapable of isolation. Any disturbance in the universe (the macrocosm) was inevitably reflected in man (the microcosm). The Fall was such a disturbance; it made a once godlike creature subject to sickness and death. But man was happily also endowed with an *Angelike spright* (2), or soul, which most theologians considered as a separate entity from the body. Physicians (as well as nascent psychologists such as Donne) thought, on the other hand, that the two were interdependent. All agreed, however, that the spirit was immaterial and immortal. Evil, the source of disorder, was for Donne *black sinne* (3), which might be pardoned only by penitence and intervention of divine grace. Symbolically, sin or uncontrolled passion was black, virtue and harmony fair. Human disorders, such as melancholy, resulted from misuse of the body, ultimately from some imbalance in the mixture of humours, which stimulated inordinate passions of the mind. Salvation being of the soul, Donne was a never-ceasing penitent, fearful lest both aspects of his world, body and soul, should die (4).

The second quatrain concerns the new Astronomy, which

Donne regarded with some apprehension. His allusion is probably to Galileo's *Sidereus Nuntius,* published in Venice in 1610. Pseudo-scientists had associated the theologian's heaven with Ptolemy's eighth sphere of the fixed stars; thus the latter were described as heavenly bodies. The sphere beyond that was the *Primum Mobile* or First Cause. In lines 5 and 6 Donne refers to Galileo's observations of new territory on the moon, and of more distant stars, the evidence of his telescope supporting the Copernican system. He suggests, somewhat extravagantly, that the new explorers of the universe might *Powre new seas* (7) into the penitent's eyes, that the world should be drowned with Donne's weeping. There is an oblique reference to Noah's deluge in the conceit of line 9, that if there should be no second flood, tears will suffice to *wash* ('purify') Donne's 'little world'.

In the five-line finale there are two biblical references. Donne supposes that the microcosm would suffer the same fate as the macrocosm, at the Day of Judgement, according to the prophecy in 2 Peter, iii 7. The poet pleads that he has already suffered in the holocaust of his earlier sins of *lust and envie* (11), which has made his little world *fouler* than before (12). The prayer is characteristically paradoxical in its ending: that these flames should retreat and consume rather his physical body, to the rescuing of his soul. Psalm 59, verses 9 and 10, reads: 'For the zeale of thine house hath eaten me up . . . 10 When I wept, and chastened my soule with fasting, that was to my reproch' (King James Bible). Even after his ordination, Donne did not always favour the Authorized Version, but sometimes the Douai translation of the Vulgate. In 1617 the latter was published in six volumes, with a commentary by Nicholas of Lyra, a medieval theologian (see M. F. Moloney, *John Donne, His Flight from Mediaevalism,* p 43).

An interpretation of the sonnet on the above lines will help to counteract the libertarian view expressed below in Chapter 3 of William Empson's *Some Versions of Pastoral* (1935), certainly not based on a close reading of the text:

> The octet, though without indifference to a universal right and wrong, takes the soul as isolated and independent; it is viewed as the world in the new astronomy, a small sphere, complete in itself, safe from interference, in the middle distance. The idea that you can get right away to America,

that human affairs are not organized round one certainly right authority (*e.g.* the Pope) is directly compared to the new idea that there are other worlds like this one, so that the inhabitants of each can live in their own way. These notions carried a considerable weight of implication, because they lead at once to a doubt either of the justice or the uniqueness of Christ. . . .

Drowning the world *no more* brings us back to Noah and an entirely pre-Copernican heaven, and there is a surprise in the first part of the line which prepares us for it; the distinction between *wash* and *drown* brought out the question as to what was to be drowned. It seems at first that the *sprite* and *elements*, spirit and body, correspond to the day and night of the imagined globe, a fine case of the fusion of soul and body which Donne often attempts. But in that case both are to be drowned; the soul is safe because sure of extinction. The flood pulls us back from this with a reminder of the final fire. . . . The symbolism of the use of fire as a punishment for heresy could not but work on a man exposed to it as it was meant to do; it produced a sort of belief. The reader is now safely recalled from the interplanetary spaces, baffled among the cramped, inverted, cannibal, appallingly tangled impulses that are his home upon the world.

The clash here shows what the globe has been used for in Donne's earlier poetry, where it is a continual metaphor; I suppose he had a globe map in his room.

Sonnet 1

Since she whome I lovd, hath payd her last debt
To Nature, and to hers, and my good is dead,
And her soule early into heaven ravishéd,
Wholy in heavenly things my mind is sett.
Here the admyring her my mind did whett   5
To seeke thee God; so streames do shew the head,
But though I have found thee, and thou my thirst hast fed,
A holy thirsty dropsy melts mee yett.
But why should I begg more love, when as thou
Dost wooe my soule, for hers offring all thine: 10

And dost not only feare least I allow
My love to saints and Angels, things divine,
But in thy tender jealosy dost doubt
Least the World, fleshe, yea Devill putt thee out.
(*from the Westmoreland MS*; *XVII in Grierson's edition*)

The three poems in the Westmoreland MS, not printed in the seventeenth-century editions of Donne's *Poems*, are of a personal nature;
Helen Gardner suggests that they did not find their way into print
because they were written after the poet was ordained. Donne lost
his wife, in her thirty-third year, in August 1617, but apparently
did not write the sonnet until some time later. Gardner offers the
date May 1619, and remarks upon the effect of the heavily-
stressed personal pronouns.

The sense of *to hers* (2) is difficult to determine; probably the
meaning is 'things appertaining to her'. Certain words and phrases,
such as *ravishéd* (3), *holy thirsty dropsy* (8), *wooe* (10) and *tender jealosy*
(13), are designed to enhance the conceit that a jealous God had
not only replaced Donne's deceased wife, but possessively guarded
him against the secular world, the flesh and the devil. Donne's
tribute to his wife is confined to lines 5 and 6, in which he claims
that the qualities of her mind induced him to a sacramental love,
which resembled Dante's. Ann was, platonically, the fountain-head
of the stream at which Donne quenched his thirst for God. Whim-
sically, Donne suggests the anthropomorphic rivalry for his love
of the Catholic *saints and Angels* (11–12), both having divine
associations.

The words *dropsy* (8) and *hydroptic* occur several times in Donne's
writings; for the adjective, see line 6 of *A Nocturnall upon S. Lucies
Day*, p 89. In *Letters to Several Persons of Honour*, 1651 (p 50), he
confessed to an '*Hydroptique* immoderate desire for humane learning and languages'; Donne's is the first use of the adjective,
meaning 'unquenchable', recorded in the OED. *Dropsy* is derived,
through Latin and French, from Greek *hudrops*. An English adaptation *ydropsi* appeared in *Cursor Mundi* (c 1300), preceded by the
aphetic form *dropesie* (c 1290), which Wyclif also used in his translation of the Gospel of St Luke.

The sense of personal loss is not mitigated by the poet's
courageous candour. Donne does not suggest that the memory of
secular love is no longer alluring; the note of resignation, not

consolation, in the spiritual outcome, flows inevitably from Ann's exemplary devotion. Wilbur Sanders says of this poem in a fine analysis:

> I don't pretend to 'understand' the mind that is at work here. To an extent, it's a mind which has moved so far beyond human foible and fretfulness that its calm seems faintly inhuman. And yet, if it is inhuman, it is also deeply natural and it is at pains to honour the natural in human feeling. . . . The equanimity is not insientence. Nor is it an 'evennesse' plagued with backward glances towards lost pleasures. It is hard-won, hard-held, and it contains real forces. It recognises the very personal route by which Donne has reached faith . . .
>
> (*John Donne's Poetry*, p 138)

John Donne's sonnets seem to confirm a preference for compact forms and patterns with minimal changes of rhyme, so that the poet might concentrate on the conflict of thought and exceptional feelings. His mingling of sensuous and biblical imagery reflects an undoubted instability of the passions. Most sonnets are meditations of a strenuous personality struggling to live up to the moral truths of religion, but falling short in real or imaginary defeat. This is not coterie poetry, but metaphysical in the patristic sense, and it requires some grounding in the teachings of the Christian Fathers and St Ignatius Loyola to understand its impact upon Donne's successors, Herbert, Crashaw and Cowley.

A Litanie
(Stanzas XXIII – XXV, lines 199–225)

XXIII

Heare us, O heare us Lord; to thee
A sinner is more musique, when he prayes,   200
 Then spheares, or Angels praises bee,
In Panegyrique Allelujaes,
  Heare us, for till thou heare us Lord
  We know not what to say.
Thine eare to'our sighes, teares, thoughts gives voice and
 word.   205

O Thou who Satan heard'st in Jobs sicke day,
Heare thy selfe now, for thou in us dost pray.

XXIV

That wee may change to evennesse
This intermitting aguish Pietie,
  That snatching cramps of wickednesse   210
And Apoplexies of fast sin, may die;
      That musique of thy promises,
      Not threats in Thunder may
Awaken us to our just offices;
What in thy booke, thou dost, or creatures say,   215
That we may heare, Lord heare us, when wee pray.

XXV

That our eares sicknesse wee may cure,
And rectifie those Labyrinths aright,
  That wee by harkning, not procure
Our praise, nor others dispraise so invite,   220
      That wee get not a slipperinesse,
      And senslesly decline,
From hearing bold wits jeast at Kings excesse,
To'admit the like of majestie divine,
That we may locke our eares, Lord open thine.   225

Helen Gardner considers that *A Litanie* was composed at Mitcham,
during a prolonged illness, in the autumn of 1608. Donne's spirits
were low, but calm and resigned, and he sought a middle way out
of his religious dilemma, through piety and patience. There are
unmistakeable indications of a leaning towards Anglicanism, in
spite of the nostalgic Catholicism that *A Litanie* also contains. The
emphasis is on self-examination for the evidence of sin, characteristically described as *snatching cramps of wickednesse* (210); but Donne
aims decisively at a compromise between Rome and Geneva. The
Thirty-Nine Articles of the Church of England were adopted only
a year before Donne was born.

The origin of the poem is explained in an undated letter to Sir
Henry Goodyer, where Donne mentions two Latin litanies, by
fourteenth-century monks; he had studied these, but dismissed
them as 'poor and barbarous'. The first litany in English was composed by Archbishop Cranmer in 1544, and published in *The King's*

Primer the following year. It retained the form of the Latin fore-bears, consisting of four parts, Invocation, Deprecation, Obsecration and Intercession, in that order. A *deprecation* was a prayer to avert or remove evil; an *obsecration* a vehement intreaty in the name of the Deity, usually beginning in Latin with *per*, in English with *by*.

In Donne's poem Gardner observes that, 'the form has had to be too much twisted to fit the material, and the material has been moulded to the form rather than expressed by it' (*Divine Poems*, Introd. p xxviii). Nevertheless, an attempt was made to preserve the structural divisions as follows: Invocation, stanzas I to XIII; Deprecation, XIV–XXII; Obsecration, XXIII–XXVII; Intercession, XXVIII. The poem's twenty-eight stanzas each have nine lines, rhyming a b a b c d c d d, a form of Donne's invention. The first five lines have, alternately, four and five feet; the sixth is a trimeter, followed by three pentameters, the dominant measure being iambic.

The word *litany* was derived from Greek *litē* (a supplication), but more specifically from *litaneia* (a prayer). It appeared in Old English in the tenth century, with radical vowel *e* instead of *i*, suggesting a borrowing from O. French and Latin. In M. English church services the *e*-spelling was preserved, as in both books of *Common Prayer* (1549 and 1552); it survived alongside the *i*-spelling until the seventeenth century.

In *A Litanie* Donne's quest for moderation takes the form of a mean between two extremes, expressed in terms of paradox. The poet's petition to be heard has an urgency that springs from a desire for the experience of a personal relationship with God. The Church made sensible use of music as an ally of worship by linking the litany to the psalms, songs of praise or petitions for succour; the English Church in Donne's time favoured Sternhold and Hopkins's settings. Donne echoes the Church in saying that *A sinner is more musique, when he prayes* (200) than choirs of Angels. A feature of these stanzas is the resonant use the litanist made of polysyllables of foreign origin, in such phrases as *Panegyrique Allelujaes* (202), *intermitting aguish Pietie* (209), *Apoplexies of fast sin* (211), *rectifie those Labyrinths* (218).

An anglicized form *panegyrike* (a laudatory song of the Greeks) was introduced, both as noun and adjective, in 1603. *Allelujaes*, from Hebrew, through Greek, was first employed in English in Wyclif's Bible (Revelation xix 6). *Apoplexie*, used by Chaucer in the *Nun's Priest's Tale* (21), was from Greek *apoplēssein* 'to strike off', hence 'afflicted with a stroke'. Although the Greek borrowing *labyrinth* (a maze) was used as early as 1387 by Higden in his translation of Trevisa, it was not found in English for the anatomy of the 'inner ear' until 1696, according to the OED.

The dissonant imagery of *A Litanie* reverts consistently to thoughts of the sick-bed, e.g. *Jobs sicke day* (206), *intermittent aguish* (209), *Apoplexies* (211), *eares sicknesse* (217). *Slipperinesse* (221) is metaphorically associated with Donne's rebuff to critics who execrate royalty in jest. The symbolism of the poem is predominantly biblical. At the beginning of Book 1, Chapter 5 of *The Imitation of Christ* (which the poet seems to have been reading) Thomas à Kempis says: 'In the holy Scriptures, truth is to be looked for rather than fair phrases. All sacred scriptures should be read in the spirit in which they were written.' This was invariably Donne's religious aim.

Goodfriday, 1613. Riding Westward

Let mans Soule be a Spheare, and then, in this,
The intelligence that moves, devotion is,
And as the other Spheares, by being growne
Subject to forraigne motions, lose their owne,
And being by others hurried every day,   5
Scarce in a yeare their naturall forme obey:
Pleasure or businesse, so, our Soules admit
For their first mover, and are whirld by it.
Hence is't, that I am carryed towards the West
This day, when my Soules forme bends toward the East.   10
There I should see a Sunne, by rising set,
And by that setting endlesse day beget;
But that Christ on this Crosse, did rise and fall,
Sinne had eternally benighted all.
Yet dare I'almost be glad, I do not see   15
That spectacle of too much weight for mee.
Who sees Gods face, that is selfe life, must dye;
What a death were it then to see God dye?
It made his owne Lieutenant Nature shrinke,
It made his footstoole crack, and the Sunne winke.   20
Could I behold those hands which span the Poles,

And tune all spheares at once, peirc'd with those holes?
Could I behold that endlesse height which is
Zenith to us, and to'our Antipodes,
Humbled below us? or that blood which is   25
The seat of all our Soules, if not of his,
Make durt of dust, or that flesh which was worne
By God, for his apparell, rag'd, and torne?
If on these things I durst not looke, durst I
Upon his miserable mother cast mine eye,   30
Who was Gods partner here, and furnish'd thus
Halfe of that Sacrifice, which ransom'd us?
Though these things, as I ride, be from mine eye,
They'are present yet unto my memory,
For that looks towards them; and thou look'st towards
    mee,   35
O Saviour, as thou hang'st upon the tree;
I turne my backe to thee, but to receive
Corrections, till thy mercies bid thee leave.
O thinke mee worth thine anger, punish mee,
Burne off my rusts, and my deformity,   40
Restore thine Image, so much, by thy grace,
That thou may'st know mee, and I'll turne my face.

Grierson adopted an alternative reading of the manuscripts, *turne*
for *tune*, in line 22.

This dramatic monologue, in pentameter couplets, was written,
without title, a year and a half before Donne was ordained. The
date is significant, not only for the author's state of mind at the
time, but for the blend of cosmic and religious subtlety that makes
the poem difficult to interpret. The occasion was a journey to
Montgomery Castle in Wales, a well-known seat of the Herbert
family. The present title was first supplied in the 1633 edition.

The poem divides itself naturally into three parts, lines 1–10,
11–32 and 33–42, the middle portion containing the heart of the
matter. The first ten lines employ an extended conceit, based on
the Ptolemaic cosmology, with the ultimate support of Plato's
Timaeus. Both in poetry and the *Sermons*, Donne drew analogies
from the latter fruitful source. He took advantage of the chaos into
which the Renaissance thinking world had been thrown by the new
astronomy of Copernicus, Galileo and Kepler.

In Plato's cosmology the Creator imposed on his universe a certain order, the first being a division of the heavens into inner and outer spheres, namely, those of the planets, and those of the supposedly fixed stars. The earth was regarded as the centre around which all moved, once in twenty-four hours. The orbits of the fixed stars took a different direction from those of the planets. The sphere of the fixed stars (called the Same) moved in a circle from left to right; the seven planets (called the Other) had contrary motion from right to left.

Aristotle in *De Anima* was the first to transfer the analogy of the spheres to man, the microcosm, likening them to the opposite tendencies of appetite and will. The medieval handbook with which Donne was probably most familiar was the *De Sphaera* of the mathematician John Holywood, who was known as Sacrobosco. This writer explained the 'rational motion' of the ninth sphere (*Primum Mobile*) as movement 'from east to west and back to east again', which he thought resembled the rational faculty in man, whose thoughts proceed from the Creator, through His creatures, back to their origin. The opposite motion, that of the planets in the firmament, he described as 'irrational' or 'sensual'. Philo Judaeus, the neo-Platonist, incidentally saw a physical resemblance between the sphere and the human head.

The relevance of this to *Goodfriday, 1613* appears in the extended conceit of the first ten lines. Having some knowledge of the new Astronomy, Donne poses a hypothetical analogy, as though it were a Euclidian proposition. Travelling to Wales on this religious festival, he became acutely aware of the Passion of Christ in relation to his Christian obligations. He was too pre-occupied with the state of inertia to attempt a reconstruction of the event in his mind, or to direct his thoughts to the East, where the Crucifixion took place. Christians, remembering the Crusades, still held the East to be a symbolic direction of importance; in Luke i 78 Christ is called 'the day-spring from on high', identified with the rising sun.

Donne observes in line 2 that the intelligence motivating his sphere (or soul) is *devotion* – he should therefore be travelling east. But as a man of the world, activated by *Pleasure or businesse* (7), he finds himself influenced by the rational soul, whose direction is westward. Why should the *Primum Mobile* urge men in an unfavourable direction? The reason seems to be that the lower sphere is under the influence of the upper one (3–6). Man gets the impression he is going the wrong way, because he believes in the infallibility of reason. Donne's purpose is to dramatize the conflict between the pragmatic business of living and man's religious duties (9–10).

Living in a mechanistic universe is depressing in contrast to the joys of the spiritual life; Donne meditates on some of the Christian paradoxes in the quatrain 11–14. Had Christ not redeemed our sins, we should be living in perpetual darkness, instead of alternate night and day. Why, then, does the pilgrim not turn his steps and face the benefactor of his salvation? Donne confesses trepidation at viewing the horrors of a physical re-enactment (15–16). *Who sees Gods face . . . must dye* (17) is a quotation from the *Summa Theologica* of Aquinas (1 xii 4); but it also recalls Exodus xxxiii 20. *Selfe life* (the vision of life in its essence) is forbidden, according to St Thomas, until man has, by grace, been united with God.

Donne next considers the awesome consequences of the Crucifixion. A characteristic Donnian metaphor is the concept of Nature (18) as 'God's Lieutenant', an officer, who takes the place of another, or 'vice-regent'. The implication of inadequacy resides in the verb *shrinke*, and may reflect Donne's disapproval of natural religion. God's *footstoole* (20) that 'cracks' is the earth (see Isaiah lxvi 1); and the 'winking' *Sunne* looks back to the three hours of darkness in Luke xxiii 44. *Those hands which span the Poles* (21) is a biblical image, with dual meaning, illustrating Donne's dignified employment of serious puns in religious symbolism.

In lines 21–8, four rhetorical questions sublimely express Donne's apprehension at the situation he could not face; he resorts to scientific images culled from his reading. *Zenith* (24), derived from Arabic *samt*, meant a 'path over the head'; but it came to be narrowly employed in medieval astronomy as a technical term for the 'highest point of a celestial sphere'. This word, and its Greek companion *Antipodes*, are found in Trevisa's fourteenth-century translation of Bartholomaeus's *De Proprietatibus Rerum*. *Durt* (27), by *metathesis* from M. English *drit*, came often to be spelt with a *u* in the fifteenth to the seventeenth centuries. The original meaning was moist excrement or filth. *Make durt of dust* refers to the mingling of earth with blood.

The agonized middle passage serves to change the tone from discursive to passionate. Donne does not suggest that Christians should avoid facing the physical tragedy of Good Friday; but its spiritual significance can be realized by another path – through the

interior vision of the memory, an adjunct of the soul. Beginning
with line 33, the argument runs thus: the eye sees only what lies
before it, but memory (traditionally located at the back of the head)
is retrospective (33–6). Through memory a sinner is reminded that
Christ, upon the Cross, observes *him*. The direction he has taken
exposes his back to the correction it deserves. The traveller asks to
be worthy of God's anger, that the dross may be purged by fire,
and mercy granted. A Christian's prayer is always to be restored to
God's image through grace, that when his soul is brought face to
face with its Maker, it will be recognized (39–42).

In *Goodfriday, 1613* Donne aims to present three important
truths: the psychological, that seeing is partially a function of the
memory; the geographical, that the map of the world is properly,
not a flat, but a round concept; and the spiritual, that man emanates
from God, and may return to Him through humility, penitence and
grace, irrespective of the rational direction his life has taken.
Donne, the humanist, has dabbled intellectually in science, but is
now ready to dedicate his life to religion. *Goodfriday* seems to have
some affinities with Blake's poem, *Morning*:

> To find the Western path,
> Right thro' the Gates of Wrath
> I urge my way;
> Sweet mercy leads me on
> With soft repentant moan:
> I see the break of day.

Hymne to God my God, in my sicknesse

This poem was first printed in the second edition of Donne's
Poems (1635). There were two manuscript versions, Stowe 961 and
in the papers of Sir Julius Caesar. A feature of the 1635 printed text
is the inconsistency of the spelling, especially the doubling of consonants e.g. *comming* (1), *come* (3); *Mapp* (7), *Maps* (14); *Flat* (8),
flatt (14); *streights* (10, 19), *straits* (11).

> Since I am comming to that Holy roome,
>   Where, with thy Quire of Saints for evermore,
> I shall be made thy Musique; As I come
>   I tune the Instrument here at the dore,
>   And what I must doe then, thinke now before.   5

Whilst my Physitians by their love are growne
  Cosmographers, and I their Mapp, who lie
Flat on this bed, that by them may be showne
    That this is my South-west discoverie
    Per fretum febris, by these streights to die,   10

I joy, that in these straits, I see my West;
  For, though theire currants yeeld returne to none,
What shall my West hurt me? As West and East
    In all flatt Maps (and I am one) are one,
    So death doth touch the Resurrection.   15

Is the Pacifique Sea my home? Or are
  The Easterne riches? Is *Jerusalem*?
Anyan, and *Magellan*, and *Gibraltare*,
    All streights, and none but streights, are wayes to them,
    Whether where *Japhet* dwelt, or *Cham*, or *Sem*.   20

We thinke that *Paradise* and *Calvarie*,
  Christs Crosse, and *Adams* tree, stood in one place;
Looke Lord, and finde both *Adams* met in me;
    As the first *Adams* sweat surrounds my face,
    May the last *Adams* blood my soule embrace.   25

So, in his purple wrapp'd receive mee Lord,
  By these his thornes give me his other Crowne;
And as to others soules I preach'd thy word,
    Be this my Text, my Sermon to mine owne,
    Therfore that he may raise the Lord throws down.   30

Walton in his *Life of Donne* gave the date of this poem as 23 March 1630 (new style 1631), for he supposed it to have been written a week before the poet died. In this view he was supported by Evelyn Simpson. John Sparrow, using citations from the *Devotions,* argued that the hymn was penned during Donne's previous illness in 1623, a date confirmed in Sir Julius Caesar's manuscript copy of the poem, and favoured by Helen Gardner. Whatever the time of the illness, Donne sincerely believed he was about to die.

The comparative metrical regularity, and even pace of the poem's five-line pentameter stanzas, rhyming a b a b b, gives this Hymn a dignity and musicality unrivalled among death-bed poems. Only one line (18), containing three proper names, offers stress difficulties:

The Divine Poems

Añyăn, añd *Măgéllăn*, añd *Gíbrăltáre,*

Anyan was the sixteenth-century name for the Bering Straits. Donne's sense of form in the *Hymne to God my God* is as remarkable as the restraint of his language.

From Walton's and the poet's own accounts, few men could have been better prepared for death than Donne; this is confirmed in lines 4 and 5. A subtle conceit vitalizes each of the first five stanzas; while in the final stanza he calls his justification of God's ways a sermon to himself, in which he supplies his own text (29).

In lines 1–5 the poet, picturing his sick-bed in an ante-room to Heaven, is among the suitors waiting to be received, himself an aspirant instrumentalist preparing for admission to the King's Music. This he describes as a *Quire of Saints* (2), having in mind an account of Heaven in the Book of Revelation. *Musique*, a dominating conceit, is placed in the middle of the stanza, harmony being the significant note of God's house.

Stanza 2 depicts the patient in the hands of *Physitians* who, *by their love*, are turned *Cosmographers*, studying the body as though it were a *Mapp* of the world, rolled out on a flat surface. The idea that love for a patient is essential to obtaining a cure was a tenet of Paracelsus, adopted by the Platonists. One of Donne's physicians, Dr Fox, was a very close friend indeed. But the poet remarks on a limitation of the physicians (8–10), who merely point to discoveries made by others; the analogy drawn is to explorations of the New World, particularly in the *South-west* (9) by Magellan. Through the narrow straits of his own fever (*Per fretum febris*), Donne maintains that he has found the path to deliverance (lines 6–10).

In stanza 3 the poet reverts to the cartographical paradox of *Goodfriday, 1613* – that *West and East/ In all flatt Maps . . . are one* (13/14). Lying prone on his sick-bed, Donne thinks of himself as such a map, and the *straits* located there as his sufferings. The patient has reached a point of no return (12), but is excited at death's triumph over the body, death being the assurance of *Resurrection* (11–15).

The conceit continues in stanza 4. The seeming reward of tribulation is the arrival at calm waters of the *Pacifique Sea* (16). But such respite is not the goal of the true explorer; nor is the wealth of the East, or Jerusalem. The straits (or perils) are means to the divine end, whether the traveller toils in Europe (*Japhet*), Africa (*Cham*) or Asia (*Sem*).

The allusions of stanza 5 are to the Old and the New Testaments. Neither Paradise nor Calvary is to be found as a location on a map; Donne thinks it immaterial whether Eden and Golgotha were in one place. *Calvarie* from Latin *Calvaria* (skull) is named as the place of crucifixion only in Luke's Gospel; the Greek Testament has *Kranion,* with the same meaning. Elsewhere the name is *Golgotha,* from Aramaic *gulgulta* (skull). Legend has it that the skull of Adam was found on the same site, a hill shaped like the human cranium. For the Christian, Donne holds that Christ and Adam are generic symbols, and in line 23 he asks God to see them as united in his impending death. He is quietly confident that he will be saved. He feels the sweat of sinning Adam upon his face, but knows that the blood of Christ (the second Adam) will bring about his redemption. Donne's thoughts were on 1 Corinthians xv 21–58, the most memorable being:

> 21 For since by man came death, by man came also the resurrection of the dead. 22 For as in Adam all die, even so in Christ shall all be made alive . . . 45 And so it is written: The first man Adam was made a living soule, the last Adam was made a quickening spirit.
>
> (King James Bible, 1611)

In stanza 6 Donne beseeches God to apotheosize his death. He is to be shrouded in purple, the colour appropriate to royal persons (originally crimson) and to receive a crown, no longer of thorns, but of glory. This is because, in his clerical office, he served as the Lord's instrument in preaching the gospel. This poem is his last sermon, its moral being that to be raised from the dead, one must have experienced the dark night of the soul. Verse 8 of Psalm 146, one of Donne's favourites, reads: 'The Lord raiseth them that are bowed down.' Walton says of Donne that he was 'alwaies preaching to himself, like an Angel from a cloud, but in none' (*Life,* p 49).

The keynote of the Hymn is serenity and theological self-sufficiency. Donne steadfastly believed in the Pauline doctrine of salvation in heaven, and prepared himself, as devout Christians still do. Modern readers have to accept this, fully to appreciate the piety of the poem, as it expresses the patristic tradition.

Donne did not dramatize his death in attuning his soul to its Christian destiny. But the undoubted music is a virtue unexpected in his theological poems. The sincerity of the language palliates the curious thinking, the paradoxes and the schematic rhetoric. Note, particularly, the pervasive employment of *ploce*: *come* (1, 3), *thinke* (5, 21), *Mapp* (7, 14), *flat* (8, 14), *West* (9, 11, 13), *East* (13, 17), *streights* (10, 11, 19 twice), *none* (12, 19), *one* (14 twice), *Adam* (22, 23, 24, 25), *Lord* (23, 30), *soule* (25, 28).

To borrow some phrases of Robert Browning, Donne employed the mediate word to breed the thought, and he attempted to 'save the soul besides'. Dealing in sacramental and other symbols, he needs an interpreter, as early Christians required biblical hermeneuts and commentators. Critics sometimes complain of a sameness of technique, and the burden of theological ideas, which the Reformation did much to put out of countenance. But neither criticism is unanswerable.

Donne began as a shrewd London observer, writing elegies and love poems ironically reminiscent of the Ovidian and Petrarchan traditions. He was nevertheless conditioned by the ingrained discipline of his early Catholic education. Not all the mature poems are debates between the soul and the body, but the best of them trade in paradoxes of doctrine, and concepts of a theologian, who is intellectual as well as emotive. His merit lies in the hard, logical language, which is as denotative as any in Bacon. His poetry has exciting vividness, especially in communicating individual relationships with a woman, with friends, or with God. Ambiguities, of words or ideas, make the poems even more meaningful in their period context.

Any poet who essays a discursive style cannot survive without colloquial rhythms and prosaic nuances of stress. Donne appears to be thinking aloud, and effectively, because his masculine abundance of monosyllables and subtle articulation are perfectly natural. The reader responds to a voice that is personable, not bookish, whatever the source of Donne's ideas. These are often abstract, but the predicative statements, the vocatives and the pronouns, have a stress individuation that creates a sense of liveliness and emotional intensity. This pressure arises from Donne's positive sense of values, especially in love and religion. The urgency is motivated, the language concise, the mood unsentimental; and

Donne sternly resists the conventional locution, in an age that was most derivative when it tried to be English.

Donne's liberties with stress were notorious, and it has been suggested that he was attempting to resuscitate the measures of Wyatt and Skelton. But what he sought was freedom within the syllable-counting tradition of Italian and Spanish poets. T. S. Eliot was just in claiming that Donne was no rebel in metrical practice; but Donne probably forced the pace of succeeding generations, who learnt from him the art of modulating a pentameter couplet. What Dryden and Pope superadded was phrasal and clausal balance, to make the couplet a self-contained unit.

Josephine Miles discovered that Donne used the proportion of 'about eight adjectives, sixteen nouns and twelve verbs in ten lines throughout most of his work (*Eras and Modes in English Poetry*, p 24). This may account for the sameness of his methods as alleged by disapproving critics; in fact, there is a designed disparity between the rhythms of the *Satyres* and those of the later *Divine Poems*. Donne's stanzaic craftsmanship was carefully studied by the Continental critic, Pierre Legouis; and Mario Praz expressed the view that, however 'crabbed and prosaic' Donne's imagery might be, his metrical originality was beyond compare. Although the poet called his experiments 'songs', in most cases they were intended to be spoken. In the Sonnets, said Praz, 'the unit is not the line . . . but the entire poem' ('Donne's Relation to the Poetry of his Time', *A Garland for John Donne*, pp 56–7).

Coventry Patmore, in his 'Essay on Metrical Law' (*Poetical Works*, Bell II, 1903, pp 221–33) has some observations that are relevant to Donne's metrical quality:

> The quality of all emotion which is not ignoble is to boast of its allegiance to law. The limits and decencies of ordinary speech will by no means declare high and strong feelings with efficiency. These must have free use of all sorts of figures and latitudes of speech; such latitudes as would at once be perceived by a delicately constituted mind to be lax and vicious, without the shackles of artistic form. What in prose would be shrieks and vulgar hyperbole, is transmuted by metre into graceful and impressive song. . . . The language should always seem to *feel,* though not to *suffer from* the bonds of verse. The very deformities produced, really

or apparently, in the phraseology of a great poet, by the confinement of metre, are beautiful ... *Perfect poetry and song are, in fact, nothing more than perfect speech upon high and moving subjects.*

Donne's imagination was powerfully influenced by his most recent reading, not of the poems of his contemporaries, but of encyclopedic treatises. Miscellaneous prose affected the structure of his dialectic verse, by engendering an interior conflict between word emphasis and the metrical requirements of the line, as envisaged by Puttenham in *The Arte of English Poesie*. That Donne experimented with forty-six different stanza forms, some highly intricate, is indeed worthy of notice; he apparently enjoyed the self-discipline, as a kind of asceticism he could turn to account. Once determined upon a pattern, he made few significant departures unconnected with the internal modulation of the lines. Unlike Browning in the dramatic monologues, he did not wait upon thought and feeling to shape the holistic design. Form was paramount; and Donne's forte was to adjust the dramatized ideas to the chosen pattern.

The appeal of Donne since the 1920s has been partly based on his honesty as a writer, the candid reporting of his emotions, and the amusingly cynical attitude towards conventional morality. For this reason his long narrative monologue, *The Extasie*, has been regarded as a test piece. Critics are by no means disposed to see this as a celebration of conjugal love; the ambiguities are cleverly introduced to conceal the private nature of the experience. In a longish composition like this, the ensuing stanzas depend largely on the emotions that shape the rhythmical design of the first. The poet is the more important of the (usually two) actors in a Donnian drama, because the responses of the lady are necessarily implicit – a principal ground for asserting that Donne's scope is more limited than Shakespeare's.

What significance the term 'metaphysical' now has is largely to distinguish Donne's contribution from that of his contemporaries, Chapman and Fulke Greville. Some aspects of metaphysical verse were undoubtedly anticipated by Sidney, and can be traced back to neo-Platonism. M. P. Ramsay has shown in 'Donne's Relation to Philosophy' (*A Garland for John Donne*, pp 100–120) that the metaphysical cult was one of several attempts to counter the authoritarianism of the medieval account of classical philosophy, aroused by the revival of interest in Aristotle. Catholic Italy, France and Spain provided the intellectual climate in which the metaphysics of individualists like Donne flowered.

Ample use of Aristotle's *Organon* and Plato's *Timaeus* was made by Thomas Aquinas, whose scholastic method became the core of revitalized education at the University of Paris. Scholasticism soon obtained the approval of the Catholic Church, and was artistically assimilated in Dante's great epic, as an official justification of the Faith. Rationally, it was explained that God had revealed Himself, if not His laws, to a body of men and women, who founded the Christian Church.

As yet there was no distinction between philosophy and science; the new philosophy that 'calls all in doubt' (*An Anatomie of the World,* 205) was natural science, typified for Donne by mathematics, astronomy, physiology and anatomy. The new discoveries were based upon observation of phenomena (even before the use of optical instruments), and specifically on motion, mass and objective measurements; they clearly undermined scholastic teaching about man and the universe, a so-called science of Being and Essence, propounded in *Summa Theologica.* The hint was now obvious that Aquinas and fellow thinkers had relied on received doctrine and fallacious reasoning, not only to replace the *prima materia* of Paracelsus, but to establish a relationship between soul and body that neither the evidence of the senses, nor logical argument could substantiate. Scholasticism had not before encountered a conflict between qualitative 'truth' and the empirical, quantitative facts; it was writers like Bacon and Galileo (trained as a Pythagorean Platonist) who discredited scholastic procedures, by insisting on the philosophical validity of science.

Donne had joined the Anglican cause before he wrote his Sonnet on the Church (No. 2 in the Westmoreland MS) depicting his dilemma about the future of Christian worship. However acute the poet's sensibilities may have been, the writings of this period do not reflect a unified personality. Donne had read much too liberally and intensely not to be moved by a sense of intellectual insecurity, despite his faith.

Philosophically, the world was in a period of transition, and Donne saw no hope in adopting either the new cosmology, or the neo-Platonist compromise with Christianity, which was largely a mystical solution, worked out in Alexandria, and transformed in

humanist Italy. Accepting the divine inspiration of the Bible, and
the Pauline necessity for grace, Donne anchored his faith in a
practising Christianity, as a means of coping with original sin, a
vital problem of patristic theologians. Donne could not share the
humanist belief in the perfectibility of man by his own efforts; the
erring faculties of men would, he felt, negate the gains of empirical
enquiry. The efficacy of all systems of knowledge was transitory,
including Paracelsian transcendental alchemy, the *tria prima,* by
which Donne explained the corruption of the world in the
Anniversaries.

From the latter source Donne likened the soul of man to the
'*Balsamum* of the Body', which had 'a natural and untaught hatred
. . . of that which is evil'. The Old and Middle English word, of
Greek origin, was revived in the 1590s by Marlowe and Shakespeare; Donne used it in many analogies, and described the nature
of this healing oil in a Sermon preached on Whitsunday 1624 (VI
v 216). For Paracelsus, the self-recuperative properties of the
Balsamum existed in all organic bodies.

The model of the unified world, described by medieval philosophers and by C. S. Lewis in *The Discarded Image* (C.U.P., 1967),
was by 1600 threatened with disintegration. Donne's theologically
orientated poems reflect the intellectual conflicts that this dissolution entailed, and in that sense the term 'metaphysical' is appropriate to the kind of discursive poetry he wrote. The secular lyrics
belong to another, the Courtly school, which had arisen from the
hierarchical structure of the Tudor monarchy. There was inevitable rivalry among literary coteries, and the circulation of compositions in manuscript was the order of the day among cynics who
were disrespectful of traditional symbols. Donne's secular re-
creations were private, as his speculative *Sermons* were public
utterances.

Robin Skelton, contributing to *Elizabethan Poetry* (Arnold,
1960), believes that very few of Donne's 'non-secular meditative
poems succeed. There is not sufficient pressure of personal
necessity' (p 218). This is true of some; but what an imperfect
impression of the range of Donne's powers one would gain from
the naturalistic lyrics in *Songs and Sonets*! The religious expression
was no less spontaneous, and valuable for the speculations and
perceptions it awakened in the devotions of others. The *Divine
Poems* of James I's reign alleviate the starkness of Donne, the

Elizabethan, and through their dignity temper the mind for the moving language of the *Sermons*. The praiseworthy grouping of poems, according to chronology, in the volumes edited by Helen Gardner for the Clarendon Press has stimulated new and valuable assessments of Donne's literary development after 1600.

Miscellaneous Prose: *Biathanatos,* *Pseudo-Martyr, Ignatius his Conclave,* and *The True Character of a Dunce*

🐚🐚🐚🐚🐚🐚

BETWEEN 1608 and 1614 Donne produced most of the miscellaneous writings, which were works of intellectual maturity, and significant steps in his progress towards faith. Though varied in theme, they bear the impress of an analytical mind, respecting ancient authority, but desiring truth with reason. It would be mistaken to regard *Biathanatos* simply as a scholastic exercise. Written in 1607 or 1608, it was an apology for suicide of which Donne was discreetly proud, though it remained unpublished until 1646. An authoritative manuscript of the work was deposited in the Bodleian Library by Donne's friend, Lord Herbert of Cherbury, in 1642.

Much research and ingenuity in interpreting canon and civil law went into the composition of *Biathanatos.* Canon law consisted of decrees issued by the Church in ecclesiastical council, and Donne felt that some of these were the fruit of prejudice or undeserved respect, rather than religious dogma. There is no doubt of Donne's frustration at the lack of purposive activity during his retirement at Mitcham, and there were signs of mental distress occasioned by depression and illness. This is borne out by the writer's confession in the Preface that he, like Beza, had a morbid inclination to take his own life, which he ascribed partly to the 'suppressed and afflicted religion' in which he was educated, and partly to a deep admiration for Christian martyrs, such as St Stephen. Martyrdom for any faith Donne regarded as 'sanctified self-homicide'; there were martyrs in plenty to remind Donne in Bede's *Ecclesiastical History* and in the medieval homilies.

Suicide was an esteemed way of dying among adherents of the Stoic philosophy, despite the belief of the school in the natural law of self-preservation. *Biathanatos* may have arisen as an enquiry into the relative position of Epicurus. But whatever the motive, Donne withheld the book from publication, because he was aware that self-murder had been declared a sin, and was therefore heretical, in the Christian faith of whatever doctrinal persuasion. Taking historical examples, he examined the role of conscience, and established that self-homicide is not cowardly, even though the Church regarded it as an unforgivable sin. This book has a place beside Burton's *Anatomy of Melancholy,* as a reflection of the temper of the times, in which cynics sometimes minimized the worth of life by affecting a contempt for its values.

In Part I Donne discusses, as a practical psychologist, the civilized and moral implications of the law of nature, to which suicide is not opposed. In Part II he examines the rational attitude of the Christian Fathers, and adds observations on the views of Aristotle and Jospehus. Part III takes into account the instances of alleged suicide in the Scriptures, among which those of Samson and Judas Iscariot are test cases; he also considers the implications of the Commandment of Moses 'Thou shalt not kill'. It is clear from a letter that Donne wrote to Sir Henry Goodyer in September 1608, that he was troubled by the problem of freedom of will, and with the duties and responsibilities of men in society:

> To chuse is to do: but to be no part of any body is to be
> nothing. At most, the greatest persons, are but great wens
> and excrescences; men of wit and delightful conversation
> but as moales for ornament, except they be so incorporated
> into the body of the world, that they contribute something
> to the sustentation of the whole.

In his last Sermon, *Death's Duel,* he spoke of life paradoxically as *hebdomada mortium,* a week of death; and it would seem from Donne's elaborate preparations for his end, after his mother's passing in 1631, that death was for him the crowning public event of his life.

One is bound, therefore, to compare *Biathanatos* with the subtler Browningesque view of life expressed in the adjurations of *Satyre* III, lines 76–84:

> To'adore, or scorne an image, or protest,   76
> May all be bad; doubt wisely; in strange way
> To stand inquiring right, is not to stray;

To sleepe, or runne wrong, is. On a huge hill,
Cragged, and steep, Truth stands, and hee that will   80
Reach her, about must, and about must goe;
And what th'hills suddennes resists, winne so;
Yet strive so, that before age, deaths twilight,
Thy Soule rest, for none can worke in that night.

The last line, an unconscious recollection of the Gospel of St John
ix 4, provides a cadence to the optimism of Donne; none of the
lines yield to the accidie of some of *Biathanatos*.

There is a note of self-criticism in Donne's letter to Sir Robert
Ker, written about April or May, 1619, in which he admits that the
manuscript was shown to 'particular friends in both universities',
the response being that 'certainly, there was a false thread in it, but
not easily to be found' (Simpson, *Selected Prose,* p 152). George
Williamson argues that *Biathanatos* is a 'libertine document', in
which Donne carried paradox to unprecedented limits. In *Seventeenth Century Contexts* he quotes the following passage to illustrate
Donne's 'relativistic philosophy'. The style is characteristic of
Donne's paradoxical mode of progression, and negligent use of
capitalized nouns:

> That light which issues from the Moone, doth best re-
> present and expresse that which in our selves we call the
> light of Nature; for as that in the Moone is permanent and
> ever there, and yet it is unequall, various, pale, and lan-
> guishing, So is our light of Nature changeable. For being
> at the first kindling at full, it wayned presently, and by
> departing further and further from God, declined by
> generall sinne, to almost a totall Eclipse: till God comming
> neerer to us, first by the Law, and then by Grace, enlightned
> and repayred it againe, conveniently to his ends, for further
> exercise of his Mercy and Justice. And then those Artificiall
> Lights, which our selves make for our use and service here,
> as Fires, Tapers, and such resemble the light of Reason, as
> wee have in our Second part accepted that Word. For
> though the light of these Fires and Tapers be not so naturall,
> as the Moone, yet because they are more domestique, and
> obedient to us, wee distinguish particular objects better by
> them, than by the Moone; So by the Arguments, and

Deductions, and Conclusions, which our selves beget and produce, as being more serviceable and under us, because they are our creatures; particular cases are made more cleare and evident to us; for these we can be bold withall, and put them to any office, and examine, and prove their truth, or likeliehood, and make them answers as long as wee will aske; whereas the light of Nature, with a solemne and supercilious Majestie, will speake but once, and give no Reason, nor endure Examination.

But because of these two kindes of light, the first is too weake, and the other false, (for onely colour is the object of sight, and we not trust candlelight to discerne Colours) we have therefore the Sunne, which is the Fountaine and Treasure of all created light, for an Embleme of that third best light of our understanding, which is the Word of God.

(*Biathanatos,* 1646, Third Part, Distinction 1, Section 1,
p 153)

In his prose, Donne is more in harmony with the practice of the time than in the poetry; the toils of stylistic convention were no less intractable for him than for Nashe, Lyly, Shakespeare and Chapman, who could write with vigour in the prose medium. The habit of aphoristic expression, and the mould of rhetorical schemes and devices, were astonishingly inflexible in determining syntactic sequences, as well as the balance of phrases and clauses. Long experience was needed to overcome lack of orderliness, concision and unity in the building of paragraphs.

In the middle period, Donne's dialectic and discursive prose was not remarkable for originality. The syntax is laboured and involved, and is not helped by whims of punctuation, one instrument of dividing thoughts; for instance, before the analogical connective *So,* which is conspicuous by its capital letter. There is a trick of redundancy in employing doublets, e.g. *represent and expresse*; *permanent and ever there*; *unequall, various*; *beget and produce*; *cleare and evident*; *examine, and prove their truth*; *Fountaine and Treasure*. In the first ten lines the changes of tense from present to past are without warrant. The scholastic method of reasoning seems to encourage haphazard afterthoughts, which destroy the integrity of the syntactic units, and end by clouding understanding with irrelevance.

Donne had not yet discovered that the organization of efficient prose is more complicated than that of verse, because it lacks the discipline of stanza or couplet form. Good prose is ordered by a sense development that appeals rhythmically to the ear. A happy sequence of vowels and consonants underscores the intonation and stress of an imagined speaking voice, and the effect is generally appealing when a writer seems to be talking naturally to a reader. Donne is at his best when he conveys an experienced emotion in symbolic language, and *Biathanatos* offers few opportunities. He can be at his dullest when the sentences are strung together by logical connectives, *so, since, but therefore,* etc.

Biathanatos has an argumentative tone of such sobriety that it is difficult for Donne to invest it with literary attractiveness. There is no audience to address, or to hang upon his dramatic utterances, as in the *Sermons.* While in theory Donne rejects the supremacy of logic in moral issues, he is unable to replace it with the lexical simplicity of Scripture, or the personal intimacy that enlivens the finest of his letters. The pages teem with borrowings from classical sources, such as *exagitate, obtrectations, umbragious* and *excribing,* all in the Preface. The curious vocabulary and learned analogues give the impression that Donne's dialectic prose is not designed for perspicuous reading. In the passage of thirty lines cited above, there are but five full-stops; and the structure of the sentences is not notably periodic.

The analogy between the law of Nature and the light of the inconstant Moon, occupying the opening ten lines, is not much improved by the elaborate images from astronomy that point the theological implications. Donne argues inconclusively that the orbital position of the heavenly body determines the observer's distance from or nearness to God.

In the second analogy, which occupies twelve lines, Reason is likened to the artificial lights that man devises; they are domestic and proximate, consequently useful for argument and conclusion. Being instruments of the mind, they continue to elucidate, as long as men ask questions. But the rational faculty has no real validity in Nature, which is imperious, and gives no reasons.

Man's third kind of light is that of the Sun, the emblem of majesty and the fountain-head of truth and understanding, symbolizing the mediate grace of God. This light enables man to discern colours, regarded by Donne as the object of sight; neither moon nor artificial light reliably distinguishes these. The full conspectus of this analogy occupies a long paragraph (here curtailed), which is metaphorical to the point of allegory.

The charge of casuistry has been levelled against *Biathanatos*, though much of it is characterized by an intellectual coldness and detachment. The word *casuist*, in the seventeenth century, was derived from Jesuit doctrine, to which Donne had been long exposed, its first appearance in the OED being from Ben Jonson's *The Silent Woman* (1609). The abstract noun *casuistry* was not, however, in literary use until Pope employed it in *The Rape of the Lock* (1725). By then the word suggested quibbling, with a theological bias, the sort of reasoning that dethrones common sense in matters of conscience. Donne's bent was to dislike dialectical hypocrisy, and the natural conclusion is that the non-serious argument in *Biathanatos* is intended as a satire on dubious justification. The identification of martyrdom with suicide can only be regarded as an error of judgement.

PSEUDO-MARTYR

Unjustifiable martyrdom is the theme of the next work, *Pseudo-Martyr* (1610), not only the longest, but also the first of Donne's prose works to be published. Donne entered the active field of polemics in defence of the Oath of Allegiance, which James I imposed upon recusants, after the disclosure of the Gunpowder Plot in 1605. Catholics who were loyal blamed the Jesuits for this enactment, which met with vigorous pamphleteering resistance. Donne admonished die-hard recusants, whom he regarded as aspirant martyrs unworthy of the name; their cause, he argued, had no moral or legal justification. *Pseudo-Martyr* was dedicated to, and approved by the King, and was partly written to secure his secular favour; in fact, it earned Donne an honorary M.A. degree from Oxford University, and a request from James I that he should join the Anglican Church.

The merits of the book are not strictly literary; but the thinking throws light on Donne's religious standpoint, and provides a background for some of his other writings. Whatever the character of the writer's religious upbringing, Jesuit doctrines must have been inculcated within the Donne family circle; there was no scope for Ignatian education in England in the 1580s, when Donne went to Oxford and Cambridge. Jesuit suppression included penalties by death or exile for immigrant missionaries. Donne's moderation in this controversy was therefore prudent, and probably inspired by the *Apologia Catholica* (1605) and other polemics of Thomas Morton, chaplain to the Earl of Rutland, who in 1607 became Dean of Gloucester. Morton, on frequent visits to London, pleaded with Donne to take holy orders, and offered him a benefice; but according to Walton, Donne declined the offer, on account of the irregularities of his youth.

Pseudo-Martyr has twelve chapters, and the substance of its plea is that English Catholics ought to take the oath, as a mark of loyalty to their country, even if allegiance to the King conflicted with the claimed supremacy of the Pope. Jesuits who failed to do so were not entitled to the dignity accorded by the Church to martyrs. Catholic opposition to the oath was based on Cardinal Bellarmine's doctrine of indirect power, which Donne refuted in the second half of the treatise. His exposition at the time was regarded as vigorous and soundly argued, and only Thomas Fitzherbert saw fit publicly to contest it. The style makes little advance on that of *Biathanatos,* the tone of the argument being unimpassioned.

The passage from the Preface, addressed 'To the Priests, and Jesuits, and to their Disciples in this Kingdom', illustrates the greater *élan* that Donne was able to muster, when he was personally involved:

If they will be content to impute to me all humane infirmi-
ties, they shall neede to faine nothing: I am, I confesse,
obnoxious enough. My naturall impatience not to digge
painefully in deepe, and stony, and sullen learnings: My
Indulgence to my freedome and libertie, as in all other   5
indifferent things, so in my studies also, not to betroth or
enthral my selfe, to any one science, which should possesse
or denominate me: My easines, to affoord a sweete and
gentle Interpretation, to all professors of Christian Religion,
if they shake not the Foundation, wherein I have in my   10
ordinary Communication and familiar writings, often expressed and declared my selfe: hath opened me enough to
their malice, and put me into their danger, and given them
advantage to impute me, whatsoever such degrees of lazi-
ness, of liberty, of irresolution, can produce. . . .   15

I had a longer worke to doe than many other men; for I was first to blot out, certaine impressions of the Romane religion, and to wrastle both against the examples and against the reasons, by which some hold was taken; ... And although I apprehended well enough, that this irreso-   20
lution not onely retarded my fortune, but also bred some scandall, and endangered my spirituall reputation, by laying me open to many mis-interpretations; yet all these respects did not transport me to any violent and sudden determina-
nation, till I had, to the measure of my poore wit and   25
judgement, survayed and digested the whole body of Divi-
nity, controverted betweene ours and the Romane Church. In which search and disquisition, that God, which awakened me then, and hath never forsaken me in that industry, as he is the Author of that purpose, so is he a witnes of this pro-   30
testation; that I behaved my selfe, and proceeded therin with humility, and diffidence in my selfe; ...

   To have alwaies abstained from this declaration of my selfe, had beene to betray, and to abandon, and prostitute my good name to their misconceivings and imputations;   35
who thinke presently, that hee hath no Religion, which dares not call his Religion by some newer name than *Christian*.

The candour of the author is disarming, but it is hampered by the mannered presentation. In Tudor English *shall* (2) remained the auxiliary of an educated writer for all persons, though *will* was in use in popular speech. *Obnoxious* (3) was employed several times by Donne in senses somewhat different from modern usage. With him, as with other writers, it did not mean 'odious', 'objectionable' or 'likely to give offence'; the word acquired these meanings only in the last quarter of the seventeenth century. The earlier sense was 'exposed to harm', 'blameworthy', 'liable to censure'; the significance was thus passive rather than active. The word appears to have been made current by Hooker's employment of it in *The Laws of Ecclesiastical Polity* (1597).

   After a lively start, in which the writer expresses impatience at delving into '*deepe*, and *stony*, and *sullen* learnings' (4) – well chosen metaphorical epithets – the syntax becomes confused in a morass of compound-complex structures, which hold up the pre-
dication, *hath opened me . . . to their malice* (12/13). The reason is

that Donne's co-ordinated subjects *impatience* (3), *Indulgence* (5) and *easines* (8) are side-tracked by qualifying phrases, which favour rhetorical synonymia, e.g. *freedom and libertie* (5), *betroth or enthral* (6/7), *possesse or denominate* (7/8), *sweete and gentle* (8/9), *expressed and declared* (11/12). Such pleonastic pairings are usually connected by *and* when their implications are more or less identical, and by *or* when there is a shade of difference in meaning. This overworked device Donne may have learnt from Bishop J. Fisher (see his *English Works* published by the EETS, 1876, p 90).

The habit of doubling, which has a doubtful origin, became a mannerism that Donne never eliminated; it resembles the rhetoricians' *schesis onomaton*, and is continued in *violent and sudden* (24), *survayed and digested* (26), *search and disquisition* (28), *humility and diffidence* (32), *betray and abandon* (34), *misconceivings and imputations* (35), where the *and/or* distinction is not so well observed. Abstract nouns in the plural, e.g. *learnings* (4) began in O. English, reached their peak in the sixteenth century, and declined in the eighteenth.

Another of Donne's notable habits is the juxtaposition of *as* and *so* phrases (or clauses) for comparison (e.g. in lines 5 and 29). The prose of Donne also encouraged literary archaism, such as the use of *hath* (12, 29, 36), then being superseded by *has*. The employment of compound relative adverbs, e.g. *wherein* (10), is a further instance. Most of the latter type of compounds date from the thirteenth century, and lasted until the eighteenth, when they passed into the jargon of officials. Donne has the alternative usage *by which* in line 19.

The piling up of subordinations invariably leads Donne into involved sentence structures, which he sometimes attempts to resolve by punctuation (e.g. a semicolon or a colon), as in line 23 before the resumptive connective *yet*. He is fond, too, of appended participial phrases, a constant source of looseness in his sentences; an awkward example occurs in *controverted betweene ours and the Romane Church* (27). Not only is the past participle a polysyllabic misfit, but *ours* would have been placed to better advantage at the end of the sentence.

The well-known conservatism of Donne's prose is well illustrated in the last paragraph. The pluperfect tense employed for hypothetical statements in the past, e.g. '*had been* to betray' (34), was still in vogue with Jacobean writers, but the modern indicative construction with *would* was overtaking it. He was also inclined to the employment of possessive personal pronouns as antecedents to relative clauses, which began in M. English with the relative *that*; e.g. 'prostitute my good name to *their* misconceivings and imputations; *who* thinke presently' (a semicolon before the relative is a Donnian idiosyncracy). Relative *which*, dating back to the twelfth century, still had common gender in Alexander Gill's *Logonomia Anglica* (1621); in line 36 of the passage the reference is to persons, but this usage fell into disuse during the seventeenth century.

Word-choice and punctuation in Donne's prose have not received the attention they deserve, except perhaps from two critics, Morris W. Croll and Joan Webber. In *Pseudo-Martyr* the so-called anti-Ciceronian style is weighted with Latin polysyllables, producing novel effects upon the rhythm of sentences. An important adjunct is the disruptive punctuation, marked by a frequency of colons and semicolons, which replace connectives. Twists and turns of thought are not conducive to the roundness and harmony that one finds in Hooker's *Laws of Ecclesiastical Polity*; rarely does one encounter a smooth, syntactic continuity in Donne's expository prose. Paragraphs seem casual, unpremeditated, unrevised, because the writer is so pre-occupied with logical process that he neglects the proportions of the final utterance. Donne aims to persuade, rather than to convince, by thorough examination of the real motives that determine religious affiliations.

Pseudo-Martyr's loose style and long paragraphs abound in interpolations and digressions from the main path. What symmetry sentences possess is a result partly of the rhetorical principles that were inculcated in Donne's youth, and partly of his imaginative use of words. But there does not seem to have been that anterior sense of a completeness of rhythm for the thoughts, which he was to develop later in the *Sermons*. The paragraphs of *Pseudo-Martyr* may be described as thoughts communicated without a visualized audience, but so related that they can rarely be isolated for quotation. There are, however, witty parentheses of disapproval, as when Donne writes:

> Those other men, who in proude humility will say *brother Thiefe*, and *brother Wolfe*, and *brother Asse* (as Saint Francis, perchance not unprophetically, is said to have done) will admit no fraternity nor fellowshippe with Princes.
>
> (*Pseudo-Martyr*, p 50)

IGNATIUS HIS CONCLAVE

The original satire, in Latin, was written in the latter half of 1610, and printed in duodecimo the following year; there is no indication of place or authorship. The Latin edition was followed by an English version (1611) printed by Nicholas Okes for Richard More. Both were widely circulated, extant copies including a quarto from an undisclosed foreign press. Three further editions appeared in the succeeding forty-two years, the second during Donne's lifetime (1626).

Parallel texts of the Latin and English versions were edited by T. S. Healy, for the Clarendon Press in 1969, the citations below being taken from his English text. This editor regarded the Latin version as superior in 'rhetorical polish' to the English, and he supports John Donne Jr in believing that the translation was made by the writer himself. The language of the English version, he maintains, falls short of 'the rich blend of Senecan and Ciceronian styles' that Donne later evolved (Introd. p xiv). The satirical and sportive tone of the piece demands a pointed and lively style, not unlike that of the *Paradoxes*.

In its 143 pages *Ignatius his Conclave* arraigns the vanity, lightness and petulance of the Jesuits, without becoming too serious a polemic. Its spontaneity is not inconsistent with its being a commissioned work, probably instigated by King James I and the religious controversialist Thomas Morton, whose defence of the Oath of Supremacy and Allegiance had been attacked in Latin by the Ignatian advocate, Cardinal Bellarmine. Donne's Latin was skilful enough to respond in a way that repudiated the Vatican thrusts, while disillusioning English Catholics. The Catholics in England principally objected to the compulsions to attend Anglican church services and to receive its Sacraments at least once a year. The mockery of Donne's diatribe imitates that of Lucian's *Dialogues of the Dead*, then in fashion; but the immediate model was the French *Satyre Menippée*, burlesquing the meeting of the Estates General in Paris in 1593. There are also echoes of the genial humour of Erasmus.

Donne's marginal references show that he had access to thirty-three publications, not freely available to non-theological readers. Healy says (op. cit. p xxviii) that citations are from Catholic sources in Latin, not English ones, Kepler being the only

Protestant quoted. Greek and Arab texts are, however, occasionally referred to. Eighteen of the sources had been published in 1609 or 1610, when Donne had not the financial resources to purchase expensive books, and Healy's conclusion is that Donne was offered the use of the library of St Paul's Deanery, where he had assisted Morton in the theological controversies of the years 1602 to 1607 (op. cit. p 171).

In *Ignatius his Conclave* Donne recounts an imaginary visit to Hell, and the famous people he found there:

> I saw a secret place, where there were not many, beside *Lucifer* himselfe; to which, onely they had title, which had so attempted any innovation in this life, that they gave an affront to all antiquitie, and induced doubts, and anxieties, and scruples, and after, a libertie of beleeving what they would; at length established opinions, directly contrary to all established before.
>
> (*Conclave,* p 9)

The principal innovators controverted are Copernicus, Paracelsus, Machiavelli, Aretino and Philip Neri, all impugned from a theological standpoint. Columbus is introduced largely because of the evil machinations of the Jesuit order in South and Central America. Ignatius is conceived as a comic disputant, whose function is to debunk those innovators who claim the honour of sitting on the right hand of Satan's throne. Each competitor is required to state his claim to be considered the most important innovator in history; Ignatius is so successful in demolishing their pleas that he rivals Lucifer in subtlety, and is sent to found a kingdom on the moon. The craftiness of Ignatius of Loyola (1491–1556), who was a Basque educated late in life, is distinguished by distortion of history and treason against kings. Donne's satire was topical, because Ignatius had recently been canonized (1609). The Jesuits had been regarded with suspicion in several countries; Venice, for instance, expelled them for fifty years, and France for nine, during Donne's lifetime.

Donne contemned the arrogance of papal intervention in secular politics, and he equally disliked scholastic methods of controversy. He also made fun of the misapplied zeal, abstruseness and historical insignificance of some theologians. Dante's Inferno was peopled with traitors, and Milton's Hell with rebellious angels. But Donne encounters in the underworld counter-reformationists who seek to undermine the divine right of kings, religious immoderates and mystics who threaten conservative stability. The idea of an established Church was older even than that of St Paul, and Donne's conception of social harmony in states is derived from prototypes in the Old and New Testaments. In several works he expresses belief in the three canonical books: God's Register of the Elect (Revelation iii 5), the Book of Life (or Bible) and the Book of Creatures (Nature's laws anterior to the Church); they were regarded as man's keys to the mystery, morality and reality of life.

Copernicus, Tycho Brahe, Kepler and Galileo are implicated in the satire, not for the reason that Donne disapproved of the new Astronomy and its use of technology and measuring instruments, but because each innovator looked to him like a new Prometheus, disturbing man's relationship to God. Religion was, for Donne, a matter of conscience and communal assent to authority, both divine and kingly; innovation was, in intention, a form of rebellion, questioning the literal truth of the Bible. Man's error was to regard the Bible as factual history; the roles of the prophet and the poet should be recognized as significant to the efficacy of both Testaments.

In *Ignatius his Conclave* Donne enumerates some of the liberties of interpretation taken by the Catholic Church, without warrant of the Bible, such as the concept of Purgatory, and the right of equivocation to protect church interests, commonly regarded as a form of Machiavellianism. The seventh-century Pope Boniface III Donne places among the innovators for destroying the early Christian church, founded on the teaching of the Gospels. Not all of Donne's overdrawn evils could be laid at the door of Ignatius Loyola; and in suggesting that Machiavelli in *The Prince* and *Discorsi* taught the Jesuits much of their cunning, the writer is less than just to both parties.

The vigour and lucidity of Donne's prose are at their best in the following excerpts, the first in the form of narrative, the second of direct address:

A. As soone as the doore creekt, I spied a certaine *Mathe-* 15
matitian, which till then had bene busied to find, to deride,
to detrude *Ptolomey*; and now with an erect countenance,
and setled pace, came to the gates, and with hands and feet

(scarce respecting *Lucifer* himselfe) beat the dores, and
cried; 'Are these shut against me, to whom all the Heavens   20
were ever open, who was a Soule to the Earth, and gave it
motion?'

By this I knew it was *Copernicus*: For though I had never
heard ill of his life, and therefore might wonder to find him
there; yet when I remembred, that the *Papists* have extended   25
the name, & the punishment of Heresie, almost to every
thing, and that as yet I used *Gregories* and Bedes spectacles,
by which one saw *Origen,* who deserved so well of the
Christian Church, burning *in Hell*, I doubted no longer, but
assured my selfe that it was *Copernicus*.   30

(*Conclave,* p 13)

B. But for you, what new thing have you invented, by
which our *Lucifer* gets any thing? What cares hee whether   15
the earth travell, or stand still? Hath your raising up of the
earth into heaven, brought men to that confidence, that they
build new towers or threaten God againe? Or do they out
of this motion of the earth conclude, that there is no hell,
or deny the punishment of sin? Do not men beleeve? do   20
they not live just, as they did before? Besides, this detracts
from the dignity of your learning, and derogates from your
right and title of comming to this place, that those opinions
of yours may very well be true. If therfore any man have
honour or title to this place in this matter, it belongs wholly   25
to our *Clavius,* who opposed himselfe opportunely against
you, and the truth, which at that time was creeping into
every mans minde. Hee only can be called the Author of all
contentions, and schoole-combats in this cause; and no
greater profit can bee hoped for heerein, but that for such   30
brabbles, more necessarie matters bee neglected. And yet
not onely for this is our *Clavius* to bee honoured, but for the
great paines also which hee tooke in the *Gregorian Calender,*
by which both the peace of the Church, & Civill businesses
have beene egregiously troubled: nor hath heaven it selfe   35
escaped his violence, but hath ever since obeied his
apointments: so that *S. Stephen, John Baptist,* & all the rest,
which have bin commanded to worke miracles at certain
appointed daies, where their Reliques are preserved, do not

now attend till the day come, as they were accustomed, but 40
are awaked ten daies sooner, and constrained by him to
come downe from heaven to do that businesse; But your
inventions can scarce bee called yours, since long before
you, *Heraclides, Ecphantus* & *Aristarchus* thrust them into
the world 45

(*Conclave*, pp 17–19)

Copernicus's *De Revolutionibus Orbium Coelestium* (1543) was not the
assertive treatise Donne implies in the word *detrude* (A 17), meaning
to 'thrust out' or 'expell by force'. According to the OED this
borrowing first appeared in Hall's *Chronicle*, 1548, concerning the
reign of Richard III, and remained in use until the nineteenth
century. One of the properties of the sensible soul, according to
scholastic philosophers, was the faculty of motion; but Copernicus
did not ascribe the movement of the earth to any metaphorical
source, such as Donne suggests (A 20/22). The allusion to Origen's
heresy (A 25–30) is taken from Bellarmine's *De Purgatorio*, II 8.
Origen (AD 185–254) held that any evil-doer who was damned
would ultimately be saved; for which opinion he was condemned
by orthodox theologians after the fifth century, though himself an
exemplary Christian.

The Clavius of B 26 was a German professor of mathematics,
Christopher Klau, who taught at the Jesuit College in Rome. He
helped reform the Catholic calendar under Gregory XIII in 1582,
when the year was reduced by ten days. The innovation, which
Klau explained in a treatise dated 1603, was not accepted in England and other Protestant countries. Ignatius refuted the innovations of Copernicus on the ground that they were actually anticipated by three Greek mathematicians. Aristarchos of Samos, born
c 300 BC, wrote a treatise on *The sizes and distances of the Sun and the
Moon*, which was based on inaccurate data; but Archimedes, a late
contemporary, placed on record that Aristarchos (known in
modern times as 'the Copernicus of antiquity') did initiate the
hypothesis that the earth revolves about the sun. Heracleides of
Pontos, slightly earlier, anticipated some of the explanations of
Tycho Brahe, his system being a compromise between the helio-
centric and Ptolemaic universe. The dates of Ecphantos are uncertain, but the Greeks traditionally associated him with the
Aristarchan school of astronomers.

The main disadvantage of Donne's prose style is the tangential activity of the ideas, reflected in the syntax. Subordinate clauses, especially in compound-complex sentences, pile up disconcertingly, and interpolations deflect attention from the logical thread of the discourse. For instance, the adjectival parenthesis in A 19, *scarce respecting Lucifer himselfe* is inconsequently placed after *feet*; while the second adjectival clause in 21/22, qualifying *me*, calls for the conjunction *and*, because the relative pronoun *who* is here used in two different case functions.

In electing to write the original in Latin, Donne created difficulties for himself in the English translation. A long complex sentence begins with *For* in line A 23 and ends with *Copernicus* in line 30. Before one arrives at the main clause *I doubted no longer* (A 29), there are two concessive subordinations, an adverbial clause of time followed by a noun clause; then another adverbial clause of time, followed by two relative clauses with different antecedents – a total of seven subordinations, necessitating the connectives *For though, and therefore, yet when, that, and that, by which, who*. Such deflections from the logical progression are too many for the grammatical memory to sustain. On page 67 of *Ignatius his Conclave*, beginning at line 2, there is a long sentence which ends in line 21; it not only defies grammatical analysis, but defeats understanding.

In passage B shorter sentences and rhetorical questions (there are six examples of *erotema* in lines 14–21) help to keep the syntax under control. Continuity of reasoning in prose depends on the choice of connectives (often compounded), such as *Besides, If therefore, but that, And yet, but for, by which* (21–34). The syntactic variety of the passage (28–45) is memorable for seven passive constructions. The sixteenth-century word *brabbles* (31), meaning 'quibbles' or 'paltry disputes', was borrowed from Dutch, but did not survive the nineteenth century, except in dialect.

Donne's satire does not favour the *style coupé* of Montaigne's essays, but displays an asymmetry typical of Renaissance prose. Note, for instance, the relative length of the five clauses, in B
39–42: 'do not now attend/ till the day come,/ as they were accustomed,/ but are awaked ten daies sooner,/ *and constrained by him to come downe from heaven to do that businesse.*' In passage B

members of the complex sentence express relationship through introductory connectives, whose significance is in proportion to that of the subordinate clauses themselves.

Donne's love of autonomous subordination displays the labyrinthine complexity of his thinking. Order is spontaneous, because matter is presented as it comes into his mind. Donne seems not to have planned the syntax or the rhythm of a paragraph before he put pen to paper, neither length nor punctuation being premeditated. He is not in this piece seriously motivated by the formality of school rhetoric.

THE TRUE CHARACTER OF A DUNCE

Four miscellaneous pieces, associated in style with the *Paradoxes and Problems*, are of considerable interest to the student of Donne's prose. Along with *An Essay of Valour*, *The True Character of a Dunce* was first published in the eleventh edition (1622) of Sir Thomas Overbury's posthumous poem *On the choice of a Wife, whereunto are added many witty characters* (1614). The additional prose sketches were by friends or associates of the author, among them Donne, and Evelyn Simpson thinks that they were written in the early part of James I's reign (*Modern Language Review* 18, p. 415).

The following extract from *The True Character of a Dunce* offers a taste of the witty and incisive quality of this short piece, the text being from John Hayward's Nonesuch edition of Donne:

The most part of the faculties of his soule lie fallow, or are like the restive Jades, that no spur can drive forwards towards the pursuit of any worthy designes. One of the most unprofitable of Gods creatures being as he is, a thing put cleane besides the right use, made fit for the cart and the flayle; and by mischance intangled amongst books and papers. . . . You shall note him oft (besides his dull eye, and lowring head, and a certain clammy benummed pace) by a faire displaied beard, a night cap, and a gowne, whose very wrinckles proclaime him the true *Genius* of formalitie. But of all others, his discourse, and compositions best speake him, both of them are much of one stuffe and fashion. He speakes just what his bookes or last company said unto him, without varying one whit, and very seldome under- 5

10

stands himselfe. You may know by his discourse where he   15
was last: for what he heard or read yesterday, hee now dis-
chargeth his memory or Note-booke of, not his understanding, for it never came there. What hee hath, he flings
abroad at all adventures without accomodating it to time,
place, persons, or occasions. He commonly loseth himselfe   20
in his tale, and flutters up and downe windlesse without
recovery, and whatsoever next presents it selfe, his heavy
conceit seizeth upon, and goeth along with, how ever
Heterogeneall to his matter in hand. His Jests are either old
flead *Proverbs*, or leane-sterv'd-hackney-*Apophthegmes*, or   25
poore verball quips, outworne by Servingmen, Tapsters,
and Milkemaides, even laid aside by Balladers. He assents to
all men that bring any shadow of reason, and you may make
him when he speakes most Dogmatically, even with one
breath, to averre poore contradictions.   30

Prose of this type has affinities with the character-writing of
Joseph Hall and Overbury himself, and the sketch was obviously a
pièce d'occasion, classified by the American critic M. W. Croll as
Senecan. The chief characteristic of this sententious style is its dis-
junctive tendency, the syntactic units being virtually autonomous.
The manner is suited to note-taking observations, of which well-
known specimens are found in the earliest edition of Bacon's
Essays.

In the passage cited, the second of the observations (3–7) has no
finite verb. Sketchiness is compensated by a bold virtuosity in the
phrase-making: *restive Jades, fit for the cart and the flayle, intangled
amongst books and papers, clammy benummed pace, true Genius of formalitie, flings abroad at all adventures, flutters up and down windlesse, Heterogeneall, flead Proverbs, leane-sterv'd-hackney-Apophthegmes.* This is
fliting in the journalistic style of Thomas Nashe and the pam-
phleteers. The ambition of the phrase-maker is to be original, and
his skill is cumulative, like the master strokes of a caricaturist.
Minimal subordination secures a concision that seldom taxes the
memory.

Another characteristic of Senecan stylists is their authoritative,
aphoristic attitude; they affect a gnomic acuteness of expression
that is well illustrated immediately before the above extract.
Example: *He sleepes as he goes, and his thoughts seldome reach an inch*

further then his eies. Donne was not fond of shaping a paragraph out of saws and maxims. Consequently, his writing seldom generalizes, or attempts didacticism. The aphoristic strait-jacket was apparently too constricting for his imagination.

CHAPTER VII

The Prose Letters

🐍🐍🐍🐍🐍🐍

DONNE'S correspondence was not published until two decades after his death, when his son collected 129 of his epistles in *Letters to Severall Persons of Honour* (1651). The title of this book was as ill-favoured as its unmethodical presentation; for the editor sometimes gave false headings, and made no attempt at establishing the chronological order. Many letters bore no date, and some lacked the name of any addressee.

In 1660 thirty-nine other letters were published in an equally chaotic *Collection* made by Sir Toby Mathew, a Catholic convert and acquaintance of Donne. Nine letters were added in 1852 from the Losely MSS, now in the Folger Library, Washington; while G. H. Finch's Burley-on-the-Hill MSS added an uncertain number in 1878. The last were of earliest date, beginning in 1597, and were reprinted by Evelyn Simpson in *A Study of the Prose Works of John Donne*. They came from a commonplace book also containing letters of Sir Henry Wotton, one of Donne's closest friends. The Clarendon Press fortunately had a transcript made, before this MS was destroyed by fire. When Logan Pearsall Smith and Grierson examined the Burley collection, they found that several letters were of doubtful authorship.

Of the 129 letters of the 1651 edition, fifty-six were addressed to Sir Henry Goodyer, twenty-four to Sir Robert Ker and seventeen to Donne's intimate friend, George Garrard. Eight of the letters in the collection had surprisingly been printed, with only minor differences, in the 1633 edition of the poems.

No Jacobean writer, except Bacon, is better represented in the field of letters than Donne. The ease and elegance of his epistolary style appear at their best after his marriage in 1601, when the correspondence reflects the diversity and fortitude of domestic life at Mitcham.

The text of the five letters cited below is from *John Donne,*

Selected Prose, ed. H. Gardner and T. Healy. Four were addressed to Goodyer, to whom Donne wrote every Tuesday during the Mitcham period. Some unexpected sides of the writer's character are revealed in this correspondence; for Goodyer was a friend to whom he could speak his thoughts frankly, and who benefited from Donne's advice on some of his religious doubts.

Both Hayward and Simpson minimize the value of Donne's letters, although the biography of the middle years is largely dependent on them. The pattern was that of Seneca, Pliny and other classical writers; but the distinction of phrase is Donne's, and it is unaffected by the topical or homiletic content of the letters. The 'slow but massive movement of Donne's mind' that Hayward found uninspiring (Nonesuch edition, p 438), is no less appropriate here than in the *Sermons*; for Donne said that his friendships meant only less to him than his religion. Among contemporaries, his reputation as a letter-writer was as respected as his wit and his passionate conviction in the pulpit. Writing to Sir Thomas Lucy in October 1607, he said that the feeling put into the letters was a 'kind of ecstacy'. He never tired of expounding the nature of the soul, or discussing the effect upon his philosophy of his frequent illnesses.

The genesis of Donne's epistolary style is difficult to trace. Like the letters in the Paston papers a century earlier, they are not familiar, except in a few lines of domestic news; there is a tone of formality that approaches the style of the persuasive essay. Prose grew in strength among five groups of writers: letter-writers, teachers of rhetoric, chroniclers, preachers and translators, the last mainly from Latin, Italian, Spanish and French texts. Many handbooks on letter-writing, from foreign as well as indigenous sources, began to be printed in the last quarter of the sixteenth century, along with collections of essays. The influence of Erasmus's *Colloquies* on both forms was considerable.

Though Donne's letters were not written with a deliberate literary aim, they differ in the length and structure of sentences from much of his other prose. There is, however, the stamp of individuality on all his writing, even when emulating the informative correspondence of Sir Henry Wotton (1568–1639), who knew Kepler, and spent seven years after studying at Oxford in Geneva, Rome, Florence, Venice, Naples and Vienna. Wotton wrote with no idea of publication in mind, and only unconsciously under the influence of rhetoric; yet his admirable concision lapses constantly into parenthetical phrases or clauses.

Letters here chosen show Donne in a congenial mood. The first, dated sometime in 1604, is addressed to Goodyer and deals with the consolation of letters:

> If you were here, you would not think me importune, if I bid you good morrow every day; and such a patience will excuse my often Letters. No other kinde of conveyance is better for knowledge, or love: What treasures of Morall knowledge are in *Senecaes* Letters to onely one *Lucilius*? and what of Naturall in *Plinies*? how much of the storie of the time, is in *Ciceroes* Letters? . . . The Italians, which are most discursive, and think the world owes them all wisdome, abound so much in this kinde of expressing, that *Michel Montaigne* saies, he hath seen, (as I remember) 400 volumes of Italian Letters. But it is the other capacity which must make mine acceptable, that they are also the best conveyors of love. But, though all knowledge be in those Authors already, yet, as some poisons, and some medicines, hurt not, nor profit, except the creature in which they reside, contribute their lively activitie, and vigor; so, much of the knowledge buried in Books perisheth, and becomes ineffectuall, if it be not applied, and refreshed by a companion, or friend. Much of their goodnesse, hath the same period, which some Physicians of *Italy* have observed to be in the biting of their *Tarentola,* that it affects no longer, than the flie lives.

Gosse thought that this letter was sent to Donne's father-in-law, Sir George More, because the (apparently false) superscription read 'To Sir G. M.'. But another part of the letter refers to an exchange of 'problems', which Donne and Goodyer penned as ironical exercises to amuse friends. Gosse's understandable error is repeated by Healy in the Commentary to *Ignatius his Conclave* (p. 153). In an article on 'Donne's *Letters to Severall Persons of Honour*', R. E. Bennett explains bogus headings, such as 'To Sir G. M.', as a desire on the part of the editor to 'create an impression of a variety of letters . . . and to obscure the fact that most of the letters were to Goodyer' (pp 137–8).

There is a lapse of memory on Donne's part in referring to

Montaigne; for Florio's translation of the French essayist records only *one* hundred volumes of Italian letters seen by that writer.

In Donne's letter-style one sees undoubted instances of 'strong lines' in Jacobean prose – a series of short sentences, loosely linked by co-ordinating conjunctions. Where necessary, simple subordination is preferred. In lines 1–5, two conditional clauses; in 6–10 two adjectival clauses, one consecutive, one noun, and one adverbial clause; in 11–15 one noun, two adverbial and one adjectival clause; in 16–22 two adverbial clauses, one adjectival and one noun clause – fifteen subordinations, all brief and direct. Donne's epistolary manner is not monotonously Senecan, but mixed, (Wiliamson's 'loose and free' style) – a thoroughly English adaptation, which progresses naturally, and modifies as it goes. In the prose of Donne and related contemporaries, the modifications are not always subordinate, in the sense of eighteenth-century grammarians. Having a greater variety of linking words, writers utilized variant means of co-ordination; take, for example, the interpolation of line 10, and the appositional noun clauses in lines 12 and 21. Donne knew only classical rules of composition, but endeavoured to guide the reader by individualistic punctuation, which the printer apparently did not always understand.

In adverbial clauses of condition or concession, Donne preferred the subjunctive mood, as in *were* (1), *be* (13 and 18) and *contribute* (15/16); and being conservative, he frequently employed linking words, such as *which* (for *who*), and *except* (for *unless*). On the other hand, in letters he favoured the colloquial use of the *-s* inflexion for the 3rd person singular present indicative of notional verbs, e.g. *owes* (8), *saies* (10), *becomes* (17), *affects* (21), *lives* (22), while retaining conventional *-th* in *hath, doth* and *perisheth,* the stem of the last ending in an affricative digraph (*sh*). *Importune* (1), as an adjective, came into the language with the English version of the *Romaunt of the Rose* (end of fourteenth century), and was still found archaically employed during the nineteenth century, e.g. in Carlyle's *Frederick the Great*; the verb, however, dates from the sixteenth century only. The OED remarks that the adjectival use of *often* (3) was common in the sixteenth and seventeenth centuries, but rare after 1688, and now archaic.

The next letter to Goodyer was written in September 1608. Donne referred in a postscript to the tragic death, from want and neglect,

of one Captain Edmund Whitlock, and his letter takes the form of
an autobiographical meditation, already quoted in connection with
Biathanatos:

> I would not that death should take me asleep. I would not
> have him meerly seise me, and onely declare me to be dead,
> but win me, and overcome me. When I must shipwrack, I
> would do it in a Sea, where mine impotencie might have
> some excuse; not in a sullen weedy lake, where I could not   5
> have so much as exercise for my swimming. Therefore I
> would fain do something; but that I cannot tell what, is no
> wonder. For to chuse, is to do: but to be no part of any
> body, is to be nothing. At most, the greatest persons, are
> but great wens, and excrescences; men of wit and delight-   10
> full conversation, but as moales for ornament, except they
> be so incorporated into the body of the world, that they
> contribute something to the sustentation of the whole.
> This I made account that I begun early, when I understood
> the study of our laws: but was diverted by the worst volup-   15
> tuousnes, which is an Hydroptique immoderate desire of
> humane learning and languages: beautifull ornaments to
> great fortunes; but mine needed an occupation, and a course
> which I thought I entred well into, when I submitted my
> self to such a service, as I thought might have imployed   20
> those poor advantages, which I had. And there I stumbled
> too, yet I would try again: for to this hour I am nothing, or
> so little, that I am scarce subject and argument good enough
> for one of mine own letters: yet I fear, that doth not ever
> proceed from a good root, that I am so well content to be   25
> lesse, that is dead. You, Sir, are farre enough from these
> descents, your vertue keeps you secure, and your naturall
> disposition to mirth will preserve you; but lose none of
> these holds, a slip is often as dangerous as a bruise, and
> though you cannot fall to my lownesse, yet in a much lesse   30
> distraction you may meet my sadnesse; for he is no safer
> which falls from an high tower into the leads, than he which
> falls from thence to the ground: make therefore to your
> self some mark, and go towards it *alegrement*. Though I be
> in such a planetary and erratique fortune, that I can do   35
> nothing constantly, yet you may finde some constancy in
> my constant advising you to it.

Donne returns to this theme in the *Devotions upon Emergent Occasions,* and sometimes in the *Sermons.* The language is poetical, compared with that of the earlier letter, partly because it is more figurative. Besides the tropes there are schemes of words that contribute to the patterning. The vocabulary of lines 10 to 16 is rich in Latin- or Greek-derived polysyllables, such as *excrescences, incorporated, sustentation, voluptuousness, Hydroptique* and *immoderate,* producing a crescendo whose resonance is impressive. The word *sustentation* was first employed in the Wyclif New Testament (Romans iii 26) with the meaning of 'bearing up', 'support', 'preservation'; the OED shows that it continued in use until the end of the nineteenth century.

The principal trope at the beginning of this selection is personification: death has the power to *take, seise, declare . . . dead, win* and *overcome.* As usual in the prose, the effect of synonyms is cumulative, and in this letter ominous. The scene is quickly shifted to death by water. Shipwreck at sea shows man in his impotency, but it also excuses his failure to survive; foundering in a *sullen, weedy lake* brings only unheroic frustration, even for a swimmer.

Donne's state of lethargy inhibits the action necessary to surmount his depressing situation, as an unemployed intellectual. The pivot of lines 6 to 13 is the gnomic balanced clause *to chuse is to do.* The form of words is antithetical, the sense is complementary. The writer is confronted with a scholastic dilemma: *essence* or *becoming.* Without the opportunity of participating fruitfully in society, man loses his essential function. In metaphorical allusions, Donne meditates upon the topical problem of 'degree'. He sees great figures as *wens,* i.e. as blemishes like 'tumours' or 'warts'. His partiality for doublets, in the additional word *excrescences,* is here pointedly cynical. The suggestion is that upper classes in aristocratic society are parasites. Bright talkers are moles on the visible body; ornamental, but in a derogatory sense, unless capable of fulfilling some useful service in the body politic.

Donne's career next comes under review, beginning with the law, from which he turns to become a voluptuary, not of the flesh, but of humanism with unquenchable thirst for learning. The metaphor *Hydroptique immoderate desire* (16) may be intended as the central image of the letter. Learning is pictured as 'a beautiful ornament to great fortunes'. Here Donne is arguing that knowledge withers without means and status. His future was sacrificed when he *stumbled* in Lord Ellesmere's service, through an impulsive marriage. Humiliation was complete when he accepted life as negation.

Defeatism is an unhealthy plant, because it is virtual death. Donne sustains the figurative language through such lexical enlargements as *descents* (27), *vertue keeps you secure* (27), *lose none of these holds* (28/9), *a slip is often as dangerous as a bruise* (29), his hortatory advice to Goodyer being couched in proverbial wisdom (*paroemia*). A tendentious metaphor is that in which Donne's luckless fortune is described as *planetary and erratique* (35), a feature of the new Astronomy being the distinction between the wandering and fixed stars. *Some constancy in my constant advising* (36/7) is interesting, because it combines three rhetorical schemes, *ploce, paranomasia*, and *polyptoton*. Elizabethan and Jacobean writers found *ploce* indispensable to sentence cohesion, as in lines 1 to 3 of this passage.

Paragraphing is invariably absent in Donne's letters, and the syntax is not helped by the idiosyncratic punctuation. In lines 15 to 24 the colons after *laws, languages* and *letters* are misleading. *This* (14) is the equivalent of *thus*, which the OED suggests is an adverbial use of the accusative singular neuter of the OE form of the demonstrative. *Made account* in the same line, meaning 'considered important', is an idiomatic combination dating from the fourteenth century. *Begun* (14) is a relict of the *u* preterites of OE class three strong verbs, an example of form-levelling from the past-participle, which came into use alongside the *a*-preterite.

The next letter, written to Goodyer in 1608 or 1609, merits close analysis; its symmetry is displayed in sentence groupings, resembling biblical verses, in order to make the rhythmical structure apparent. Donne was familiar with the prose of Augustine, Erasmus and More, and admired the well-proportioned dignity of certain books of the Old Testament. The passage below is unparagraphed in *Letters to Severall Persons of Honour*, but the syntactic groupings are indicated in its punctuation, where the colons are significant:

1.   It should be nó interrúption to your *pleásures,|* to héar *m*e óften sáy that I lóve you,| and that yóu are as *m*úch *m*y meditátions as *m*y sélf:

2. I *óften* compáre nót yoú and *mé*,/ but the sphéar in which your resolútions áre, and *mý* whéel;/ bóth I hópe *c*oncéntrique to *Gód*:

3. for *m*e *th*ínks the néw *A*strónomie is *th*ús *a*pplíable wéll,/ *th*at wé which are a líttle *eárth*, should ráther *móve towards Gód*,/ *th*an *th*at hé which is fulfílling, and can cóme no whíther, should *móve towards* ús . . .

4.   You knów,/ théy which *d*wéll fárthest from the Sún,/ if in ány convénient *d*ístance,/ have *lónger d*áies, *bétter* áppetites, *bétter d*igéstion, *bétter* gRówth, and *lónger l*ífe:

5. And *á*ll these *a*dvántages have théir *m*índes/ who are wéll remóved/ from the *scórch*ings,/ and *d*ázlings,/ and exháling of the wórlds *glóry*:

6. *but* neíther of our *líves* are in súch extrémes;/ for yóu *lív*ing at *Cóurt* without ambítion,/ *which would* búrn yóu,/ or without énvy,/ *which would d*evést óthers,/ *lí*ve in the Sún,/ nót in the fíre:

7. And Í *which lí*ve in the *Cóuntry without* stúpefying,/ am *nót* in *d*árknesse,/ *but* in *shádow*,/ which is *nót* no líght,/ *but* a pállid,/ wáterish, and *d*ilúted one.

8.   As *áll shádows* are of one *c*ólour,/ if you *r*espéct the bódy from which they are *c*ást/ (for our *shádows* upon *c*láy will be dírty,/ and in a *g*árden gréen, and flówery)

9. so *áll* retírings into a *shádowy life* are *alíke* from áll *c*áuses,/ and *alíke* subject to the bárbarousnesse and insípid *d*úlnesse of the *Cóuntry*:

10. ónely the emploíments,/ and thát upon which you *c*ást and bestów your *pléasure*, *b*úsinesse, or *b*óoks,/ gíves it the tíncture, and *b*eáuty.

11.   *But trúly* wheresoéver *we* áre,/ if *we* cán *but t*éll oursélves *trúly* whát and whére we woúld be,/ we may máke ány *s*táte and pláce *s*úch;

12. for we are só *c*ompósed,/ that if abúndance, or *glóry scórch* and mélt us,/ we have an *eárthly c*áve, our *b*ódies, to *g*ó ínto by consíderation,/ and *c*oól our sélves:

13. and if we be *f*rózen, and *c*ontrácted with lowér and *d*árk *f*ortunes,/ we have *w*ithín us a tórch, a sóul,/ líghter and *w*ármer than ány *w*ithóut:

14. we are thérefore *our own* umbrélla's,/ and *our ówn* súns.

15.   Thése, Sir, are the sállads and ónions of *M*ícham,/ sént to

you with as whólesome afféction/ as your óther fríends send
Mélons and Quélque-choses from *Cóurt* and Lóndon.

Set out in fifteen rhythmical units, the pattern of the writing becomes conspicuously clear; the formal balance is not perfect, but
basic. Its asymmetrical relief is designed to conceal the art of
varying within a pattern that is not dictated by custom, to make it
appear artless. Moreover, the present arrangement assists reading
by suggesting the distribution of stress upon the significant words;
and it has the advantage of determining paragraphs, of which
there are five, each devoted to a new turn of thinking or feeling.
One finds similar principles at work in the Proverbs and in the
Song of Moses (Deuteronomy, xxxii). That the punctuation was
Donne's, not the printer's, is not manifest; but what we have
suggests an elocutionary purpose, whose source may be liturgical;
time-stops, it should be observed, do not imply any conventional
length.

The importance of the grouping is its triadic pattern. The first
and third paragraphs have three verses; the second and fourth have
four; while the fifth serves as a coda. I regard *You know* at the
beginning of verse 4 as a kind of *anacrusis* (extra syllables preceding
the normal rhythm). In each paragraph, the later units are amplified
by parallelistic enlargement, in which balanced phrases or clauses
are the instruments. This involves much repetition of words, the
personal pronouns being used over forty times. The groupings
would not have been so effective without this constant resort to
ploce; many of the examples are shown in italics, and the observation applies with equal force to pervasive alliteration, the consonants principally affected being, *b, c, d, f, g, l, m, r, s, t* and *w*.

Because the guiding principle is rhythmical balance, the syntax
favours co-ordination (note the predominance of linking words
and and *but*); the use of subordinate clauses is only of the simplest
kind. Each paragraph has a rhythm complete in itself; yet there is
a pleasing continuity in this personal style. But the tone of this
passage is not conversational. The letters, as a whole, are consciously phrased, yet homely; ample in their utterance, yet not
diffuse.

Every syllable in this passage contributes to the rhythmical
organization. Runs of lightly stressed syllables, occur only in
verses 2, 7, 9, 10, 12 and 15). There are fewer syntactic inversions,

one occurring at the beginning of verse 5. Donne's preference for the relative *which* when referring to persons is more common than in most prose writers of this time, and was probably the result of his familiarity with the Bible. The King James version (1611) was not yet available when this letter was written, but it shows that the relative of common gender was still preserved.

There is one suggested improvement to the received text, namely that *resolutions* in verse 2, should read *revolutions*. *Wheel* in the same line is a witty metonymy for 'fortune'. *Appliable*, in verse 3, was an adjective common in More and Tyndale, that did not survive the seventeenth century, when the latinism *applicable* succeeded it. Donne used the French borrowing *Quelque-choses* in the plural, as did most writers, though he must have realized that the correct form is the singular. Florio first recorded the word in 1598, meaning a 'fancy dish', a 'dainty' of French cuisine. Shakespeare, following popular custom, had already corrupted it in *2 Henry IV* (v i 29) to *Kick-shawes*, the form that is still in use.

In Walton's words (at the end of his biography) Donne was 'a great lover of the offices of humanity', and this appears in the following passage on religious tolerance, from a letter written to Goodyer in about 1609:

> You knów | I néver féttered | nor imprísoned | the wórd Relígion; | nót stráightning it | Fríerly, | *ad Religiónes factítias,* | (as the *Rómans* cáll wéll | their órders of Relígion) | nor immúring it | in a *Róme,* | or a *Wittemberg,* | or a *Genéva;* | they are áll | vírtuall béams | of óne Sún, | and wheresoéver 5 they fínde | cláy heárts, | they hárden them, | and móulder them | into dúst; | and they enténder | and móllifie wáxen. | They are nót so cóntrary | as the Nórth and Sóuth Póles; | and that they are connáturall píeces | of óne círcle. | Relígion is Christiánity, | which being tóo spírituall | to be 10 séen by ús, | doth thérefore táke | an appárent bódy | of góod lífe and wórks, | so salvátion requíres | an hónest Chrístian. | Thése are the twó Élements, | and hé which élemented from thése, | hath the compléxion | of a góod mán, | and a fít Fríend. | The diséases áre, | tóo múch 15 inténtion | into índiscreet zéal, | and tóo múch remísnesse | and négligence | by gíving scándall: | for our condítion |

and státe in thís, | is as ínfírm | as in our bódies; | where
physítians consíder | only twó degrées; | sícknesse, | and
neutrálity; | for there ís nó héalth in us. | Thís ,Sír, | I úse to   20
sáy to you, | ráther to háve | so góod a wítnesse | and
corréctor of my meditátions, | than to advíse; | and yét to do
thát tóo, | since it is párdonable | in a fríend: | Nót to sláck
you | towárds thóse fríends | which are relígious | in óther
clóthes than wé;   25

The passage is short enough to consider from several aspects:
vocabulary, choice of epithets, tropes, stress grouping (with relevant punctuation) and schematic rhetoric.

First should be noticed the already-mentioned pairing of words
of approximate, but not real, semantic identity: *fettered/imprisoned,
entender/mollifie, remisnesse/negligence, condition/state, witnesse/corrector*.
This is a use of parallelism so characteristic of Donne's style as to
be a mannerism.

In Elizabethan English the different senses of the words
straighten and *straiten* were not orthographically distinguished. The
meaning of the former spelling in line 2 is to 'narrow' or 'restrict'.
Frierly in the same line, has not the sometimes sinister significance
of 'deceitful', associated with the mendicant orders of the Middle
Ages; here it is used theologically, as the succeeding Latin phrase
shows. *Ad Religiones factitias* ('to agreed principles'), suggests
merely that the stricter *Romans* (i.e. Catholics) laid down rules for
the observance of their religion. *Entender* (7), meaning 'weaken'or
'enervate', was introduced into the English language by the
Catholic writer Southwell in 1594, according to the OED, which
reminds us that the word did not re-appear after Goldsmith's
employment of it in an essay of 1765. *Connaturall* (9), 'having the
same nature from birth', had its origin in the second elegy of Sir
John Davies's *Nosce teipsum* (1592); a word seldom found in the
seventeenth century, it has been largely superseded by *cognate*. The
preterite *elemented* (14), here employed as an intransitive verb, in
the sense of 'compounded of the four elements', was a usage much
favoured by Donne in verse and prose; it entered the language in
the Late Middle English period, but the OED has no examples
later than 1662.

Epithets either qualify or predicate, and Donne's practice bespeaks the conservative tenor of his writing. As a humanist, he did

not favour the attributive adjectives of natural description; as a poet, he tended to use some epithets metaphorically, as in *'clay* hearts' that are hardened, as distinguished from hearts which are *waxen* and mollified (6–7). Syntactically, the attributive adjective *virtuall* (5) has the value of an adverb. Predicative adjectives are the words *contrary* (8), *connaturall* (9), *spirituall* (10), *infirm* (18), *pardonable* (23), *religious* (24), all having ethical connotations. The epithets, indeed, sustain the burden of Donne's moral purpose in this letter, not hesitating at the common clichés of the pastoral message; examples are *apparent* body (because Christianity is alleged to be 'too spiritual'), *good* life/man/witnesse, *honest* Christian, *fit* friend. In *'indiscreet* zeal' we have an instance of transferred epithet, because 'indiscretion' properly resides in the *person* who abuses religion.

The tropes in Donne's epistolary language are not as outlandish as they often are in the poetry; the writer's purpose is not to invite notice by witty originality, but to vitalize the expressions in a somewhat allegorical way. The chief instruments are metaphor and personification, for instance: 'I never *fettered* or *imprisoned* Religion . . . nor *immuring* it' (1–4); 'they are virtuall *beams of one Sun*' (5); 'wheresoever they finde *clay hearts,* they *harden* them, and *moulder them into dust*' (5–7); 'they are connaturall *pieces of one circle*' (9); 'religious in *other clothes* than we' (24/5). A more prominent figure is *synecdoche* exemplified in 'a *Rome,* or a *Wittemberg,* or a *Geneva*' (4), places symbolic of the Catholic, Protestant and Calvinistic creeds.

The intimate tone of Donne's writing makes the stress grouping of successive phrases as significant as the syntax. The phrasal groups segmented in the above passage correspond to the natural progression of the speaking voice, and are not intended as counterparts of scansion in verse; the principles involved in each medium are distinct. Occasionally it happens that there are more than two stresses in a phrasal group; but there are rarely more than three, and they have no essential place or incidence. It becomes apparent that light syllables outnumber those with primary accentuation by as much as two or three to one. The unequal measure of phrasal groups speeds the utterance of prose, but it is also subject to natural fluctuations of speech rhythm, as in verse. The rhythm of prose can be more lively and animated (in a temporal sense) than that of poetry; and Donne was apparently conscious of this, for he did not confuse the principles proper to each. Readers of prose who locate phrasing in the above way, may find their rendering of it more persuasive.

Comprehending the phrase group is the clause, and beyond that there is the grammatical sentence, with the main clause strategically placed to secure a complex movement designed to hold the reader's attention. The principle of paragraphing, which Donne found superfluous in the letters, is to link clauses by rhythmical continuity, until an aspect of the theme becomes exhausted, accompanying the close with a gradual retardation of the movement. Since the time of Chaucer the word *cadence* has been cavalierly employed without much precise meaning. L. Murray in his *English Grammar* (1824) does not clarify it by suggesting that *cadence* is a closing pause, not to be confused with the fall of voice, uniformly practised by readers to complete a sentence.

If rhythm constitutes the movement pattern of phrasal groups, it seems also to provide emotional satisfaction from the progression and relation of syllables, especially the stressed ones. Dispositions of certain sounds may actually suggest and illuminate the meaning, the mind of the reader actively perceiving what the writer intends him to accept.

Donne intends the punctuation to point the rhythm; therefore stops have an important part to play in his expressive groupings. His rhythmical use of four semicolons in the first eight lines, to separate or enlarge ideas, is noteworthy, whether the groups contain finite verbs or not. With the exception of the full stop, the pointing has little time function, because it is elocutionary. The colons after *scandall* (17) and *friend* (23) are arbitrary; they may even be the work of the printer, who had exhausted his stock of semicolons, of which Donne was a spendthrift user; see further employments of this stop after *bodies*, *degrees* and *neutrality* and *advise* (18–22).

Rhythm is skilfully modulated by Donne in the use of parallel constructions, sometimes deflected by digressions and interpolations. But the underlying pattern, initiated by coupled substantives and verbs, is there to observe for the sensitive reader: e.g. *not straightening it . . . nor immuring it*; *a good man*, and *a fit friend*; *too much intention . . . and too much remisnesse*. Donne's letters represent a prose of thought; the movement develops as spontaneously as the thinking, and with great individuality. The style is neither Senecan, nor Ciceronian, nor Euphuistic, but an amalgam, with repetition maintaining a bell-like insistence. In the passage cited,

Religion or *religious* is used five times, *Christianity* or *Christian* twice, *Element* or *elemented* twice, *Rome* or *Romans* twice and *friend* again twice. Donne paid as much attention to *ploce* as he did to tempo in the mind's ear; he realized that the advantage to be gained from the prose medium is flexibility, for here the quantitative values of syllables come into their own.

The last of the selected letters was written in 1611 or 1612 to a recusant Catholic who was abroad. The recipient is thought by Donne specialists to have been Toby Mathew, friend of Francis Bacon, and son of the Bishop of Durham. Mathew was knighted in 1623, and later became a collector of Donne's letters. In this one, religious toleration is once more the theme. Written before Donne entered the ministry, the letter reveals the amiable exchange of views which he cultivated with friends of both the Anglican and Catholic faiths:

> ... as in D*iv*ine, | so in Morall things, | where the beginning is from *ot*hers, | the assistance, | and co-operation, | is in our *sél*ves. | Í therefore, | who could do nothing | towards the begetting, | would fain do somewhat | towards the *bree*ding | and cherishing | of such degrees of friendship, | as for- 5
> merly | I had the honour | to hold with *yóu*. | If Letters be not able | to do that office, | they are yet able, | at *least* to *te*stifie, | that he, | who sends them, | would be glad | to do more, | if he could. | Í have a great de*sire*, | not without some *hope*, | to see yóu | this Summer *thére*; | and Í have 10
> more *hope* | and more de*sire*, | to see yóu | this next Winter *hére*; | and Í have abundantly | more of both, | that, at *least*, | wé shall meet | in H*eav*en. | That we differ | in our *Wa*yes, | I hope we pardon | one another. | Men go to C*hin*a, | both by the Straights, | and by the *Cape*. | I néver | misinterpreted | 15
> yoúr way; | nor suffered it | to be so, | wheresoever I found it | in discourse. | For I was *sure*, | yóu took not up | yóur Religion | upon trust, | but payed | ready money | for it, | and at a high *Rate*. | And this taste of mine | towards *yóu*, | makes me hope for, | and *claime* | the same disposition | in 20
> yóu | towards *mé*. |

Most of Donne's letters are in the style of personal essays; this one, however, exudes a cautious sympathy intended to preserve human relations, despite differences in religious outlook. Donne was still hoping for secular employment, pondering his conversion and probably contemplating the second of his *Anniversaries*.

This was a crucial period in Donne's life; he was attracted more to the essential need for Christianity than to the articles of particular creeds, about which his mind was open. It was disturbing to hear that Mathew, born in the Anglican faith, had tried to convince Donne's friend, Sir Henry Goodyer, of the wisdom of following Rome. Yet four years after he was ordained deacon and priest of St Paul's, he wrote as follows to Mathew (September 1619):

> Forms of Religion destroy not moralitie, nor civill offices.
> ... We are fallen into so slack and negligent times, that I
> have been sometimes glad to hear, that some of my friends
> have differed from me in Religion. It is some degree of an
> union to be united in a serious meditation of God, and to
> make any Religion the rule of our actions.

Donne clearly believed that the differences between *honest* Christians were not fundamental, but verbal, and that self-interest induced doctrinalists to magnify them.

That Donne's overtures are tentative and hesitant, is shown not only in the twists and turns of thought, (cf the conditional clauses of lines 6–9), but in the punctuation. There are 27 commas, 3 semicolons and 8 full-stops in 20 lines. This is excessive, even if one grants that there may have been contributions from the printer. In the count of syllables, the phrasal groups are shorter than in the previous letter; but connectives are more numerous (26, of which co-ordinating *and* occurs 8 times).

The choice of words is plainer, and the style Senecan in its abruptness. That the attitude is tentative is shown by the number of negative words. Donne's characteristic pairing of words is again present, e.g. *assistance/co-operation* (2); *begetting/breeding* (4); *towards you/towards me* (19/21). Also present is repetition of words, such as *desire, more* and *hope* (9–12), though neither habit is obtrusive. It is in the central group of lines (9–12) that syntactic parallelism is most conspicuous. Throughout, the relationship between the correspondents is marked by the appropriate emphasis upon the personal pronouns *I, me, we* and *you, your, ourselves*.

'Attack' in the rendering of a prose passage depends not alone upon phrase-stress, but on variations of tempo, which Donne regulated by syllable weight and pause. In his book on *Style* (Arnold, 1898, p 26) Walter Raleigh wrote: 'Words carry with them all the meanings they have worn, and the writer shall be judged by those he selects for prominence in the train of his thought.' Finding the lexical message through emphasis is an instructive exercise, and I have tried to indicate some expressive syllables in italics. They have quantitative value, as in Di*vine*, (though not necessarily containing long vowels or diphthongs); and they occur usually in the last word of phrases, which is invariably succeeded by a pause.

The force of key words and syllables is instrumental in securing modulation of a prose rhythm, but characteristics of a style are not determined by rhythm alone. There are, for instance, frequencies of sound to which R. L. Stevenson drew attention (without precise phonetic knowledge) in his essay 'On Some Technical Elements of Style in Literature' (*Essays in the Art of Writing*, Heinemann, 1923, p 35-45):

> The motive and end of any art whatever, is to make a pattern; . . . Music and literature, the two temporal arts, contrive their pattern of sounds in time; or, in other words, of sounds and pauses. . . . Pattern and argument live in each other . . .
>
> Style is synthetic; . . . That style is therefore the most perfect . . . which attains the highest degree of elegant and pregnant implication unobtrusively; or if obtrusively, then with the greatest gain to sense and vigour. . . .
>
> The prose phrase is greatly longer and is much more nonchalantly uttered than the group in verse; so that not only is there a greater interval of continuous sound between the pauses, but, for that very reason, word is linked more readily to word by a more summary enunciation. . . .
> The beauty of the contents of a phrase, or of a sentence, depends implicitly upon alliteration and upon assonance. The vowel demands to be repeated; the consonant demands to be repeated; and both cry aloud to be perpetually varied.

If one, at random, examines the first six and the last six, of the phrase groups, each constituting a complete sentence, the literal repetitions are immediately apparent; but there is far from phonetic identity in every occurrence of this phenomenon:

A. Phrases 1–3, vowel *i*; consonants *n, ng, th*
   Phrases 4–6, vowels *i, a*; consonants *n, s, t*

B. Phrases 1–3, vowel *a*; consonants *m, t*
   Phrases 4–6, vowels *i, a*; consonants *m, s*

Josephine Miles's observation quoted on p 190, that the proportion of parts of speech in Donne is about eight adjectives to sixteen nouns and twelve verbs in every ten lines of verse, prompts comparative figures for the above eighteen lines of prose. They are respectively 15, 31, 36; and this would suggest that, while the proportion of adjectives and nouns in epistolary prose remains constant, the verbs increase considerably. The significance of this is diminished, however, by the fact that the substantives contain four verbal nouns, and the verb 'to be' is repeated seven times.

J. Middleton Murry (lectures on *Style*, O.U.P., 1922, p 51) maintained that prose in the age of Bacon and Donne had not attained 'the absolute precision of statement', nor 'the flexible non-insistent rhythm' which it later evolved in its maturity. To agree to this is to accept his dubious generalization that the King James Bible, and the prose of Milton and Thomas Browne should be excluded on the ground that they are poetic prose. Donne's *Letters*, for the most part, are not in this category. Murry was merely echoing Raleigh in claiming that style, in its aesthetic aspect, is organic, and should not be regarded analogically as the clothing of ideas. A critic, whose pre-occupation is the organization of ideas about literary history, can hardly give a comprehensive account of an author's style by the arbitrary selection of a few supporting lines.

CHAPTER VIII

Essayes in Divinity
and Devotions upon Emergent Occasions

𝕊𝕊𝕊𝕊𝕊𝕊

DONNE's *Essayes in Divinity*, first published in his son's edition of
1651, were composed at different times between 1611 and 1614, to
clarify the author's mind on contentious issues of religion before
his ordination. The opening verses of Genesis and Exodus were
merely the pretexts of these dissertations, mingled with prayers
and meditations, that reveal Donne's endeavour to arrive at a
reasonable orthodoxy. A second edition, published in 1652, in-
appropriately included the *Paradoxes* and *Problems*. The edition of
the *Essayes* cited is that of the Clarendon Press, 1952, edited by
Evelyn Simpson, who had considered their origin and purpose in
Chapter IX of *A Study of the Prose Works of John Donne*.

A letter to Goodyer, written on 14 March 1614, affirms that
Donne had been in touch with the Cambridge scholar Dr John
Layfield, rector of St Clement Danes, a Hebraist who had served
on the panel to revise books of the Pentateuch for the King James
Bible. This association may account for Donne's special theological
interest in Genesis and Exodus, which he must have read in
Hebrew with Layfield. Many allusions, and most of the imagery in
the *Essayes* and accompanying prayers, are drawn from these two
books. Three of the prayers at the end of the book were public
supplications, which, according to Izaak Walton, preceded sermons; they would therefore be of a later date than the essays.

In his second essay, 'Of Moses', Donne discusses the antiquity
of the Israelite leader's testimony, concluding that God himself
was the author of the Ten Commandments. Book I, part 1, seeks
to establish that the first two books of the Pentateuch are authentic,
on both historical and moral grounds. That the world was created
by God out of chaos, or nothingness, was for Donne a simple act
of faith.

191

Donne annotates in the margin the source of numerous biblical and other quotations. For the former he used either the Vulgate or Geneva text, not the Hebrew, though he does cite from the Greek Septuagint. He did not care to refer to the King James Bible (1611) until the preparation of the *Sermons*, and then only sporadically. In Book II, part 2 (Exodus), Donne writes: 'God hath not, or is not such an Omnipotence, as can do all things . . . The word *Omnipotence* is not found in all the Bible; nor *Omnipotent* in the New Testament. And where it is in the Old, it would rather be interpreted *All-sufficient*, than *Almighty*, between which there is much difference' (Simpson, *Essayes*, p 79, lines 23-4, 37-9; p 80, 1-2). Donne is, however, mistaken. The Greek word *pantokrator* occurs in Revelation xix 6, and is correctly rendered as *almyghti* in the Wyclif Bible, and *omnipotent* in the Tyndale, Great Bible, Geneva, Rheims and King James translations.

The commentaries of Augustine, Nicholas of Lyra (a medieval professor in Paris), Calvin and the Spanish Jesuit, Pererius of Rome, were always at Donne's elbow, and so was the *Summa Theologica* of Thomas Aquinas. Among Renaissance scholars, the references are most frequently to Pico della Mirandola and Reuchlin, a German humanist and Hebrew specialist. Allusions to classical writers, to Cicero, Horace, Seneca and others, are abundant; but, curiously, two references were all that were made to Lucretius's *De Rerum Natura*.

A significant influence on Donne's thinking was the Spanish philosopher, Raymond of Sebund, who taught at Toulouse; his *Liber Naturae sive Creaturarum* was the subject of Montaigne's longest essay, 'An Apology for Raymond de Sebonde'. Donne's first essay provides evidence that he knew of and reacted to Montaigne's sceptical attitude towards the comments of the Christian Fathers. Raymond, who died in the early fifteenth century, had maintained that the Book of Creatures was of divine inspiration, like the Bible, and deserved equal attention, because it could not 'be falsified by Hereticks' (*Essayes*, p 7, line 37). Donne saw in the book of Genesis a possible way to refute this doctrine.

Despite the heterogeneous character of the *Essayes in Divinity*, which precludes the appearance of a coherent stylistic picture, the book throws light on the related theme of the *Anniversaries*. It is also biographically illuminating, since it exposes Donne's mind grappling with some major problems of theology.

Some of the *Essayes* discuss the commentators' interpretations of obscure passages, and reveal judgements that are open-minded, generous, impersonal and anxious not to arouse controversy, for instance by arguments from the new Astronomy, or by ironical gibes, like those of Donne's *Catalogus Librorum Satyricus* (*c* 1605). The *Essayes in Divinity* proved a more than useful preparation for the *Sermons,* the first of which was probably delivered on 30 April 1615.

The first passage to be considered is taken from the essay 'Of Genesis', part I (p 19 of the Simpson edition):

> Truly, ‖ the *Creation* and the *last Judgement,* | are the *Diluculum* and *Crepusculum,* | the *Morning* and the *Evening* twi-lights | of the long day of this world. ‖ Which times, | though they be not utterly dark, | yet they are but of un-certain, | doubtfull, and conjecturall light. ‖ Yet not equally; ‖ for the break of the day, | because it hath a succession of more and more light, | is clearer then the shutting in, | which is overtaken with more and more darknesse; ‖ so is the birth of the world more discernable then the death, | because upon this God hath cast more clouds.

There is a likeness between this excerpt and the prose of Sir Thomas Browne. The alliterative interplay of vowels and consonants; the smoothness achieved by the liquids, nasals, and sibilants; the grouping and balancing of phrases and sentences; all undoubtedly anticipate the author of *Urn Burial.* Four sentences of different grammatical structure (the second being relative to the first) are of similar scope and gradation; two of them are poised on either side of the middle phrase 'Yet not equally', matching the opening adverb 'Truly'.

The divisions marked are units of rhythm in the sentences, and the punctuation invites attention to them. Paired or opposed words and phrases are perceived more readily than the sound variations, e.g. in 'though they be not utterly dark, yet they are but of *un-certain, doubtful,* and *conjecturall* light'. Here the phonemic sequence nearly exhausts the gamut of vowel sounds peculiar to the language.

Each of Donne's sentences has a memorable rhythm, partly because the voice falls in English polysyllables from a stressed to an unstressed syllable; when occasion arises the stress elements are cunningly matched; e.g. in *Crèátĭŏn, làst Júdgemĕ̆nt*; *Mórnĭ̆ng, Év(e)nĭ̆ng*. Eleven Latin polysyllables blend with more numerous Anglo-Saxonisms. Sir Thomas Elyot was in the van of the borrowing from Latin to improve the fertility and mobility of Renaissance ideas.

It is worth observing that *Diluculum* (break of day) and *Crepusculum* (evening twilight) were respectively in the vocabulary of Cicero and Ovid, two of the most admired authors of the Renaissance. The word *dilucidity* was apparently coined by Philemon Holland in his translation of Plutarch's *Morals* in 1603. *Crepusculum* is found in Trevisa's translation of Bartholmaeus's *De Proprietatibus Rerum* (1398), and *Crepuscule* in Chaucer's *Treatise on the Astrolabe* (*c* 1391). Donne's defence of the historicity of Genesis includes the unusual plural *Chineses* (Simpson, p 18, line 28).

Allegorically, *Creation* and *last Judgement* allude to the first and last books of the Bible, and by implication, to the beginning and end of the world, the one more cloudy than the other. Donne suggests that 'we must return again to our strong hold, *faith,* and end with this' (p 19, lines 24–6).

Ciceronian roundness and fulness were not easily adaptable to the analytical progression of Elizabethan English, the patterns of subordinate linking being different; and long periods invariably resulted in cloudiness of thought. Donne is rarely in the ornate school of seventeenth-century prose writers. Like the English churchmen, Tyndale, Coverdale, Cranmer, Latimer and Hooker, he developed a style of different sentence-lengths and idiomatic rhythm that is essentially English.

In the next excerpt the writer is in moralistic mood, to which his style is carefully adapted. Donne had two principal attributes: ability to express his thoughts vigorously and memorably, and the will to think individually, even when the matter was closest to 'the bosoms and business of men'. He would have agreed with Thomas Nashe that sounder arts for the writer existed than 'exornation by colours', appraised by Thomas Wilson in the *Arte of Rhetorique* (1553). The passage below is from Book II, part 2, of the *Essayes in Divinity* (Simpson, p 66, lines 25–36):

Let no smalnesse retard thee: || if thou beest not a Cedar to
help towards a palace, | if thou beest not Amber, Bezoar,

nor liquid gold, to restore Princes; || yet thou art a shrub to
shelter a lambe, | or to feed a bird; | or thou art a plantane,
to ease a childs smart; | or a grasse to cure a sick dog. ||| 5
Love an asker better then a giver: | which was good *Agape-*
tus counsel to *Justinian*: || Yea rather, prevent the asking; |
and do not so much joyn and concur with misery, | as to
suffer it to grow to that strength, | that it shall make thy
brother ask, | and put him to the danger of a denyall.   10

In *Studies in Words* (C.U.P. 1961, pp 218–19) C. S. Lewis offers
sensible advice to the neophyte: 'Avoid all epithets which are
merely emotional . . . You must go quite a different way to work
. . . by secretly evoking powerful associations, by offering the
right stimuli to our nerves (in the right degree and the right order),
and by the very beat and vowel melody and length and brevity of
your sentences.' Donne is actuated by similar principles, when his
persuasion aims, above all, at lucidity.

In this passage there is only one epithet, *good*, a qualifier that is
factual, and probably derived from the *Histories* or *Anecdotes* of
Procopius. The evocative associations are at their liveliest in lines
2–5, where images of healing are mainly of folk origin. *Bezoar,* a
corruption of Arabic *bāzahr,* is found in Gerard's *Herbal* (1597),
where it is described as an antidote to poisons, supposedly obtained
from stones in the intestines of the wild goat of Persia. The
plantane, or 'waybread', is earlier, being mentioned in both
Chaucer and Gower. This was a broad-leaved herb, whose juice
had medicinal properties, applied to ulcers.

The *Essayes in Divinity* are the most objective, and regarded on
that account as the least original, of Donne's prose writings. It is
quite likely that these chamber homilies were not intended for
publication. A sequence of brief balanced sentences was rhythmically appropriate to the homiletic writing of this excerpt, where
the thoughts are associative, rather than logical. Indeed, the continuity of ideas and long paragraphs of most of the *Essayes* make it
difficult to assess an extract without reference to its context. The
purpose of the *Essayes* was to study biblical pronouncements in the
situations that engendered them, and to avoid the tangential
temptations of a spoken sermon.

A homily is an exhortation addressed directly to hearers, to
induce moral behaviour; like an apostrophe in a demagogic

harangue, it comes at a point where the speaker abandons exposition in order to promote action. Magnanimity is the theme of this adjuration, which consists of three main clauses in the imperative, with a medial pause of considerable duration before *Love* (line 6). This pause is the fulcrum to the parallelism of the subordinate clauses. The first part of the exhortation has a pair of conditional clauses, balanced by the common words *if thou beest*; to these the ritual responses are *yet thou art,* complemented by alternative infinitival phrases. The *if*-clauses, in the subjunctive, are negative; the responses in the indicative, are positive.

The principal exhortation constitutes the second half, an appeal for the Pauline conception of *caritas*; on 'divine love' Agapetus is the counsellor to Emperor Justinian (a collocation in history of some importance). The gradation of the three imperatives is emphasized by the biblical expletive *Yea* (7). The verb *prevent* in this line has the contemporary sense of 'anticipate'. Retardation of the rhythm comes through a succession of adverbial phrases (or clauses) of comparison, in which the infinitives are most significant. Like the instances of *ploce,* alliterative words, such as *danger* and *denyall* (10), *shrub* and *shelter* (3/4), are seldom conspicuous in Donne; but their rhythmical effect is as subtle as the underlying sequence of lateral, nasal and sibilant consonants.

In the short homily of ten lines, notional verbs are paramount. They are: *retard, help, restore, shelter, feed, ease, cure, love, prevent, joyn, concur, suffer, grow, ask* and *put* (to danger), fifteen words characteristically operative in the Christian gospels. The figurative importance of the nouns is to contrast different states in society, to which Christ became a leveller. On the one hand we have *smalnesse, shrub, lamb, bird, plantane, child, smart, dog* and *grass*; on the other, *Cedar, palace, Amber, Bezoar, liquid gold, Princes, Agapetus* and *Justinian.* The passage neatly demonstrates Donne's dependence, for his eloquence, on the choice of words and images, and the relative duration of the pauses.

The final excerpt from Book II, part 2 (Simpson, *Essayes,* p 75, lines 26–38) is, in reality, a prayer of thanksgiving for deliverance; Christ is here compared with Moses, liberator of the Israelites from the servitude of Egypt:

Thou hast delivered me, | O God, | from the Egypt of confidence and presumption, | by interrupting my fortunes, |

and intercepting my hopes; || And from the Egypt of
despair | by contemplation of thine abundant treasures, |
and my portion therein; || from the Egypt of lust, | by con-   5
fining my affections; || and from the monstrous and un-
naturall Egypt | of painfull and wearisome idleness, | by the
necessities of domestick and familiar cares and duties. |||
Yet as an Eagle, | though she enjoy her wing and beak, | is
wholly prisoner, | if she be held by but one talon; || so are   10
we, | though we could be delivered of all habit of sin, | in
bondage still, | if Vanity hold us but by a silken thred.

This 'meditation' (Donne's description in line 21) expresses gratitude for the writer's personal salvation from the sin of vanity.
Egypt is a metonym for different aspects of evil: *presumption* (2),
despair (4), *lust* (5) and *idleness* (7). Donne recalls his expectations of
worldly success, now replaced by contrition. The dashing of his
hopes was the first step to the recovery of faith; others were a
realization of God's goodness and mercy, his constancy in marriage,
and the obligations of domestic duty.

These acknowledgements occupy the first movement of the
supplication. The second expands the illusion of captivity by an
extended simile in which the Eagle (lord of the skies) is a symbol
of regeneration. The pride of this mythological bird was cast down
for aspiring to outstare the sun; but Donne's metaphor images a
noble creature sacrificed for a minor misdemeanour. Even so, a
man who may have shed the habit of sin, is held captive by the
silken thred of his own vanity.

Structurally, the pattern resembles that of the previous passage.
Parallelism at first consists of adverbial phrases of manner, in
which co-ordinated substantives are poised against each other.
Enforced *idleness* is the offence, *monstrous* and *unnaturall*, to which
Donne gives unusual emphasis by adding the epithets, *painfull* and
wearisome. Only eight qualifiers appear in this passage, all polysyllables; their effect in drawing out the rhythm is deliberate.

The long pause after *duties* in line 8 introduces into the second
half a Euphuistic modification – the elaborate similitude reminiscent of Lyly's borrowings from the natural history of Pliny, in
which the principal statements are interrupted by corresponding
concessive clauses.

Vestiges of the Ciceronian period are still visible in the *Essayes*, though the fashion was outmoded after Bacon's intellectual prose. With it went the not very precise theory of English prose cadence. This rhetorical convention allowed no member of a prose period to exceed twenty syllables and four emphatic stresses. Cadence in seventeenth-century prose was not, however, confined to a completed sentence, or form of words comprehensible in itself; in the English practice it became appropriate at any significant point, before breathing pauses.

The rhythm of prayers obviously demanded euphonious utterance, and this was achieved in Latin versions of the Hebrew psalmody by an adaptation of the Ciceronian *cursus* (or 'run'), in which a falling rhythm was axiomatic in the closing five or six syllables. Little attempt was made to reproduce the same cadence in English prayer-books, partly because stress had replaced the classical quantitative measures of oratorical prose.

Donne's marginal notes indicate that he had read Psalms 105 and 106, which recapitulate the several deliverances of the Israelites. Psalm 106 was a festival song of thanksgiving, composed in exile during the captivity in Babylon; but its interest in English translation lies in the units of rhythm, similar to those in Donne's prayer.

The rhythm of the passage quoted was conceived in two periods, indicated by the punctuation, and separated by the pause in line 8. Omitting the interpolated invocation of the Deity, the first period has twelve members, and the second eight. The number of syllables in each varies from four to eighteen, and the number of stresses from two to five. The length of members, as well as their grammatical status and function, is not arbitrary, so long as oral presentation is borne in mind. The theory of periodicity seems to have arisen from a desire to balance syntax and stress in related members, and to enable the writer, who is also a speaker, consciously to vary the pattern as the thought requires. Too precise a parallelism of words, phrases and stresses leads, however, to the artifice of Euphuism.

Considered as units of rhythmical flow, Donne's phrases offer many instances of internal cadence, which bear no relation to the ends of sentences in the classical *cursus*. Examples in the above passage are: *Egýpt ŏf cónfidĕnce* (1), and *weárĭsŏme ídlĕnĕss* (7). Classical rhetoricians called members that contained such phrases *cola* or *commata,* according to the length of pause that succeeded them.

Cadenced phrases in Donne's prayer are effectively employed for amplification in *mŏnstrŏus aňd ŭnnátŭrăll* (6/7). There is thus a rhetorical explanation for his taste in nearly synonymous words, in poetry as well as prose.

English prose in the hands of divines developed alternative sentence-closures to the Latin *cursus*, one of which ends the cadence with a final stressed syllable e.g. *silken thrèd*. The classical influence is preserved in the penultimate word *silkĕn*. Retardation of the rhythm in English begins, however, at an earlier point than the sixth syllable, as Donne's final sentence illustrates. *Vănĭtÿ*, the most emphasized word in it, begins the slowing down; and on some such heavily-stressed syllable the English cadence, of whatever kind, invariably turns (cf. in period 1, *fămĭlĭăr căres aňd dŭtĭĕs*).

Repetition and balance are thus fundamental aspects of rhythmical writing; and both extend to the unobtrusive subdivisions of words (syllables), to the emphasis they bear, and to the pauses that set limits to holistic utterance.

THE DEVOTIONS

Devotions upon Emergent Occasions, most esteemed of Donne's prose in his lifetime, appeared in February 1624, and was republished in 1626 and 1627. *Emergent*, in this context, means 'pressing' or 'urgent', the earliest known use being by Bishop Thomas Bilson in *The Perpetual Government of Christ's Church* (1593). In November 1623, Donne was taken seriously ill with relapsing fever, which was raging in epidemic proportions in London. The disease became critical during the first week, and a large number of citizens succumbed. From Donne's correspondence it is apparent that the twenty-three penitential *Devotions* were written within a month, during convalescence, and that the *Hymn to God the Father* belongs to the same period.

Each devotion is in three parts, consisting of a meditation on the human condition, an expostulation (or dramatic deliberation with God), and a prayer, at first in expiation of sins, then of thanksgiving for deliverance. Only the last two exercises incorporate quotations, actual or adapted, from the Old and New Testaments, the version used being mainly the King James Bible. The meditations provide step-by-step accounts of Donne's illness, in which medical details are sometimes allegorically treated. Nervous tension, induced by morbid interest in the psycho-pathology of his own case, and a grotesque use of the historical imagination, provide the literary equivalent of Dürer's etchings. There was no lack of response by contemporary readers to the introspective, impassioned language.

Andrewes and Taylor wrote devotions remarkable for their extrovert understanding of the Christian philosophy, but not as revealing or unconventional as Donne's. Margaret Bottrall in *Every Man a Phoenix* (p 25) has this to say in her assessment:

> It cannot be denied that self-display was as powerful a motive with Donne as self-scrutiny. . . . Up to the last moment of his life, he wanted to make the image and likeness of John Donne memorable, striking, unique.

Donne's immense lexical and rhetorical resource, mingled with Job-like querulousness, does not impair the sincerity of his language. Most striking is the biblical learning he brings to the relation of physical to mental disharmony. There is a graphic narrative in the meditations that Donne did not elsewhere achieve; an instance is the macabre humour used to describe the diagnoses of physicians, among them the King's own medical adviser.

Ignatian concreteness in Donne's *Devotions* has an attractiveness that does not invalidate their depth of feeling. While the clinical facts are realistic, the rational style is reminiscent of Thomas Aquinas; the combined gifts arouse emotions similar to those produced by the *Sermons*. In the most original exercises, the meditations, there is little doctrinal matter to distract the reader from Donne's overmastering assurance of faith, and theocentric intellect. The text quoted is from the edition prepared by Anthony Raspa (McGill-Queens U.P., 1975):

> *Earth* is the *center* of my *body, Heaven* is the *center* of my *Soule*; these two are the naturall places of those two; but those goe not to these two, in an equall pace: My *body* falls downe without pushing, my *Soule* does not go up without pulling: *Ascension* is my *Soules* pace & measure, but *precipitation* my *bodies*.

(*Devotions, Meditation* 2, p 11, lines 17–21)

The italicized words of the original editions imply several things besides allusions to other works; here the purpose is speech emphasis.

Donne's *Devotions* reveal a sympathy with St Augustine's fundamental maxim: 'I believe, in order that I may understand.' In his
book *De Trinitate* (x xi 17–18) Augustine argues that three levels
of reality are possible, in memory, understanding and will, all
central to the unity of life and mind. The tripartite division of
Donne's meditations corresponds to these levels. Augustine
further enunciates the principle that 'God works through Nature'
(iii v 11–16), and is visible in his Creation. Donne's references to
the 'Book of Creatures' aim to return thanks to the Creator, and to
remind Christians of the companion Book of Life; the salvation
promised by the Scriptures was thought to provide the key to both.
The Bible, for Donne, was the work of God's amanuenses; its
divine ideas have no other end than to serve mankind as prototypes. He refers to the three 'books' in the ninth Expostulation:

> ... al the way, *O my God*, (ever constant to thine owne
> wayes) thou hast proceeded *openly, intelligibly, manifestly, by
> the book*. From thy first *book*, the book of *life*, never shut to
> thee, but never throughly open to us; from thy second
> *book*, the *booke* of *Nature*, where though subobscurely, and
> in shadows, thou hast expressed thine own *Image*; from thy
> third *booke*; the *Scriptures*, where thou hadst written all in
> the *Old*, and then lightedst us a candle to read it by, in the
> *New Testament*; To these thou hadst added the *booke* of just,
> and usefull *Lawes*, established by them, to whom thou hast
> committed thy people
>
> (*Devotions,* p 49, lines 1–10)

The rhetoric of Donne's *Devotions* is palpable in the cumulative
style, reinforced by metaphysical imagery, similar to that in the
Divine Poems. In a letter accompanying a copy sent to the exiled
Princess Elizabeth of Bohemia, Donne admits to 'open parentheses' and 'sentences within sentences'; while in Meditation 11 he
returns to the observation figuratively: '*Eternity* is not an everlasting flux of *Tyme*; but Tyme is as a short *parenthesis* in a long
period.' Many sentences have a loose, but not undisciplined,
fluidity, characteristic of the writing of visionaries. The expostulations and prayers show the exegetical expertise of the sermons,
flowering with a moral clarity of considerable aesthetic value.
Using Luke xi, 5–8, as his text, Donne reaches a scriptural dignity
in the sixth Expostulation, which is deeply moving:

Pray in thy bed at midnight, and God wil not say, I will
heare thee to morrow upon thy knees, at thy bed side; pray
upon thy knees there, then, & God will not say, I will
heare thee on *Sunday*, at *Church*; *God* is no *dilatory God*, no
froward *God*; Praier is never *unseasonable*, *God* is never
asleep nor absent.

(Devotions, p 31, lines 7–11)

Notice the persuasive effect of the polysyllables *dilatory* and
unseasonable.

Studious planning and concentration went into the design of
these exercises; the spontaneity in the associations was due in
large part to the physicians' ban upon reading during Donne's
convalescence. He was compelled to write from his innermost resources, and fresh personal experiences, in a way that was excus-
ably egocentric. In Meditation 21, he saw condemnation of self as
one of his sins, which encouraged 'faintnesses of Spirit'; he had
lost none of the self-abasement that produced *Biathanatos*.

Donne's self-evaluation, often physical, commences with negation, and moves by Thomistic reasoning, and the repetition of key
words, to a positive article of faith. To begin a spiritual exercise
with acknowledged self-devaluation was in accord with the Jesuit
practice, though humility was not confined to that order. This
procedure led to ironic situations, quite unlike those of the sceptical Montaigne. Perhaps the most ironic of Donne's meditations is
that which opens the series; here he contemplates disease as a con-
tradiction of the order and providence of God's Book of Creatures.
Two passages are examined below, for diction, rhetoric and symbolic imagery:

Is this the honour which Man hath by being a *little world*,
That he hath these *earthquakes* in him selfe, sodaine
shakings; these *lightnings*, sodaine flashes; these *thunders*,
sodaine noises; these *Eclypses*, sodain offuscations, &
darknings of his senses; these *blazing stars*, sodaine fiery
exhalations; these *rivers of blood*, sodaine red waters? Is he a
world to himselfe onely therefore, that he hath inough in
himself, not only to destroy, and execute himselfe, but to
presage that execution upon himselfe; to assist the sicknes,
to antidate the sicknes, to make the sicknes the more irre-
mediable, by sad apprehensions, and as if hee would make

a fire the more vehement, by sprinkling water upon the
coales, so to wrap a hote fever in cold Melancholy.

(*Devotions, Meditation* 1, p 7, lines 31–3 and p 8, lines 1–9)

Dominating this excerpt are two long rhetorical questions
(*erotema*), and prolific parallelism and word repetition; examples of
the last are: *world, hath, these, sodaine, himselfe, execute* and *sicknes.*
The impressive vocabulary often consists of polysyllables, which
are not all latinisms. The eloquent association, linking *earthquakes,
lightnings* and *thunders*; *Eclypses* and *offuscations, blazing stars* and *fiery
exhalations*, is exhausted when it reaches *rivers of blood*; for the
necessary cadence is secured by the feebler parallelism of *sodaine red
waters*. Paired phenomena, by means of near synonyms, are again
in evidence; and the principle is applied with equal force to
occasional epithets, such as *blazing* and *fiery*.

In the second extended question, *destroy* and *execute* have very
different shades of meaning; for here the schematic parallels have
shifted to verbs. The Greek rhetoricians gave the name *hyrmos* to
this unfashioned ordering of words, continuing to the end of the
conceptual pattern, with appropriate variations. In the complex
first question, images of disorder yield to a subtle use of crossed
metaphors, in which *hote fever*, becomes *fire the more vehement* and
cold Melancholy is analogous to *sprinkling water upon the coales*. The
intellectual skill of this is surprising from an ailing man.

Every now and then the prolusion of reason is broken by an
outburst of *ecphonesis* (exclamation), mingled with other forms of
rhetoric:

O miserable abundance, O beggarly riches! how much doe
wee lacke of having *remedies* for everie disease, when as yet
we have not *names* for them? But wee have a *Hercules*
against these *Gyants*, these *Monsters*; that is the *Phisician*;
hee musters up al the forces of the other world, to succour
this; all Nature to relieve Man.

(*Devotions, Meditation* 4, p 20, lines 17–22)

The exclamations are notable for being ironic instances of oxymo-
ron; while there is humour in the metonymic use of *Hercules,
Gyants* and *Monsters*.

The pathetic fallacy is vindicated in the dramatic episode of the
tolling bells, which climaxes the sick man's dilemma. As *Devotions*
16–18 show, the persistent bells of the neighbouring Church of St

Gregory deeply agitated the troubled state of Donne during an attack of insomnia. Ruskin in *Modern Painters* III 4 XII 5 said that violent feelings may produce a misleading impression of external phenomena; and Donne was so affected, when the epidemic caused daily deaths and burials. The following is a selected sequence of Donne's reactions and recollections:

> *Meditation 16*: We have a *Convenient Author*, who writ a *Discourse of Bells* when hee was Prisoner in *Turky*. How would hee have enlarged himselfe, if he had beene my *fellow Prisoner* in this *sicke bed*, so neere to that *steeple*, which never ceases, no more than the *harmony of the spheres*, but is more heard. . . . We scarce heare of any man *preferred*, but wee thinke of our selves, that wee might very well have beene that *Man*; Why might not I have beene that *Man*, that is carried to his *grave* now? Could I fit my selfe, to *stand*, or *sit* in any Mans *place*, & not to lie in any mans *grave*? I may lacke much of the *good parts* of the meanest, but I lacke nothing of the *mortality* of the weakest.

> *Expostulation 16*: O my *God*, my *God*, doe I, that have this *feaver*, need other *remembrances* of my *Mortalitie*? Is not mine owne *hollow voice*, voice enough to pronounce that to me? Need I looke upon a *Deaths-head* in a *Ring* that, have one in my *face*? or goe for *death* to my *Neighbours* house, that have him in my *bosome*?

> *Prayer 16*: O eternall and most gracious *God* . . . I make account that I heare this dead brother of ours, who is now carried out to his *buriall*, to speake to mee, and to *preach* my *funerall Sermon*, in the voice of these *Bells*. In him, O *God*, thou has accomplished to mee, even the request of *Dives* to *Abraham*; *Thou hast sent one from the dead to speake unto mee*. He speakes to mee aloud from that *steeple*; hee whispers to mee at these *Curtaines*, and hee speaks thy words; *Blessed are the dead which die in the Lord, from henceforth. Let this praier* therfore, O my *God*, be as my *last gaspe*, my *expiring*, my *dying* in *thee*; That if this bee the houre of my *transmigration*, I may die the *death* of a *sinner* . . .

> *Meditation 17*: The *Church* is *Catholike, universall*, so are all her *Actions*; *All* that she does, belongs to *all*. When she

baptizes a child, that action concernes mee; for that child is thereby connected to that *Head* which is my *Head* too, and engraffed into that *body,* whereof I am a *member.* And when she *buries a Man,* that action concernes me; All *mankinde* is of one *Author,* and is one *volume;* when one Man dies, one *Chapter* is not *torne* out of the *booke,* but *translated* into a better *language;* and every *Chapter* must be so *translated;* . . . No Man is an *Iland,* intire of it selfe; every man is a peece of the *Continent,* a part of the *maine;* if a *Clod* bee washed away by the *Sea, Europe* is the lesse, as well as if a *Promontorie* were, as well as if a *Mannor* of thy *friends,* or of *thine owne* were; Any Mans *death* diminishes *me,* because I am involved in *Mankinde;* And therefore never send to know for whom the *bell* tolls; It tolls for *thee.*

Meditation 18: If I will aske meere *Philosophers,* what the *soule* is, I shall finde amongst them, that will tell me, it is nothing, but the *temperament* and *harmony,* and *just and equall composition of the Elements in the body,* which produces all those *faculties* which we ascribe to the *soule;* and so, in it selfe is *nothing,* no *seperable substance,* that overlives the *body.* They see the *soule* is nothing else in other *Creatures,* and they affect an *impious humilitie,* to think *as low* of Man. But if my *soule* were no more than the soule of a *beast,* I could not thinke so; that *soule* that can *reflect* upon it selfe, *consider* it selfe, is *more* than so.

(Devotions 16–18, pp 81–91)

The moods of depression, despair and resignation are dramatic in the sense that Mrs Bottrall supposed. For Donne could also make disturbing use of his acquaintance with the Book of Creatures. Phrases are illumined with flashes of insight that enable the reader to share the agony, as well as the consolations, of his *Devotions.*

The *Convenient Author* to whom he refers was the Venetian fortifications engineer, Hieronimus Magius, who was captured by the Turks in Cyprus, and died at Constantinople in 1572; his treatise *De Tintinnabulis* was written during his final captivity. In the *Constitutions and Canons* of the Anglican Church, a parish priest was supposed to ring three bells in approved sequence, on behalf of a dying member of the congregation: for the time of passing, for the actual death, and for the funeral rites. In a style

simple and impressive, Donne elects to deal with the last of these
first. The parallelism of the final adversative sentences (Med. 16)
is the only scheme of words that is rhetorical.

The expostulations, on the other hand, are essentially oratorical;
Donne puts many questions that call for no answer. No. 16 has
four instantces of *erotema* in six lines; and the repetitive uses of
ecphonesis show also his fondness for *ploce*. A *Deaths-head in a Ring*
was a type of jewellery commonly worn by mourners; and the
use of metonymy in the third rhetorical question suggests all the
trappings of mortality.

In Prayer 16 *Thou hast sent one from the dead to speake unto mee* looks
back to Luke xvi 24; while *Blessed are the dead which die in the Lord,
from henceforth* is a direct quotation from Revelation xiv 13 (King
James Bible). 'As my *last gaspe*, my *expiring*, my *dying*', is an extravagant simile, less attractive for being so emotive. *Transmigration*,
an unusual word in a prayer, is found in biblical contexts from the
late thirteenth century; but its reference is generally to the Baby-
lonian captivity of the Jews. Examples in the OED indicate that
the term was not much employed for 'the passage of the soul after
death', until the end of the sixteenth century. Conventional
language, especially archaism, tends to recur in prayers; a deliberate
movement encouraged uncomplicated phrasal units, with emphasis
on loaded words, as well as defined pauses (see David Crystal
and Derek Davy, *Investigating English Style,* Longman, 1969,
Chapter 6).

The passage from Meditation 17 begins with the language of
liturgical symbolism, initiated by the Bible; Donne's employment
of the words *Head, body* and *member* is analogical, and owes something to the Church Fathers. A strictly metaphorical sense attaches
to *Author, volume, Chapter, booke, translated* and *language*; the work in
the writer's mind is not a literary creation, but *All mankinde. Torne
out of the booke* (i.e. removed by death) is metaphysically figurative,
conceived under the influence of Tertullian and Augustine. The
cultural impact of such religious leaders was still considerable in
the sixteenth and seventeenth centuries, but not so well remembered in men's private devotions. Donne's aptitude for employing
words with ambivalent meanings, one spiritual, the other worldly,
is shown in the special significance here attached to the word
translated. Punningly, it suggests both the biblical sense of 'transferred from this world to the next', and the more familiar one,

'turned into another language', also current in the fourteenth century, when *translate* first appeared in English.

In the excerpt beginning 'No Man is an *Iland*' the theme is ephemerality – the irrelevance of size (*Clod, Promontorie* or *Mannor*) to man's equality in the sight of God. The loss of another affects us all, if religion means anything; and Donne therefore regards the death-knell as a proper reminder to Everyman of his mortality. The spiritual implications are so profound that the reader may be unaware of the rhetorical devices of Donne's peroration; for instance, the emphatic repetitions of phrase, even when the key nouns are sporadically italicized: 'entire' and 'of it selfe'; 'a peece of the *Continent*, a part of the *maine*.' The semantic value that Donne attached to personal pronouns is syntactically demonstrated in the emphatic final position of the word *thee*.

Donne's attitude to the secular philosophy of the ancients was not unconventional. He was aware of the extent to which the latter's thinking had been absorbed into the work of such writers as Philo, Origen, Tertullian, Augustine and Aquinas. In the excerpt from Meditation 18, defence of the immortality of the human soul rested upon Aquinas's *Summa Theologica,* just as he borrowed from Aristotle's *De Anima*. Donne would have known, too, Sir John Davies's *Nosce Teipsum* (1597), the third edition of which appeared in the *Poems* published in 1622.

Aquinas explained the soul (*anima*) as 'the first principle of life' (*S.T.* 1a, 75 1), equating it with Aristotle's *psyche,* which was responsible for all vital activities. According to the acknowledged hierarchies, the rational, sensitive and vegetative souls were conferred respectively on men, animals and plants, this inheritance enabling them to sustain life. Each order was thought to incorporate the powers of those below. The atheistical view, which Donne and Aquinas rejected, maintained that the soul was a function of matter, without potential except through the body. Donne phrases this argument differently, attributing the soul to '*temperament* and *harmony*, and the *just and equall composition of the Elements in the body*.'

Aquinas admitted the sensory experience that the soul acquired through the body; but he thought that spiritual knowledge, not imaginary, transcended matter, could serve the soul after death. *Impious humility* is Donne's description of the endeavour to degrade humans to the level of non-spiritual Creatures. The soul of man 'can *reflect* upon it selfe, *consider* it selfe'. Donne offers alternative accounts of the origin of the soul, but concludes that they are less important than its end, which is salvation, the ground of Augustine's faith in Christian charity.

Dr Johnson's complaint, in his Life of Cowley, that the metaphysical poets 'broke every image into fragments', is indifferently true of the *Devotions upon Emergent Occasions*. In tone and imagery, the prayers are the most temperate of the compositions. The allusive intensity of the expostulations, belongs to that neglected body of medieval colloquy, religious fantasy. Much of the meditations is untheological. Concentrating upon Man and life's demands upon him, Donne shows the distortion of reality that arises from reflections on his parlous condition. Amplification, antithesis and parallelism are ever-present mannerisms in this mixed kind of writing, but they are eloquently handled and help build tension. The style is mixed, because it is ornate as well as pointed. The emotional pressure of Donne's ideas in the *Devotions* could not, however, have been conveyed so readably, without the arts of rhetoric to dignify the meditations.

CHAPTER IX

The *Sermons*

𝕨𝕨𝕨𝕨𝕨𝕨

DONNE'S one hundred and sixty extant *Sermons* were delivered between 1615 and 1630, a decade and a half of progressive accomplishment that earned popular acclaim. According to his biographers, he would have written a sermon a week, and the loss of his work must therefore have been considerable. Individual sermons and small groups were published during Donne's lifetime; but the authoritative text of one hundred and forty-five surviving examples depends largely on three folio volumes collected by John Donne Jr; these are: *LXXX Sermons* (1640), *Fifty Sermons* (1649), and *XXVI Sermons* (1661). Twenty-three sermons survive in more than one text, and sixteen of these are found also in manuscript. Unfortunately no holograph copies are known to exist.

Between 1953 and 1962 the University of California Press published the standard ten-volume edition of the *Sermons,* edited by G. R. Potter and E. M. Simpson; the headings, which record appropriate festivals or places of delivery, were taken from the three folio volumes mentioned. The inestimable value of this edition, which is cited in the following pages, is that it dates the majority of the sermons, and prints them, as circumstances permit, in chronological order.

Donne's method of preparing the sermons, after choosing the text, has some bearing on the language of the final product, preserved in the folios. According to Walton's *Life,* the preacher divided his text into sections of key words, and meditated on these, after consulting the works of Church Fathers and commentators. The sermon was then outlined in notes, and the line of presentation memorized. Some time after the preaching, Donne found occasion to polish and improve the draft, with a view to ultimate publication. This was the procedure adopted by most eminent preachers of the seventeenth century; it gave a degree of spontaneity at the time of address, but also accounts for the literariness of sermons in print. A lack of opportunity or wish to remodel early sermons may explain the non-survival of much of Donne's output. In a letter Donne discloses that, during the outbreak of plague in 1625, he resided in the home of Sir John Danvers in Chelsea, and there revised eighty of the sermons (no doubt from earlier notes); but which these are is unknown.

Donne's preferment as a Divinity Reader at Lincoln's Inn from 1616 to 1622 was an influential step in his development as a preacher. In 1624 he succeeded to the vicarage of St Dunstans-in-the-West, where his biographer, Izaak Walton, was one of his parishioners. As his reputation grew, Donne was afforded opportunities of addressing many varied congregations. The most notable sermons were preached after his election as Dean of St Paul's in November, 1621. A year later he addressed the first missionary sermon to the Virginia Company, to whose Council he had recently been elected. The Virginia Plantation had been founded by Sir Walter Raleigh in 1584, and forty years later became a royal colony. Donne had a personal interest in this English colony, because in 1609 he had applied unsuccessfully to become the Company's secretary. His address to the Virginia merchants is full of the humanitarian and statesmanlike wisdom for which the *Sermons* are remarkable.

St Paul's Cross, where Donne preached frequently, was an open-air auditorium, with a canopied pulpit; it had been the scene of religious contention since 1389. The heterogeneous audience, which included women, was better behaved than in the disturbances described in John Foxe's *Actes and Monuments* (1563). Queen Elizabeth had had to restrain the extempore zeal of separatist reformers, whose pulpit-drum eloquence was anathema to the dignified Anglican divines of her reign. By the turn of the century, the best preachers, such as Andrewes and Parker, had instilled orderliness and respect, one of Richard Hooker's ideals in Church government.

Among the attractive assets of Donne's sermons are their reasonableness, relevance to social experience, and understanding of human frailty. A greater merit, however, is tolerance of outlook, in an age when the ardour of religion was prone to bigotry. There is evidence of learning in plenty, without pedantic scholarship; Donne seems merely to have transferred his imaginative gifts from poetry to oratory. Sermons were commissioned for special occasions and select audiences, and the astonishing variety of styles is not obscured by the opulent phrasing of the pleading.

In the sermons Donne was not as indifferent to literary fame as he appeared to be in other ventures. He wrote for posterity, and regarded each biblical text as an intellectual challenge. He engaged the attention of listeners by firmly, yet humbly, appealing to reason, as well as pious emotions. In a letter to the Countess of Montgomery, dated April 1619, he wrote, not in his best style:

> I know what dead carkasses things written are, in respect of things spoken. But in things of this kinde, that soul that inanimates them, receives debts from them: The Spirit of God that dictates them in the speaker or writer, and is present in his tongue or hand, meets himself again (as we meet ourselves in a glass) in the eies and hearts of the hearers and readers.

The concision of the poetry is often missed in the amplitude of the prose; but the sermons enable the reader to get nearer to the mind and personality of the artist.

The sermons display, in the fulness of his mature mind, Donne's exceptional range of reading in Astronomy, Mathematics, Medicine, Geography and Natural History. The figurative use the writer made of this knowledge is obvious in many analogies. But the Bible was the dominating incentive of ideas, and the principal source of theocratic utterances. The printed texts of Donne's sermons have the quotations in italics, while chapter and verse references are provided in the margin. Donne consulted the Hebrew and Greek Bibles when he wanted to remark on the inadequacy of English translators, especially in the Geneva and King James versions. In arbitrating, however, he was influenced by the reading in Jerome's Latin Vulgate. The usual practice of citation is to quote from the Vulgate first, then to follow up with the reading in the Authorized Version; but occasionally Donne prefers his own translation.

Like Blake, Donne believed that the New Jerusalem had found a home in Britain; the English monarchy was, indeed, based on the history of the Hebrew kingdoms, beginning with Saul. The Old Testament was Donne's authority for faith in the Divine Right of Kings. In the anniversary Sermon on England's deliverance from the Gunpowder Plot (St Paul's, 5 November 1622) he said: 'God himself, in his Unity, *is* the Modell, He *is* the Type of Monarchy' (IV ix 240). Nearly three years later, he exclaimed: 'How cheaply doth he sell his Princes favour, that hath nothing for it, but the peoples breath?' (IV xv 305, St Paul's, 8 May 1625).

In this 1625 Sermon, Donne also reveals his repeated conviction that Scripture is 'the language of the Holy Ghost' (ibid, p 301):

> It hath been observed amongst Philosophers, that *Plato* speaks probably, and *Aristotle* positively; *Platoes* way is, It may be thus, and *Aristotles,* It must be thus. The like hath been noted amongst Divines, between *Calvin,* and *Melanchthon*; *Calvin* will say, *Videtur,* It seemes to be thus, *Melanchthon,* It can be no otherwise but thus. But the best men are but Problemticall, Onely the Holy Ghost is Dogmaticall; Onely he subscribes this *surely,* and onely he seales with Infallibility. Our dealings are appointed to be in yea, yea, and nay, nay, and no farther; But *all the promises of God are yea, and Amen,* that is, surely, verily; for that is his Name; ... The nearer we come to the consideration of God, the farther we are removed from all contingencies, and all inclination to Error, and the more is this *Amen, verily, surely,* multiplied and established unto us.

One of Donne's principal concerns here is with the middle and lower strata of society, the people with whom Christ and his apostles mingled, and to whom they expounded the non-political ideal of the Kingdom of Heaven. Under God's guidance, mankind would be united in amity, when the earthly kingdom gave place to the universal. *Amen,* repeated in this passage, was the Hebrew asseveration of truth and certainty, appended to prayers, a talisman of the faith.

Evelyn Simpson estimates that Donne's references in the *Sermons* to the Bible exceed seven thousand, the greatest number being to the Psalms, on which there are no less than thirty-four sermons. As twenty-one of these are undated, the assumption is that they were early compositions. The biblical texts were studied in the languages of their earliest versions, Hebrew, Greek, Aramaic and Latin, with which Donne had varying acquaintance; he makes reference to the 'Complutense' or polyglot bible of Arias Montanus, published at Antwerp between 1571 and 1573. One hundred and forty Hebrew words or phrases are discussed in the sermons, which is taken to indicate that Donne was more familiar with Hebrew than Greek.

In 'Dean Donne Sets His Text' (*ELH* 10, pp 208–29) Don Cameron Allen investigated Donne's acquaintance with the principal biblical languages, and concluded as follows:

At no time does Donne seem to know as much Hebrew as Andrewes or even Hall although he is more ostentatious in his use of it than either of them. My impression is that Donne had 'small Hebrew and less Greek.' . . . It is quite evident to me that Donne read the Sixth and Thirty-second Psalms in the original; in fact, his sermons on the Penitential Psalms seem to be the high point of his use of the Hebrew. . . . Besides defining the Hebrew word of the text or offering variant readings, Donne sometimes plunges into philological difficulties that are probably beyond his depth. . . .

His use of the Septuagint and the Greek New Testament is very limited. In the collected sermons of other Anglican divines, we come constantly upon the Greek letter, but in the eight hundred folio pages of the *LXXX Sermons,* there are exactly seven different Greek words. . . .

Donne's method of treating the Latin and English versions of the Bible are similar. Often he quotes verbatim, but at other times he clips, condenses, paraphrases, alters the word order, changes the case and number of nouns, and the tense and number of verbs. Sometimes he even alters the words themselves. . . . Like most preachers of his time, he apparently thought of the Bible not as a rigid and fixed authority, but as something pliable that a preacher might bend to his will. . . .

It was not Donne's habit to compare the English versions with any regularity. We should like to see some uniformity in these comparisons, but it does not exist. He compares the texts when the mood strikes him, and for no apparent reason save whim. . . . Like the traditional Renaissance bee, he gathered his honey from flower and weed. He certainly lacked the scholarly approach of the great divines to the Holy Word, but he undoubtedly was more careful in his inspection of texts than the average preacher.

Donne's secondary sources were the Church Fathers of the period AD 160–600; he refers most frequently to Augustine, Tertullian, Jerome, Chrysostom, Ambrose, Basil and Gregory the Great, all men of great intellect. Tertullian, Jerome and Augustine were also masters of rhetoric, steeped in what they regarded as trustworthy skills of persuasion, inspired by Christian doctrine. Donne became a literalist largely through the impact of these commentators; he preferred evidence that could be tested upon the pulses to the philosophically abstract. He employs abstract nouns emotively to communicate a state of mind, but usually by analogy with some concrete experience.

The climactic prose rhythms of the sermons are largely managed through periodic structures of some complexity, which subordinate clauses freely, without destroying organic unity. Development of the idea, even in direct writing, is so intricate that a passage cannot be curtailed, without dismembering its cumulative significance. In the following from a Sermon preached at Lincoln's Inn (II i 49–50), it was possible to excise only three lines and retain the logic of the conception:

> If a man be asked a reason why he loves one meat better then another, where all are equally good, (as the books of Scripture are) he will at least, finde a reason in some good example, that he sees some man of good tast, and temperate withall, so do: And for my Diet, I have Saint *Augustines* protestation, that he loved the *Book of Psalms*, and Saint *Chrysostomes*, that he loved Saint *Pauls Epistles*, with a particular devotion. . . . God gives us, not onely that which is meerly necessary, but that which is convenient too; He does not onely feed us, but *feed us with marrow, and with fat-nesse*; he gives us our instruction in cheerfull forms, not in a sowre, and sullen, and angry, and unacceptable way, but cheerfully, in *Psalms*, which is also a limited, and a restrained form; Not in an *Oration*, not in *Prose*, but in *Psalms*; which is such a form as is both curious, and requires diligence in the making, and then when it is made, can have nothing, no syllable taken from it, nor added to it: Therefore is God will delivered to us in *Psalms*, that we might have it the more

cheerfully, and that we might have it the more certainly, because where all the words are numbred, and measured, and weighed, the whole work is the lesse subject to falsification, either by substraction or addition.

Substraction must be a printer's error; no such spelling is recorded in the OED.

Walton's conception of Donne as a baroque artist 'preaching to himself like an Angel from a cloud' is wide of the mark in this passage, which is a simple declaration of delight by a reader who appreciates the Scriptures for their 'delicacy, and harmony, and melody of language' (VI i 55). A characteristic example of metaphysical wit is inherent in the Psalmist's association of *food* with spiritual sustenance. The metaphor *Diet* is capitalized, and the figure is sustained in *meat* and *feed us with marrow and with fatnesse*; the latter being an adaptation of Psalm 63 5. In the King James Bible this verse begins: 'My soul shall be satisfied as with marrow and fatnesse;' but a marginal note states that there is no mention of *marrow* in the Hebrew text. *Sowre*, and *sullen* (an alliterative coupling) is in contradistinction to the earlier word *cheerfull*.

Donne had great admiration for the 'cheerfull' forms of the Psalter, the making of which he described in a Sermon on the Penitential Psalms, preached in Spring 1623 (VI i 41):

It is easie to observe, that in all Metricall compositions, of which kinde the booke of Psalmes is, the force of the whole piece, is for the most part left to the shutting up; the whole frame of the Poem is a beating out of a piece of gold, but the last clause is as the impression of the stamp, and that is it that makes it currant.

Sermons on the Psalms are rich in examples of phrasal balance, one of the forms of 'exornation': e.g. (A) 'that we might have it more *cheerfully*, that we might have it more *certainly*', and (B) 'where all the words are *numbred*, and *measured*, and *weighed*, the whole work is the lesse subject to *falsification*, either by *substraction* or *addition.*'

Allegorical interpretation of the Bible was an outcome of the fusion of Platonism and Christianity, which began with Philo Judaeus, and was continued by the patristic hermeneuts, even later than Augustine. In the reign of Elizabeth, allegorists were challenged by historical literalists, as Donne hints at the beginning of his Easter Sermon at St Paul's in 1624, an explication of Revelation xx 6 (vɪ ii 62–3):

> The literall sense is alwayes to be preserved; but the literall sense is not alwayes to be discerned: for the literall sense is not alwayes that, which the very Letter and Grammer of the place presents, as where it is literally said, *That Christ is a Vine* . . . But the literall sense of every place, is the principall intention of the Holy Ghost, in that place: And his principall intention in many places, is to expresse things by allegories, by figures; so that in many places of Scripture, a figurative sense is the literall sense, and more in this book then in any other. . . . That Expositor is not to be blamed, who not destroying the literall sense, proposes such a figurative sense, as may exalt our devotion, and advance our edification.

This Sermon is of later date than that on the Psalms, preached at Lincoln's Inn. Donne, the thinker, was now at the height of his powers. Philological parallelism and paradox were two methods of handling the theme of the Resurrection, as the following passage from the Sermon shows (p 73):

> Now every repentance is not a resurrection; It is rather a waking out of a dreame, then a rising to a new life: Nay it is rather a startling in our sleep, then any awaking at all, to have a sudden remorse, a sudden flash, and no constant perseverance. *Awake thou that sleepest*, says the Apostle, out of the Prophet: First *awake*, come to a sense of thy state; and then *arise from the dead*, sayes he, from the practise of dead works; and then, *Christ shall give thee light*: life and strength to walk in new wayes. It is a long work, and hath many steps; *Awake, arise*, and *walke*, and therefore set out betimes; At the last day, in those, which shall be found alive upon the earth, we say there shall be a sudden death, and a sudden resurrection, *In raptu, in transitu, in ictu oculi*, In an instant, in the twinckling of an eye; but do not thou trust to have this first Resurrection *In raptu, in transitu, in ictu oculi*, In thy last passage upon thy death-bed, when the twinckling of the eye, must be the closing of thine eyes: But as we assign to glorified bodies after the last Resurrection, certain *Dotes*, (as we call them in the Schoole) certaine

Endowments, so labour thou to finde those endowments,
in thy soule here, if thou beest come to this first Resurrection.

The rapturous style of this writing is not the offspring of looseness,
but of confidence in the propriety of transplanting wit to expressions of the emotions. This is mistakenly regarded as a whim of
metaphysical preachers; it was, in reality, a fundamental principle
of Book IV of Augustine's *De Doctrina Christiana,* which describes
elocutio as the elucidation of scriptural truth. Augustine held that
the central message of Christianity was the doctrine of Love, and
that imparting it was a separate art from dialectics. For Donne it
was thus feasible to consider the *resurrection* in the different mystical
senses.

St Paul in Ephesians v.14 spoke of the *resurrection* from sin,
which he saw as a preliminary to *resurrection* of the Church from
persecution, and he invoked the prophet in Isaiah lx 1, with the
rallying admonition: 'Awake, thou that sleepest, and arise from
the dead, and Christ shall give thee light.' Members of the Church
at Ephesus were advised to be circumspect, and to redeem the
time, because the days were evil. In the first part of the excerpt
Donne uses *resurrection* analogically, and adds the caveat that
impulsive repentance is not enough, unless kept alive by *constant
perseverance.*

This sermon was preached on 28 March 1624, when Donne had
just recovered from a near-fatal illness; there is a clear link between
it and the twenty-first Expostulation and Prayer of the *Devotions,*
in which Donne wrote:

[thou] hast also made this *bodily rising,* by thy *grace,* an
earnest of a *second* resurrection from *sinne,* and of a *third* to
everlasting glory.

Here we have the plural *resurrections* referred to in the second part
of the passage from Donne's Sermon at St Paul's.

The tone of the passage is in the homiletic tradition of St
Augustine and St Bernard. Donne usually moulded the style of the
sermon to the spirit of his text. He was susceptible to the influence
of the Reformation, but refrained from subordination of the argument to evangelical appeal. Memory was, for Donne, the key to
both kinds of knowledge, of self and of God; its principal instrument of association was metaphor, sometimes original, sometimes

a mere biblical vehicle, as in *the practise of dead works* and *in the twinckling of an eye*.

The Stuart kings all disapproved of the reading of sermons, and reprimanded preachers who delivered them in that way. James I complained of a sermon (not Donne's) that seemed 'negligently and extemporally spoken' (see Donne's letter to Sir Robert Ker, April 1627). Charles I called for a copy of the Sermon delivered at Whitehall in April 1627, and Donne confessed to a 'post-cribrated' version 'set down with . . . much study, and diligence, and labour of syllables'; in short a revision to placate his censorious ruler. Few sermons could have been preached in the 'exscribed' language Donne finally adorned them with for the press. (*Cribrate* [to sift], was a verb presumably coined by Donne; it must be one of the shortest-lived in English, since its life from the OED's three examples is thirty-eight years. *Exscribe* [to write out] appeared in 1607, and its span of use was a mere hundred and twenty years.)

Walton's description of Donne in the pulpit is relevant to his style. He writes that Donne preached 'the Word so, as showed his own heart was possest with those very thoughts and joys that he laboured to distill into others: A Preacher in earnest; weeping sometimes for his Auditory, sometimes with them . . . and all this with a most particular grace and an unexpressible addition of comeliness' (p 49). As an acknowledged master of eloquence, Donne's word-choice matched the emotive power of his presence. His imagery was the 'penumbra of associations' (to borrow a phrase from Joan Bennett), and, over all, the rhythmical tension and release aroused universally responsive feelings. The Sermon preached at St Paul's in 1624/5, on the text of Acts ix 4, is a good example of argument illustrated by proofs from the Bible. Note the homogeneity of figures of sound in the following passage, and the associations that gather about such metaphorical words as *Thunder*, *harmonious promises*, *Trumpet* and *Organ*.

How often does God speake, and nobody heares the voyce? He speaks in his Canon, in Thunder, and he speaks in our Canon, in the rumour of warres. He speaks in his musique, in the harmonious promises of the Gospel, and in our musique, in the temporall blessings of peace, and plenty; And we heare a noyse in his Judgements, and wee heare a sound in his mercies; but we heare no voyce, we doe not discern that this noyse, or this sound comes from any certain person; we do not feele them to be mercies, nor to be judgements uttered from God, but naturall accidents, casuall occurencies, emergent contingencies, which as an Atheist might think, would fall out though there were no God, or no commerce, no dealing, no speaking between God and Man. Though *Saul* came not instantly to a perfect discerning who spoke, yet he saw instantly, it was a Person above nature, and therefore speakes to him in that phrase of submission, *Quis es Domine? Lord who art thou?* And after, with trembling and astonishment (as the Text sayes) *Domine quid me vis facere? Lord what wilt thou have me to do?* Then we are truliest said to hear, when we know from whence the voyce comes. Princes are Gods Trumpet, and the Church is Gods Organ, but Christ Jesus is his voyce. When he speaks in the Prince, when he speaks in the Church, there we are bound to heare, and happy if we doe hear. Man hath a natural way to come to God, by the eie, by the creature; So *Visible things* shew the *Invisible God*: But then, God hath superinduced a supernaturall way, by the eare. For, though hearing be naturall, yet that faith in God should come by hearing a man preach, is supernatural. God shut up the naturall way, in *Saul*, Seeing; He struck him blind; But he opened the super-naturall way, he inabled him to heare, and to heare him. God would have us beholden to grace, and not to nature, and to come for our salvation, to his Ordinances, to the preaching of his Word, and not to any other meanes.

The entire passage is a series of ingenious analogues, presented in gracious rhythms, and mounting to a crescendo in the sentence that begins *Then we are truliest said to hear*. Donne was convinced that an inspired preacher speaks with a supernatural voice; he preached to move a living audience, he only revised for the benefit of posterity. There could have been no change in the substance of a sermon, unless it was 'exscribed' at a later date; the final gloss, however, was achieved by polishing. The mainsprings of his sermonizing were clarification of text (*sub specie aeternitatis*) and edification of the moral personality.

Logan Pearsall Smith, in the Introduction to selections of *Donne's*

Sermons (p. xxxv) attributes the preacher's baffling, hortatory and dogmatic utterances to his poignant and personal manner. In an article on 'Lancelot Andrewes' (*Essays Ancient and Modern*), T. S. Eliot suggests that a shadow hangs over Donne because of 'impure motive', spiritual indiscipline, and 'facile success' (p 15). Donne, he says, found 'refuge in religion from the tumults of a strong emotional temperament', and 'accepted a benefice because he had no other way of making a living' (p 27). This can only be a prejudicial view. Donne's methods in the *Sermons* were undoubtedly the outcome of his practice and reputation as a Renaissance poet, interested in the discovery of his own personality. A consciousness of sin made him compassionate towards the shortcomings of others; and the preaching made a lasting impression on auditors because of his long commerce with the world of men, and knowledge of new developments in science and philosophy.

Donne's Renaissance humanism should not be underestimated, because it differs in Christian outlook from the secular contribution of Shakespeare, Jonson and Bacon. In the Easter Sermon of 1624, Donne interpolated a note that *Dotes* (endowment) was a term familiar to the *Schoole*, meaning by the latter not simply the theological (and philosophic) doctrines of Aquinas, but the trend of religious thought since Augustine, covering a period of nearly a millenium. A scholarly facility in Latin was essential to the study of this body of work, written by adherents to the universal Catholic Church. With the literature of this *school*, Donne was thoroughly acquainted, and the fascination in the *Sermons* of such topics as God's creation of the world and the fall of the Angels is parallelled in Dante's *Divina Commedia* and Milton's *Paradise Lost*. To blink disparagingly at theories of the origin and destination of the soul does not minimize their impact on biblical eschatology, or Christian belief that Heaven and Hell were realities, not states of mind.

Ideas from patristic sources, as well as science, provide the bulk of Donne's conceits and metaphysical wit. Imagery that is analogical strikes a practical or sensory note, as in the Lent Sermon of 1630 (ix ix 217 and 226):

> God windes us off the Skein, that he may weave us into the whole peece.

> Crack a shell, to tast the kernell, cleare the words, to gaine the Doctrine.

The books of Scripture are the eloquentest ... every word in them hath ... his taste and verdure [*Verdure* in this context does not mean 'greenness', but 'sharpness of flavour', e.g. in the juice of fruit].

The Lent Sermon was preached on Job xvi 17–19, and Donne, as was his custom, preserved the style of the original language. He always claimed the privilege of a preacher to modify the actual words of Scripture, in order to emulate the Bible's eloquence.

Donne's pietistic eloquence did not prevent outbursts of admonitory satire, for instance, when he queried the defeatism that accompanies self-deception. The following is an example from the Sermon preached before the King at Whitehall on 24 February 1625, (VII ii 86–8):

I knowe how frivolous a tale that is, That Saint *Gregorie* drew *Trajans soule* out of *Hell*, after it was there; and I know, how groundlesse an opinion it is, that is ascrib'd to *Origen*, that at last, *the Devill shall be sav'd*; but if they could perswade mee one halfe, that *Trajan*, or that the *Devill* came to *Repentance* in *hell*, I should not be hard, in beleeving the other halfe, that they might be delivered out of *hell*. *What meane you*, says *God almighty, that yee use this Proverbe, the Fathers have eate soure grapes, and the childrens teeth are set on edge?* Doe ye meane, that because your *Fathers* have sinn'd, you must *perish*? ... And would God pretend to send thee a *gracious Messadge*, and send thee a *Divorce*? God is *Love*, and the *Holy Ghost* is amorous in his *Metaphors*; everie where his *Scriptures* abound with the notions of *Love*, of *Spouse*, and *Husband*, and *Marriadge Songs*, and *Marriadge Supper*, and *Marriadge-Bedde*. ... Every where in the *Scriptures*, we meet with *Gods venites*, in every *Prophets* mouth, invitations to come unto *God*; There is a *Venite de circuitu*, Come, though you come from compassing the Earth, which is *Satans perambulation*; though you have walkd in his wayes, yet come unto *God*.

The italicized allusions to '*soure grapes*' and '*Satans perambulation*' are respectively from Ezekiel xviii 2 and Job ii 2. 'The *Holy Ghost* is amorous in his *Metaphors*' is a touch characteristic of Donne, and *Venite de circuitu* is the kind of borrowing from the Latin Bible that Andrewes and Donne freely incorporated. When Donne follows a

Latin quotation with the English version, he often introduces a
new rhythm or tone to the movement of his paragraph. Several
students of Donne's sermons have observed that an accumulation
of *that*-clauses (noun, adjectival or adverbial), such as occurs at the
beginning of this passage, is a pervasive feature of his preaching
practice.

In the previous chapter (the last passage from the *Essayes on
Divinity*), some aspects of periodicity were considered particularly
relevant to Donne's prose. It was seen that his individual style,
varied to suit particular contexts, is not easily classified; even the
significant factor of syntax takes second place to the organic unity
of the writer's conception. Donne's paragraphs, as he elected to
use the divisions in the sermons, develop in a circular movement,
beginning with a self-generating observation, and ending when the
germinal thought has been artfully elaborated, if not materially
advanced. His writing is a tacit denial that cumulative periods,
with grammatical subordination of thought to thought, are much
of an aid to a meaningful literary style.

Donne employs articulated members, with abundant connectives, as well as paratactic structures, but as instruments of emotive
coherence, not steps in a tidily proportioned traditional pattern.
Periods are loosened in the interests of rhythmical climax and
naturalness. He is not adept at the limiting 'period', which requires
meaning to be kept in suspense until the last word. The turns and
changes of direction in Donne's thinking are marked by a greater
frequency of breaks and pauses than is customary with writers like
Hooker, who favoured the modified classical period, accommodated to the English system of pronunciation and loss of inflexion.
Here is a paragraph from a sermon preached at Whitehall on 8
March 1621, which exemplifies Donne's use of paradox in the so-
called loose period; the passage actually begins with the short
sentences of the *style coupé* (IV i 51):

> *Surge & descende in domum figuli*, sayes the Prophet *Ieremy*,
> that is, say the Expositors, to the consideration of thy
> Mortality. It is *Surge, descende, Arise and go down*: A descent
> with an ascension: Our grave is upward, and our heart is
> upon *Iacobs* Ladder, in the way, and nearer to heaven. Our
> daily Funerals are some Emblemes of that; for though we
> be laid down in the earth after, yet we are lifted up upon

mens shoulders before. We rise in the descent to death, and so we do in the descent to the contemplation of it. In all the Potters house, is there one vessell made of better stuffe then clay? There is his matter. And of all formes, a Circle is the perfectest, and art thou loath to make up that Circle, with returning to the earth again?

The Latin word *figuli*, genitive singular of *figulus*, is the 'potter', whose moulding of clay is one of the central figures of this highly emblematic utterance. Note the heavy emphasis on *There* at the beginning of the short sentence, '*There* is his matter'. The *Circle* was regarded as the symbol of perfection; in the *Devotions* Donne called it one of the *Hieroglyphicks of God*, who is conceived as the 'Geometer', a notion derived from Pythagoras and Plato. In oriental mysticism, the circle represented a serpent with its tail in its mouth, the beginning and end, or completion, of all things.

Donne's partiality for the 'loose period' is often described as the most characteristic of his traits in the *Sermons*. What this term implies is that the pattern of associations, the mutuality of thought and feeling, chiefly conditions the flexible dislocation of the syntactic order, through elements such as parenthesis, inversion and elliptical phrasing. Less care is given to grammatical relationships than to the climactic and unitary effects, in short, to the spoken appeal of the paragraph as a rhythm in completion. In prose Donne's aim seems to have been to keep the structural options open for nuances of imaginative thought appropriate to his religious emotions.

The preacher advances many arguments, but logical demonstration is not his principal purpose. Complex elaboration of an idea is at the core of Donne's circling round the meaning of a word, and testing its semantic aspects. When he has exhausted its possibilities in context, there is little more that can be said. What is remarkable of Donne's individualistic style, however, is that it seldom obscures what he has to say, one reason being that he is skilled in the rhetoric of word-position for stress and emphasis. In dignified prose, he can switch from *oratio obliqua* to direct speech with the ease of an intelligent conversationalist, whose fragmentation of syntax, and shifting points of view, are scarcely noticed. He asks and answers questions with the air of a man, not of superior intelligence, but of a teacher who has taken the trouble to enquire into moral and linguistic problems that the practical man tends to skirt.

Donne's rhetorical appeal is due in part to his consciousness of the quality of language, its referential and evocative aspects. When he Englishes Hebrew or Greek words from the Bible, he intends objectivity, while preparing to be assertive; this is shown in the curious conjunction of his associations. The sermon becomes a voyage of discovery for the listener, through the processes of meditation; definitions are offered, discarded or improved, until the truth emerges in a characteristically Donnian light. The word 'libertinism', applied to Donne, seldom refers to his early life, but to the free style he made his own.

Donne reached his audience by the warmth and sincerity of his feelings, the solemnity and power of his words, values that cannot be adequately assessed in linguistic terms. Critics have spoken, analogically, of Donne's faculty of prose orchestration; rightly, because the ensemble of many effects includes, among other things, immense resources of imagery. The imagination in prose is in no way surpassed by similar evidences in the *Divine Poems*. The word *imagination* was in recognized literary use by the sixteenth century; and *imagery* as a collective noun for rhetorical tropes was known to Puttenham, Dryden and Boswell in the *Life of Johnson*. But *image*, as a critical term for 'figurative language', did not appear until Dr Johnson's fourth *Rambler* paper. Yet Donne throughout his writings exploits the functions of the word in such modern senses as 'resemblance', 'emblem', 'symbol'.

The fecundity of Donne's imagination is revealed in the chain-effect he sustains in a figurative line of thought. When he thinks allegorically, there is an immense richness to draw upon in the Bible. Three related extracts from the Easter Sermon, preached at St Paul's in 1626, illustrate this aspect of Donne's practice (VII iii 108–15):

> There was a time, when we had a Spikenard, and a sweet savour of our own, when our own Naturall faculties, in that state as God infused them, in *Adam*, had a power to apprehend, and lay hold upon the graces of God. Man hath a reasonable soule capable of Gods grace, so hath no creature but man; man hath naturall faculties, which may be employed by God in his service, so hath no creature but

man. Onely man was made so, as that he might be better; whereas all other creatures were but to consist in that degree of goodnesse, in which they entred. Miserable fall! Only man was made to mend, and only man does grow worse; Only man was made capable of a spirituall soveraignty, and only man hath enthralled, and mancipated himselfe to a spirituall slavery. . . .

As *the eyes of a foole are in the corners of the earth,* so is the heart and soule of a sinner. The wanton and licentious man, sighs out his soule, weeps out his soule, sweares out his soule, in every place, where his lust, or his custome, or the glory of victory, in overcomming, and deluding, puts him upon such solicitations . . .

Thus it is, when a soule is scattered upon the daily practise of any one predominant, and habituall sin, but when it is indifferently scattered upon all, how much more is it so? In him, that swallowes sins in the world, as he would doe meats at a feast; passes through every dish, and never askes Physitian the nature, the quality, the danger, the offence of any dish: That baits at every sin that rises, and poures himselfe into every sinfull mold he meets: That knowes not when he began to spend his soule, nor where, nor upon what sin he laid it out; no, nor whether he have, whether ever he had any soule, or no; but hath lost his soule so long agoe, in rusty, and in incoherent sins, (not sins that produced one another, as in *Davids* case (and yet that is a fearfull state, that concatenation of sins, that pedegree of sins) but in sins which he embraces, meerely out of an easinesse to sin, and not out of a love, no, nor out of a tentation to that sin in particular) that in these incoherent sins hath so scattered his soule, as that he hath not soule enough left, to seek out the rest.

The *Spikenard* metaphor is taken from the Song of Solomon i 12: 'While the king sitteth at his table, my spikenard hath given forth her sweet savour'. The quotation italicized at the beginning of the second paragraph comes from Proverbs xvii 24. Donne appears to have been using a Latin text; in neither case is the English translation from the King James Bible.

The diversity of figures is worth noticing, employing nouns, verbs and adjectives. The first paragraph contains *Spikenard, sweet savour* and *infused*, used analogically for man's 'Naturall faculties'. The word *fall* is cognate with original sin, but had lost its metaphorical significance by Donne's time. *Soveraignty, enthralled* and *slavery* have figurative implications for Adam's loss of moral freedom.

In the second paragraph, *soule* symbolizes 'spiritual endowments', which wanton man squanders in different ways, represented in the metaphors *sighs, weeps* and *sweares*. The comparison is emphasized by triple repetition of phrases, a finesse to which Donne was extremely partial.

In the third paragraph, the figures present self-indulgence and moral incoherence; man stupifies himself with sin. The verbs *scattered, swallowes, passes, baits, poures, spend*, the nouns *mold* and *pedegree*, the adjectives *rusty* and *incoherent*, all with metaphorical significance, are a jeremiad of denunciations. A graphic listing of evils held as much fascination for Donne as the morbid ever-presence of death.

The methods employed in such pulpit eloquence deserve closer examination. Loose periods are careless of syntax, for example in the use of inner and outer parentheses; circumlocutory *that*-clauses are autonomously developed; and the abandonment of logical for emotive persuasion adds to symptoms of disproportionate paragraph building. There is no point in detailed comment on the network of rhetorical schemes – for instance, the colloquial repetition of *no, nor*, linking some of Donne's piled-up afterthoughts.

The evocativeness of Donne's imagery is usually the result of its realistic concreteness. At the end of the Sermon preached at St Paul's on 29 January 1625 (VII i 71) the preacher thunders, in abstract polysyllables, on the bliss of the life hereafter. He tells us that joy is 'perfected, *sealed*'; it 'shall no more *evaporate*', and 'shall ... *put on a more glorious garment*'; 'every thing shall be a *glasse*, to *reflect God.*' In Donne's imagination, the supernatural is always infinite, and the ultimate source of the sensuous imagery is the Bible. The Church Fathers, who perpetuated hyperbole of image, were careful to clothe metaphysical truths in naturalistic forms.

Another fruitful source of Donne's imagery was science; astronomy and cartography, in particular, seemed to expand space and give a new location, as well as dimension, to physical objects. The emotion aroused is wonder, which the preacher evoked in bizarre conceptions, such as 'the *spirituall Antipodes* of this world, the Sons of God, that *walk with feet opposed* in wayes contrary to the sons of men' (IV i 59). Donne was not so disturbed by the new Philosophy as to refrain from using its seeming outlandishness with ironic and comic effect. For contrast, here are two excerpts from *Devotions upon Emergent Occasions* (*Meditation* 4, p 19–21):

> Our *creatures* are our *thoughts, creatures* that are borne *Gyants*; that reach from *East* to *West*, from *Earth* to *Heaven*, that doe not onely bestride all the *Sea*, and *Land*, but span the *Sunn and Firmament* at once; My thoughts reach all, comprehend all. Inexplicable mistery . . . Call back therefore thy Meditation again, and bring it downe; whats become of mans great extent and proportion, when himselfe shrinkes himselfe, and consumes himselfe to a handfull of dust? whats become of his soaring thoughts, his compassing thoughts, when himselfe brings himselfe to the ignorance, to the thoughtlessnesse of the *Grave*?

Metaphor is said to be the discerning of similitude in things apparently dissimilar, and Donne's image-making faculty has a high degree of fantasy. The metaphorical relation of macrocosm to microcosm (the mundane to the human) encouraged his insight for analogy, for images of enlargement, contraction and distortion, which warp man's judgement. The prose expresses the *discordia concors* of superhuman forces that Donne could not reconcile, except through metaphysical speculation.

Despite the empirical philosophy of Bacon and Hobbes that was trying to eliminate the ambiguities of words (the latter actually described metaphors as *ignes fatui* in *Leviathan* I iv 22), Donne was in commendable company in literally interpreting the Bible. To him concrete images were not realities of perception, but instruments for making ethical truths aesthetically luminous. The mythopoeic value of words was as essential to Donne as to the fathers of biblical exegesis. As the sermons grew in intellectual power, they became less addicted to image-clusters; and some reveal a surprising rationalism in handling the layman's problems of belief. Unlike Maul in *Pilgrim's Progress* (Part 2), Donne did not 'spoil young Pilgrims with sophistry'. Here are his observations on miracles, taken from the Easter Sermon, 1627 (VII xv 373–4):

There is nothing that God hath established in a constant course of nature, and which therefore is done every day, but would seeme a Miracle, and exercise our admiration, if it were done but once; Nay, the ordinary things in Nature, would be greater miracles, then the extraordinary, which we admire most, if they were done but once; The standing still of the Sun, for *Iosuahs* use, was not, in it selfe, so wonderfull a thing, as that so vast and immense a body as the Sun, should run so many miles, in a minute; The motion of the Sun were a greater wonder then the standing still, if all were to begin againe; And onely the daily doing takes off the admiration. But then God having, as it were, concluded himself in a course of nature, and written downe in the booke of Creatures, Thus and thus all things shall be carried, though he glorifie himselfe sometimes, in doing a miracle, yet there is in every miracle, a silent chiding of the world, and a tacite reprehension of them, who require, or who need miracles.

The only allegorical figures in this are *the booke of Creatures* and God's *silent chiding of the world*. The abstract phrase *tacite reprehension* has a modern ring; it repeats the significance of *silent chiding*, as *need* reinforces *require*. No one is, however, deceived as to the period of this passage, on account of its eccentric punctuation, its syntactic involution, and (to modern ears) the archaism of words and phrases. As examples of the latter there are: *admiration* in the sense of 'wonder'; the subjunctive singular *were* for 'would be'; and the reflexive usage *concluded himself*, meaning 'decided upon'. Finally, there is the passive employment of *carried*, implying 'conducted', as Shakespeare first conceived it in *A Midsummer Night's Dream* III ii 240, and Bacon in the essay *Of Seditions and Troubles*, some years before Donne's sermon.

Donne modelled the sermons on the teaching of St Paul and St Augustine, but sincerity of expression should be evaluated in the appropriate Jacobean setting. The ingredients are those of the *Devotions*, namely meditation, expostulation and prayer; but by intent the expostulatory parts are the most dramatic. The pulpit was Donne's stage, and some of the preaching techniques were acquired in the Lincoln's Inn period when Donne was a frequenter of the theatre. The sermons abound in imaginary scenes and dialogues, in asides and apostrophes that await the histrionic nuances of the thinking voice. The Bible offers words of wisdom through dialogue, drama of the mind in the complaining of Job, and tense occasions in the Acts of the Apostles. But the tone of Donne's pleading, questioning and denunciation, belongs to the law-courts as much as the stage. Accounts of Donne's pulpit demeanour vary; but Walton, who heard him often, assured readers that the preacher was dignified in his bearing and eloquent of voice.

It should not be assumed that Donne's power over his audience was of an evangelical kind. Spiritually, he was not above his congregation, but with it, talking, persuading, but seldom haranguing with 'menaces of damnation' (T. S. Eliot, *Essays Ancient and Modern*, p 28). Donne's secret was introspective depth, a readiness to draw upon personal experience and private emotions. Original sin and the Last Judgement are no longer durable themes of the Anglican pulpit; but Eliot's observations (op. cit. pp 16–17) that Donne's zeal to communicate was 'vague and unformed', that he became 'a sorcerer of the emotions', are unfortunate. The sermons that survive were carefully re-thought, and suggest a nervous spirituality, coupled with resolute calm and deep gratitude for his religious vocation.

The great Puritan preacher, Thomas Adams (Donne's neighbour at St Gregory's) had a more pragmatic approach to the meaning of words, but that did not make him a better reasoner. Preachers were not usually of a philosophic turn of mind; but they realized that the account of Creation in Genesis was meaningless, unless perceived as a symbolic event. Donne expounded the faith in the spirit of the Church Fathers, accepting the Word in the Bible as the genuine language of the Holy Spirit. The difference between Donne and Adams was the ritual of the established church, including a symbolic re-enactment of the Man-God sacrifice that founded the Christian church. The following passage from the Sermon preached at St Paul's on Christmas Day, 1621 (III xvii 357–62) offers the most reasonable argument against contingency:

It is but a slacke opinion, it is not *Beliefe*, that is not grounded upon reason. . . .
The *reason* therefore of Man, must first be satisfied, but the way of such satisfaction must be *this*, to make him see,

That this World, a frame of so much harmony, so much concinnitie and conveniencie, and such a correspondence, and subordination in the parts thereof, must necessarily have had a workeman, for nothing can make it selfe: That no such workeman would deliver over a frame, and worke, of so much Majestie, to be governed by *Fortune*, casually, but would still retain the Administration thereof in his owne hands: That if he doe so, if he made the World, and *sustaine* it still by his watchfull Providence, there belongeth a worship and service to him, for doing so: That therefore he hath certainly revealed to man, what kinde of worship, and service, shall be acceptable to him: That this manifestation of his Will, must be permanent, it must be *written*, there must be a *Scripture*, which is his *Word* and his *Will*: And that therefore, from that Scripture, from that Word of God, all Articles of our Beliefe are to bee drawne. . . .

Knowledge cannot save us, but we cannot be saved without Knowledge; Faith is not on this side Knowledge, but beyond it; we must necessarily come to *Knowledge* first, though we must not stay at it, when we are come thither. For, a regenerate Christian, being now a *new Creature*, hath also *a new facultie of Reason*: and so believeth the Mysteries of Religion, out of another Reason, then as a meere naturall Man, he believed naturall and morall things. . . .

Reason is that first, and primogeniall light, and goes no farther in a naturall man; but in a man regenerate by faith, that light does all that reason did, *and more*; and all his *Morall*, and *Civill*, and *Domestique*, and indifferent actions (though they be never done *without Reason*) yet their principall scope, and marke is the glory of God. . . .

The key words are surely the 'Mysteries of Religion' and the 'glory of God'. Donne's opinion is that the essential, i.e. the God-given meaning of a word is partly to be gleaned by searching the generations of commentators, but truly found by the grace of understanding, whereby faith illumines Scripture. He has limitless faith in the integrity of the written word, when compared with the slipperiness of the spoken.

The images of the second paragraph, in words such as *frame*, *harmony*, *concinnitie* (concord, skilful arrangement), *correspondence*,

subordinate, Administration, watchfull, Articles, are concerned principally with the technical arts, with business and government.
Fortune is one of the commonest uses of personification. *Concinnitie*
was introduced by Sir Thomas Elyot in *The Book named the Governor*
(1531) to describe co-ordination of movement in dancing. *Primogeniall,* in the last paragraph, is said in the OED to be an erroneous
form of *primigenial* ('original'); no citation is recorded as early as
Donne's.

Two syntactic constructions in the passage are worthy of note:
A, paragraph 2 – 'if he *doe* so, if he *made* the World, and *sustaine* it
still' (confusion of tenses); B, paragraph 3 – 'out of another
Reason, then as a meere naturall Man, he believed naturall and
morall things' (*anacoluthon* – the sense seems to be 'for a reason
other than he did as a natural man, when he believed natural and
moral things').

The purpose of Donne's sermons is seldom didactic; they aim
at reminding Anglicans of their duties as Christians, and at re-
moving doubts about the validity of the Scriptures as practical rules
for the conduct of men in society. For Donne, religious truths are
mysteries that do not admit of philosophical speculation; but they
may be appreciated by poetic analogy, illustrated by allegory, and
digested in the mind by meditation. The Anglican fraternity to
which Donne belonged was a body of intellectuals, whose culture
was European, not insular, nor dissociated from the theological
background in which they were reared. There was no division between literature and religion, one enduring proof being the excellence of the Authorized Version of the Bible, which was sponsored
by the King. In 1622 *Directions Concerning Preachers* were proclaimed
by King James I, largely to prevent the pulpit from becoming a
platform for sedition. Donne preached a sermon of approval (IV vii
178–209), so highly esteemed that it was circulated in published
form. Donne's sermons were thus given an air of authority, and he
was certainly fortunate in having the backing of the Establishment
for his commitment to divine sanctions, as one of the instruments
of a stable order.

Although Donne put little trust in logic, the *Sermons* are rich in
definitions, especially of words that are central to his chosen texts.
Definition begins with the literal meaning, and is amplified in unforeseen ways, giving centripetal strength to the biblical inspiration. Formality is found only in the framework of a sermon; in

general, the theme unfolds intuitively; even pedestrian matters, such as style and syntax, are clothed on occasion in the garment of allegory. The Sermon preached at St Paul's on 23 November 1628 (VIII xii 271) alludes to Proverbs xvi 24 on the subject of diction. Here is Donne's analogy:

> *Verba composita,* saith *Solomon,* chosen words, *studied,* pre-meditated words, *pleasing* words, (so we translate it) are *as a Hony-combe.* . . . And of this Hony-combe is wax, wax apt for *sealing,* derived too. The distribution of this Hony to the Congregation, The sealing of this Hony to the Conscience, is in the *outward Ordinance of God,* and in the labour of the *Minister,* and his conscionable fitting of himselfe for so great a service.

Donne's imagination was fertile in figures of this kind. The periodic structure of the sentence 'And of this Hony-combe is *wax, wax* apt for *sealing,* derived too' seems contrived, the object being to secure the contiguity of identical words, the rhetorical scheme called *anadiplosis.*

This passage is a characteristic example of metaphysical wit, which was admired by Ben Jonson. At the end of a note on the epistolary style (*Discoveries,* lines 2286–9) Jonson praises self-discernment and the perspicuity that can adapt a theme fittingly to the judgement of an audience. 'Ripeness of judgement', he opines, 'is gotten by foure meanes, *God, Nature, Diligence, and Conversation.* Serve the first well, and the rest will serve you.' Such is the ripeness that is found in Donne's mature sermons.

CHAPTER X

Conclusions

ⓖⓖⓖⓖⓖⓖ

DONNE, like Shakespeare, was the product of his age, and conservative. Critics who study the poetry or prose in isolation tend to forget that they are the product of a unified personality. The scepticism of the *Elegies, Paradoxes* and *Problems* was a novelty that resulted from Donne's youthful pursuit of the outrageous, and dissatisfaction with the family religion. The anti-Petrarchan imagery was one mark of Donne's individuality; another was the suspicion of scholastic logic. By 1597, both were restrained, without loss of that mental resilience, which is the source of Donne's metaphysical wit.

The ingenuity of Donne's mind was soon appreciated by his contemporaries, who thought the *Elegies* and *Satyres* his most original works. Even in the controversial writings, Donne's persona was never abandoned; and it survived in the *Sermons*, which the public accepted as Donne's crowning achievement. As Dean of St Paul's he acknowledged that he devoted more time, study and learning to these orations than to any other of his writings. One cannot say whether Jacobean taste endorsed the modern preference for the *Songs and Sonets*, because the lyrical poems were in private circulation only.

To communicate his thoughts and experiences with passionate conviction, Donne gave considerable attention to the meaning of words, and one of his prose merits is the solicitude to define terms, and ensure understanding. Analogy and definition are, indeed, the true signs of Donne's originality. Since O. English, *wit* had acquired the primary meaning of 'intellect' and 'good sense'; Donne enlarged this to include a 'cleverness' that is innate. The essence of Donne's literary personality is invention, and the commonest mode of it is the conceit. This is broadly word-play that employs some rhetorical trope with a view to contrast or surprise.

Wit in the sense of 'dexterity in reply', the staple of comedies

such as *Much Ado about Nothing*, was not an end in polite conversation until after the Restoration. The *wit* of Donne seldom
sparkles with epigram or repartee; but he favoured the pun, as a
distinguishing mark of the quick thinker. The *Devotions* and *Sermons*
exploit wit with no loss of reverence or dignity, and can serve as
a needed corrective to *avant garde* interpretations of the poetry.

Some readers are nevertheless unhappy about the taste or timing
of Donne's verbal wit, and regard the cynical erudition of the
earlier works as immature. While a scholar at Lincoln's Inn, Donne
was apt to throw caution to the winds, and give full rein to his
questing imagination. Consider, for example, the conceits in *Elegie*
VI (Recusance), lines 15–20:

> So, carelesse flowers strow'd on the waters face,
> The curléd whirlepooles suck, smack, and embrace,
> Yet drowne them; so, the tapers beamie eye
> Amorously twinkling, beckens the giddie flie,
> Yet burnes his wings; and such the devill is,
> Scarce visiting them, who are intirely his.

This is a curious instance of Donne's observation of nature.
Though intrigued with natural science, he used it principally for
analogies with the human situation. The Renaissance preoccupation with mutability was more at home in a Ptolemaic universe
than a Copernican one.

There is less of the mystic and more of the pagan in Donne than
in St Augustine; and this was in accord with the humanist's sense
of liberation. A mystic is one who surrenders selfhood to attain
union with God, through contemplation; but no mystical code
would have approved the pugnacity of mind encountered in
Donne's *Paradoxes*:

> *Discord* is never so barren that it affords no fruit; for the *fall*
> of one *estate* is at the worst the *increaser* of another, because
> it is as impossible to finde a *discommodity* without *advantage*,
> as to finde *Corruption* without *Generation*: ... In a *troubled*
> *misery* Men are alwaies more *Religious* than in a *secure peace*.
> The number of *good* men, the onely charitable nourishers of
> *Concord*, wee see is thinne, and daily melts and waines ...
> Wee are ascertained of all *Disputable* doubts, onely by
> *arguing* and differing in *Opinion* ...
> ('That by Discord things increase', *Selected Prose*, p 9)

Conclusions

Evelyn Simpson regards 'intensity' and transcendancy of purpose as mystical qualities, and cites Donne's 'mineral' symbolism in *Resurrection, imperfect* (Gardner, *Divine Poems*, p 28). The intellectual discernment of 'Hee was all gold when he lay downe, but rose/ All tincture' scarcely betokens the imagery of a neo-Platonist. Though Donne accepted divine immanence, the egotism of his mind is not reconcilable with the spirit of mysticism. Donne's religious primitivism, emerging boldly into the Renaissance, resembled Giotto's in the world of art; but it was given a subtler emphasis by the intervention of the Reformation.

Donne's meddling intellect, indeed, prevented him from becoming a disciplined theologian. He perceived no clash of loyalties in his devotion, both to naturalistic truth, and to the Christian faith. His private brand of Anglicanism was a compromise with inherited Catholicism.

The Renaissance was not yet in a position to distinguish philosophy from science; but Donne was not troubled by the so-called 'new Philosophy', because, in the academic acceptance of the term, he was no philosopher. The logic of his verse is not syllogistic, but rhetorical, and inordinately given to word-play; for instance in *The Crosse,* lines 51–61 (Gardner, *Divine Poems,* pp 27–8):

And crosse thy heart: for that in man alone
Points downewards, and hath palpitation.
Crosse those dejections, when it downeward tends,
And when it to forbidden heights pretends.
And as thy braine through bony walls doth vent
By sutures, which a Crosses forme present,
So when thy braine workes, ere thou utter it,
Crosse and correct concupiscence of witt.
Be covetous of Crosses, let none fall.
Crosse no man else, but crosse thy selfe in all.
Then doth the Crosse of Christ worke fruitfully.

Dialectical manipulation points to this being one of the earliest of the *Divine Poems.* The medical knowledge appears to have come from Aristotle; but Donne was familiar also with the works of Hippocrates and Paracelsus, deriving from the latter his theory of the *Balsamum naturale.*

By a process of critical elimination, one is compelled to regard Donne purely as poet and prose-artist, and to note how emblematic his practice is. Emblem books were among the principal sources of Donne's conceits, as well as Shakespeare's. Illustrated books, emanating from Continental presses, had as their principal aim the making of abstract morality concrete. Each emblem in Jesuit handbooks explicated a motto, in the form of a quotation or a few lines of verse. Man's mortality was a common theme of the simplistic symbolism often employed by Donne in the sermons, for instance in no. 8 preached before the Countess of Bedford on 7 January 1621 (III, p 202):

> *It is appointed to all men, that they shall once dye.* . . . If thou behold a *Tree*, then *Job* gives thee a comparison of thy selfe; A *Tree* is an *embleme* of thy selfe; nay a Tree is the *originall,* thou art but the *copy,* thou are not so good as it: for, *There is hope of a tree* (as you reade there) *if the roote wax old, if the stock be dead, if it be cut down, yet by the scent of the waters, it will bud, but man is sick, and dyeth, and where is he?* he shall not wake againe, till heaven be no more.

Like its counterpart in aesthetics, baroque poetry was religious in inspiration, and apparently derived from biblical examples, such as the Psalms of David and the Song of Solomon. Baroque writing often takes the form of a meditation, on the theme of illusion or transience. Time made reality impermanent, and the soul was uppermost in the writer's thoughts; but the paradox of the baroque is invariably the sensuous language deployed for spiritual ends. Love, death and immortality are perennial dichotomies, imaged in naturalistic metaphors.

As a generalization, this view of the baroque seems to fit Donne, until a closer examination is made of lyrics such as *The Crosse,* or the meditations contained in the *Devotions.* The baroque is a figment of the same kind as T. S. Eliot's observation in *The Sacred Wood,* that the metaphysical poets 'feel their thought as immediately as the odour of a rose'. Critics are too apt to take seriously the provocative poems, and to dismiss the verse epistles and panegyrics, to appreciate that the rhetoric is functional and that its emphasis is a much solider merit than romantic vagueness.

Donne's thinking was so strongly entrenched in the meditative tradition that the Anniversaries, Expostulations, and Valedictions are seldom seen as candid expressions of an anguished heart, comparable to Augustine's *Confessions.* Donne was unashamed of candour that helped to the understanding of his experience; his motive was the restoration of harmony. The world is his place of retribution, not a Dantesque vision, but a battle-ground of the self, calling for immense discipline of mind, if order is to be created out of one's personal confusions. Belief in the immortality of the righteous soul gave Donne's later life a purpose, which he never doubted would be realized.

From the dual aspect of God in the writings of St Paul – on the one hand a deity withdrawn, on the other hand the soul of merciful love – Donne drew much of the symbolism of his meditations. Philo Judaeus studied the *Timaeus* and *Phaedo* for a solution of this paradox; but Plato, always guarded about abstractions, told him no more than that 'being' and 'essence' are difficult words. Committed to the theory that ideas are formal concepts behind natural laws, Plato suggested that God was the Master Mind controlling Nature's uniformity. Thus Plato's Deity was taken as the withdrawn One, Paul's as the merciful and unifying. Plato was the father of 'natural theology', Paul of 'spiritual essence', which he regarded as the birthright of every Christian worshipper.

Philosophers like Plato were conscious that uniformity was far from perfect, and attributed exceptions to Fate. This notion died hard among Christian apologists; but the theory of Nature's striving for oneness had less missionary appeal than Paul's doctrine of righteousness.

Donne's symbolic language made not very precise use of the experience of 'ecstasy', which meant 'union with the Absolute' in the *Enneads* of Plotinus and the writings of Marsilio Ficino. Geometry played a significant role in Donne's symbolic equipment. When he spoke of the world's 'concinnity of parts', he had in mind its three-dimensional form. In the following passage he is concerned with the concept of divine perfection:

> O Soule, O circle, why so quickly bee
> Thy ends, thy birth and death, clos'd up in thee?
> Since one foot of thy compasse still was plac'd
> In heav'n, the other might securely'have pac'd
> In the most large extent, through every path,
> Which the whole world, or man the abridgment hath.
> Thou knowst, that though the tropique circles have
> (Yea and those small ones which the Poles engrave,)

All the same roundnesse, evennesse, and all
The endlesnesse of the equinoctiall;
Yet, when we come to measure distances,
How here, how there, the Sunne affected is,
When he doth faintly worke, and when prevaile,
Onely great circles, than can be our scale.
(*Obsequies to the Lord Harrington,* Grierson, 1, pp 274–5)

An infinite circle was the symbol of eternity, and a spiral was thought to resolve the mystery of time, as linear extension; returning upon itself, on a higher plane, it described for Christian Platonists the motion of ascending love.

In the employment of images, metaphor is the particular, symbol the universal. In the post-Cartesian world, religious symbols lost much of their significance. Original sin, a concept meaningful to Donne and Milton, was not so to Hobbes and Hume. If Donne was among the metaphysical poets who 'felt' their thoughts, he did so as a soul in conflict; and he experienced especial difficulty with a poem of a hundred or more lines. In the clash between the old and the new worlds, the *Songs and Sonets* are the better poems, because in a limited space Donne achieved greater internal harmony. Beside the directness of these lyrical meditations, the *Anniversaries* have a tantalizing obliqueness, and the compliments to noble ladies arouse a suspicion of obsequiousness.

A scale of balance, on which to weigh Donne's excesses, is sometimes provided in poems to men before 1608, to Woodward, Wotton and Goodyer, and in prose epistles to loyal friends. Horatian sanity in praising virtue, and the graces of civility and courtesy, are not substitutes for the vitality and pointedness of the *Songs and Sonets*; but they are reminders that Donne admired Montaigne's *Essays* and Castiglione's *The Courtier,* as well as Ficino's translations of Plato. Thus he begins a letter to Rowland Woodward (August 1597):

If, as mine is, thy life a slumber be,
Seeme, when thou read'st these lines, to dreame of me,
Never did Morpheus nor his brother weare
Shapes soe like those Shapes, whom they would appeare,
As this my letter is like me, for it
Hath my name, words, hand, feet, heart, minde and wit;

It is my deed of gift of mee to thee,
It is my Will, my selfe the Legacie.

(Milgate, p 64, lines 1–8)

The term 'paradox', one of the most useful of the rhetorical schemes, needs clarifying in regard to Donne's practice. Cleanth Brooks, analysing *The Canonization* (extracted below), from which *The Well Wrought Urn* takes its title, says that the paradox of this poem is associated with irony and wonder, as it is in both biblical Testaments; moreover, that the attraction for a reader is the unravelling of the paradox in terms of facts identifiable with one's personal experience. In this poem, which emulates Ovid's *Amores* II 10, emblematic conceit, irony, hyperbole and rhetorical question are as amusing as in the prototype. The disciplined form has a circular movement, secured by making the first and last lines of each stanza terminate in *love,* with three other rhyme-words at least in visual accord. The steps to sainthood are treated with a pseudo-seriousness and detachment that is comic. The central paradoxes are found in thirteen lines of the last three stanzas:

STANZA 3 (LINES 23–7)
The Phoenix ridle hath more wit
By us, we two being one, are it,
So, to one neutrall thing both sexes fit.
Wee dye and rise the same, and prove
Mysterious by this love.

STANZA 4 (LINES 28 AND 33–4)
Wee can dye by it, if not live by love, . . .
As well a well wrought urne becomes
The greatest ashes, as halfe-acre tombes, . . .

STANZA 5 (LINES 39–43)
You, to whom love was peace, that now is rage;
Who did the whole worlds soule extract, and drove
Into the glasses of your eyes,
So made such mirrors, and such spies,
That they did all to you epitomize

A paradox for Donne was nothing as jejune as the flouting of accepted opinion; it was rather a demonstration that dialectic can emerge as nonsense, once it is exposed to the existential facts. Since the intellect is shadowy and undependable, it invites the wit of disillusion. Behind the most surprising paradoxes of Donne lies the Thomistic refutation of Plato's theory of ideas, a process natural enough when speculative thoughts are replaced by sensible objects.

The first of the paradoxes cited, the 'Phoenix ridle' (23), was suggested by an illustration in an Emblem book, with accompanying motto. The legend of the Phoenix, a bird unique in propagating itself, explains line 25 'So, to one *neutrall thing* both sexes fit.' The next line 'Wee dye and rise the same' has sexual overtones. The poem is dedicated to the thesis that physical love can be both vivifying and destroying according to restraint, or indulgence of desire; analogues appear to be 'a well wrought urne' and a 'halfe-acre' tomb (33–4). Line 39 suggests figuratively that love fulfilled brings 'peace', love frustrated 'rage'. The unnamed alchemist (40) who distils the world's *soul* into the lovers' eyes, uses retorts described as *glasses* (41); in line 42 the meaning is punningly transferred to 'mirrors', the metaphorical *spies* of lovers' actions.

From a close reading of the most difficult of the *Songs and Sonets,* it becomes evident that Donne's skill in rhetoric is not conventional, and sometimes obscure. The flexibility of his mind is shown in the extraordinary range and eclecticism of his interests. In other circumstances, he might have become the Montaigne of English verse, living in retirement at Mitcham. The fascination of the cosmopolitan life of London was in paradoxical contrast with his Augustinian theological understanding.

Rhetoric had its uses when literature was not in circulation, except among the wealthy, and was made public largely by the spoken word. Izaak Walton reported that Donne was an impressive speaker, and the 'invention' for which he was famous, matched his ability to articulate it vividly and cogently. The fertility of his mind sets up a chain reaction in which words and visual images generate similitudes, which give birth to new discoveries. Dynamic coherence does more for Donne's argument than logic, and the lure of mimetic diversion is a temptation he had constantly to resist. In *An Anatomie of the World* (lines 275–88), the inventive imagination is as colourful and emblematic as that of the French symbolist Rimbaud:

So, of the Starres which boast that they doe runne   275
In Circle still, none ends where he begun.

All their proportion's lame, it sinkes, it swels.
For of Meridians, and Parallels,
Man hath weav'd out a net, and this net throwne
Upon the Heavens, and now they are his owne.   280
Loth to goe up the hill, or labour thus
To goe to heaven, we make heaven come to us.
We spur, we reine the starres, and in their race
They're diversly content t'obey our pace.
But keepes the earth her round proportion still?   285
Doth not a Tenarif, or higher Hill
Rise so high like a Rocke, that one might thinke
The floating Moone would shipwracke there, and sinke?

Single-word metaphors are not found in lines 278–80, 283–4, and 288, but plurisigns of hyperbole, in which the imagery is closer to allegory. The function of the plurisign is implied in its context, the complex symbolism being evocative rather than referential.

Donne's discursive poems invariably require a second reading to discover the effective rhythm, which is closely associated with the meaning of the words, and relies minimally on the formal base of an iambic line. Verse as speech is indubitably the aim of his rarified, imagist language. The organic unit of the *Anniversaries* is neither the foot, nor the metrical line, but the paragraph; in nonstanzaic verse this is of indeterminate length. The couplet style of the *Anniversaries* is unlike Pope's well-turned thoughts, compressed into groups of two or three lines. Incisive balancing of parts was not Donne's ideal; his syntactic enjambements overstep the limits of Augustan seemliness, and the result is a more prosaic rhythm. The difference emerges clearly in Pope's rewriting of two of Donne's *Satyres*, in which he strove hard to avoid invertebrate lines such as 284 of *An Anatomie of the World*: 'They're diversly content t'obey our pace.'

Donne modulates for meaning as often as he does for rhythmical variation. Emphatic words are stressed for semantic effect in the following lines of *An Anatomie*:

278 For of | Merí | dians, | and Pá | rallèls (two primary stresses)
284 They're dí | versly | contént | t'obéy | our páce (four primary stresses)
287 Ríse só | high like | a Rócke, | that óne | mìght thínke (six primary stresses)

The last of these lines employs only monosyllables, a device that nearly always increases the primary stresses in the iambic line.

The psychology of imagination was not affected by the medium Donne chose; he wished to persuade vividly, by whatever means at his disposal. Some loss of imagery occurs in the later sermons, but is compensated by schematic resources that ensure unusual balance and proportion. In elaborate rhythms, Donne sometimes transcends the ordinary use of words. The clever collusion of sound modulation with stress and intonation, was apparently instinctive; and the management of clauses invariably enforces the interest of their content. Here is a passage from the funeral Sermon for Sir William Cokayne, dated 12 December 1626 (VII x 271):

> Consider the smallest bodies upon Earth, The haires of our head, Objects, which one would thinke, Destiny would not observe, or could not discerne; And yet Destiny, (to speak to a naturall man) And God, (to speake to a Christian) is no more troubled to make a Monarchy ruinous, than to make a haire gray. Nay, nothing needs be done to either, by God, or Destiny; A Monarchy will ruine, as a haire will grow gray, of it selfe. In the Elements themselves, of which all sub-elementary things are composed, there is no acquiescence, but a vicissitudinary transmutation into one another.

Donne was at the summit of his powers. In clarity, concision and point, the above style is modern and well-controlled, despite its Jacobean reasoning. Repetition is actuated by a design to balance the phrases, so that Donne attains the well-disposed proportions that Pope aspired to in verse. Initially, words are common; but in the final complex sentence Donne achieves a climax of poly-syllabic grandeur, found in words such as *sub-elementary*, *acquiescence*, and *vicissitudinary transmutation*.

The parallelism of this excerpt is characteristic of Donne's prose practice; there are many pages of the *Sermons* in which he employs it with variety and distinction. The inspiration was the poetry of the Old Testament, especially the Psalms and Proverbs, which he read in Hebrew, Latin and English. Donne came to a thorough understanding of the principles on which these songs of suffering and jubilation were composed; he merges quotations from the Psalms into prose paragraphs, as though they were part of his thoughts – as indeed they were. Though, in general, he chose the 'loose and free style' approved by Burton in the preface to the *Anatomy of Melancholy*, there was no deliberate design to abandon the ample Ciceronian period. He discarded involved subordinate clauses, because he preferred co-ordinate linkings, parallel structures and such groupings as do not tax the memory.

Donne's delight in Job, the Psalms and the Books of Wisdom may be used as a springboard for assessing his prevailing attitude to the Scriptures. C. S. Lewis, also an Anglican, offers in chapters xi and xii of *Reflections on the Psalms* a theological view altogether different from Donne's:

> One can respect, and at moments envy, both the Fundamentalist's view of the Bible and the Roman Catholic's view of the Church. But there is one argument which we should beware of using for either position: God must have done what is best, this is best, therefore God has done this. For we are mortals and do not know what is best for us, and it is dangerous to prescribe what God must have done.

The modern reader's reluctance to take seriously the reasoning in Donne's *Sermons* may stem from such a cause. Lewis makes a further observation, more relevant to preachers like Donne, when he writes (p 109):

> A vocation is a terrible thing. To be called out of nature into the supernatural life is . . . a costly honour. Even to be called from one natural level to another is loss as well as gain.

The present neglect of much of Donne's prose has not been because of *odium theologicum* or critical insensitivity, but of alleged limitations in the writer's religious experience. It is true that the sermons accord with the restless spirit of the age; they are intense and vigorous in movement, astounding in their explorations of words, but not always emotionally satisfying. There appears to be a sentiment, which this writer does not share, that Donne's preoccupation with sin and death was unhealthy, that the expostulations and hopeful pleas for redemption may have been without reasonable prospect of being answered.

Bibliography

༄ ༄ ༄ ༄ ༄ ༄

A. TEXTS

Donne, John. *The Poems,* ed. H. J. C. Grierson, 2 vols. London: Oxford University Press, 1912.

The Complete Poems, ed. R. E. Bennett. Chicago: 1942.

The Complete English Poems, ed. A. J. Smith. London: Penguin, 1971.

The Divine Poems, ed. Helen Gardner. Oxford: Oxford English Texts, 1952.

The Elegies and the Songs and Sonnets, ed. Helen Gardner. Oxford: Oxford English Texts, 1965.

The Satires, Epigrams and Verse Letters, ed. W. Milgate. Oxford: Oxford English Texts, 1967.

The Songs and Sonets, ed. T. Redpath. London: Methuen, 1967. (First edn, 1956.)

The Anniversaries, ed. F. Manley. Baltimore: Johns Hopkins Press, 1963.

Poems, with elegies on the author's death, 1633. London: Scolar Facsimile, 1969.

John Donne's holograph of 'A letter to the Lady Carey and Mrs. Essex Riche', 1612, ed. Helen Gardner. London: Scolar Facsimile, 1972.

Ignatius his Conclave, ed. T. S. Healy. Oxford: Clarendon Press, 1969.

Essayes in Divinity, ed. Evelyn M. Simpson. Oxford: Clarendon Press, 1952.

The Sermons, ed. G. R. Potter and E. M. Simpson, 10 vols. Berkeley and Los Angeles: University of California Press, 1953–62.

Sermons on the Psalms and Gospels, ed. E. M. Simpson. Berkeley and Los Angeles: University of California Press, 1963.

Prebend Sermons, ed. J. M. Mueller. Cambridge, Mass: Harvard University Press, 1971.

Devotions Upon Emergent Occasions, ed. John Sparrow. Cambridge: University Press, 1923.

Devotions Upon Emergent Occasions, ed. A. Raspa. Montreal and London: McGill – Queens University Press, 1975.

Bibliography

John Donne's Complete Poetry and Selected Prose, ed. J. Hayward. London: Nonesuch Press, 1929, repr. 1942.
Selected Prose, chosen by E. Simpson, ed. H. Gardner and T. Healy. Oxford: Clarendon Press, 1967.
Deaths duell, or, a consolation to the soule, 1632. London: Scolar Facsimile, 1969.
Five sermons upon speciall occasions, 1626. London: Scolar Facsimile, 1970.
Sermons, Selected Passages, ed. Logan Pearsall Smith. Oxford: Clarendon Press, 1932.

B. OTHER SOURCES

Bacon, Francis. *The Proficiencie and Advancement of Learning,* ed. W. Aldis Wright. Cambridge: University Press, 1873.
Bald, R. C. *Donne and the Drurys.* Cambridge: University Press, 1959. *John Donne, a Life.* Oxford: Clarendon Press, 1970.
Gosse, Edmund. *The Life and Letters of John Donne,* 2 vols. Gloucester, Mass: Peter Smith, 1959. Reprint of Dodd Mead, 1899.
Keynes, Geoffrey. *Bibliography of the Works of Dr. John Donne, Dean of St. Paul's.* Cambridge: University Press, 1958.
Roberts, John R. *John Donne, An Annotated Bibliography of Modern Criticism.* Columbia: University of Missouri Press, 1973.
Elizabethan Critical Essays, ed. G. Gregory Smith, 2 vols. London: Oxford University Press, 1904.
Critical Essays of the Seventeenth Century, ed. J. E. Springarn, 3 vols. London: Oxford University Press, 1907.
Walton, Izaak. *Lives of Donne, Wotton, Hooker, Herbert and Sanderson.* London: Oxford University Press, 1936.

C. MONOGRAPHS AND SPECIAL STUDIES

Hardy, Evelyn. *Donne, A Spirit in Conflict.* London: Constable, 1942.
Hunt, Clay. *Donne's Poetry.* New Haven: Yale University Press, 1954.
Legouis, Pierre. *Donne the Craftsman.* New York: Russell and Russell, 1962. Reprint of Didier, 1928.
Leishman, J. B. *The Monarch of Wit.* London: Hutchinson, 1951.
Louthan, Doniphan. *The Poetry of John Donne.* New York: Bookman Associates, 1951.
Matsuura, Kaichi. *A Study of Donne's Imagery.* Tokyo: Kenkyusha Press, 1953.
Moloney, M. F. *John Donne, His Flight from Mediaevalism.* New York: Russell and Russell, 1965. Reprint of Univ. of Illinois, 1944.

Partridge, A. C. *The Tribe of Ben*. London: Arnold, 1966.
Roston, Murray. *The Soul of Wit, A Study of John Donne*. Oxford: Clarendon Press, 1974.
Rugoff, M. A. *Donne's Imagery*. New York: Russell and Russell, 1962.
Saunders, Wilbur. *John Donne's Poetry*. Cambridge: University Press, 1971.
Simpson, E. M. *A Study of the Prose Works of John Donne*. Oxford: Clarendon Press, 1924.
Smith, A. J. *John Donne: The Songs and Sonets*. London: Arnold, 1964. Reprint of the Corporate Press, 1939.
Stampfer, Judith. *John Donne and the Metaphysical Gesture*. New York: Simon and Schuster, 1971.
Stein, Arnold. *John Donne's Lyrics, The Eloquence of Action*. Minneapolis: University of Minnesota Press, 1962.
Unger, Leonard. *Donne's Poetry and Modern Criticism*. New York: Russell and Russell, 1962. Reprint of Regnery, 1950.
Webber, Joan. *Contrary Music – The Prose Style of John Donne*. Madison: University of Wisconsin Press, 1963.

D. CRITICAL SYMPOSIA

Elizabethan Poetry, Modern Essays in Criticism, ed. P. J. Alpers. London: Oxford University Press, 1967.
Elizabethan Poetry, ed. J. R. Brown and B. Harris. London: Arnold, 1960.
Just so Much Honor, ed. P. A. Fiore. Pennsylvania State University Press, 1972.
John Donne, ed. Helen Gardner. Englewood Cliffs: Prentice-Hall, 1962.
Discussions of John Donne, ed. F. Kermode. Boston: Heath and Co., 1962.
Donne, Songs and Sonets, A Casebook, ed. J. Lovelock. London: Macmillan, 1973.
Elizabethan and Jacobean Studies Presented to F. P. Wilson, ed. H. Davis and H. Gardner. Oxford: Clarendon Press, 1959.
Essential Articles for the Study of John Donne's Poetry, ed. John R. Roberts. Hamden: Archon Books, 1975.
John Donne, Essays in Celebration, ed. A. J. Smith. London: Methuen, 1972.
John Donne, The Critical Heritage, ed. A. J. Smith. London: Routledge and Kegan Paul, 1975.
A Garland for John Donne, 1631–1931, ed. Theodore Spencer. Gloucester: Peter Smith, 1958. Reprint of Harvard U. P., 1931.
Interpretations, ed. John Wain. London: Routledge and Kegan Paul, 1955.

Bibliography

E. LITERARY SURVEYS

From Donne to Marvell, ed. Boris Ford. Harmondsworth: Pelican,1963.
Grierson, H. J. C. *Cross Currents in English Literature of the Seventeenth Century.* London: Chatto and Windus, 1929.

F. LANGUAGE STUDIES

Jones, R. F. *The Triumph of the English Language.* London: Oxford University Press, 1953.
Moore, J. L. *Tudor-Stuart Views on the Growth, Status and Destiny of the English Language.* Halle: Max Niemeyer, 1910.
Partridge, A. C. *The Accidence of Ben Jonson's Plays, Masques and Entertainments.* Cambridge: Bowes and Bowes, 1953.
Studies in the Syntax of Ben Jonson's Plays. Cambridge: Bowes and Bowes, 1953.
Tudor to Augustan English. London: Deutsch, 1969.
The Language of Renaissance Poetry. London: Deutsch, 1971.
Vickers, Brian. *Classical Rhetoric in English Poetry.* London: Macmillan, 1970.
Wyld, H. C. *Studies in English Rhymes from Surrey to Pope.* London: John Murray, 1923.

G. MISCELLANEOUS

Alvarez, A. *The School of Donne.* London: Chatto and Windus, 1962.
Bald, R. C. *Donne's Influence in English Literature.* Morpeth: St John's College Press, 1932.
Bamborough, J. B. *The Little World of Man.* London: Longmans Green, 1952.
Baum, Paul F. *The Other Harmony of Prose.* Durham N. C.: Duke University Press, 1952.
Bennett, Joan. *Four Metaphysical Poets.* Cambridge: University Press, 1934.
Bottrall, Margaret. *Every Man a Phoenix.* London: Murray, 1958.
Buxton, John. *Elizabethan Taste.* London: Macmillan, 1963.
Croll, Morris W. *Style, Rhetoric, and Rhythm.* Princeton: University Press, 1966.
Eliot, T. S. *The Sacred Wood,* London: Methuen, 1920.
Eliot, T. S. *Essays Ancient and Modern.* London: Faber and Faber, 1936.
Hamilton, K. G. *The Two Harmonies.* Oxford: Clarendon Press, 1963.
Hardison, O. B. *The Enduring Monument. A Study of the Idea of Praise in Renaissance Literary Theory and Practice.* Chapel Hill: University of North Carolina. 1962.

Husain, Itrat. *The Mystical Element in the Metaphysical Poets of the Seventeenth Century.* Edinburgh: Oliver and Boyd, 1948.

Lewis, C. S. *Reflections on the Psalms.* London: Bles, 1958.

Mahood, M. M. *Poetry and Humanism.* London: Cape, 1950.

Martz, Louis L. *The Poetry of Meditation.* New Haven: Yale University Press, 1954.

Miles, Josephine. *Eras and Modes in English Poetry.* Berkeley and Los Angeles: California University Press, 1957.

Mitchell, W. F. *English Pulpit Oratory from Andrewes to Tillotson.* London: S.P.C.K., 1932.

Nicolson, M. H. *The Breaking of the Circle.* New York: Columbia University Press, 1962.

Praz, Mario. *The Flaming Heart.* New York: Doubleday, 1958.

Partridge, A. C. *Orthography in Shakespeare and Elizabethan Drama.* London: Arnold, 1964.

English Biblical Translation. London: Deutsch, 1973.

Saintsbury, G. *A History of English Prosody,* vol. 2. New York: Russell and Russell, 1961. Reprint.

Stapleton, Laurence. *The Elected Circle.* Princeton: University Press, 1973.

Tuve, Rosemond. *Elizabethan and Metaphysical Imagery.* Chicago: University Press, 1947.

Vickers, Brian. *Francis Bacon and Renaissance Prose.* Cambridge: University Press, 1968.

Wallerstein, Ruth. *Studies in Seventeenth-Century Poetic.* Madison: Wisconsin University Press, 1950.

Williamson, George. *The Donne Tradition.* Cambridge, Mass.: Harvard University Press, 1930.

The Proper Wit of Poetry. London: Faber and Faber, 1961.

Seventeenth Century Contexts. London: Faber and Faber, 1960.

The Senecan Amble. Chicago: University Press, 1966.

Woodhouse, A. S. P. *The Poet and his Faith.* Chicago: University Press, 1965.

H. JOURNALS AND ANNUALS

Allen, Don Cameron. 'Dean Donne Sets His Text'. *ELH* 10 (1943): 208–29.

Bennett, Joan. 'An Aspect of the Evolution of Seventeenth-Century Prose'. *Review of English Studies* 17 (1941): 281–97.

Bennett, R. E. 'Donne's *Letters to Severall Persons of Honour*'. *PMLA* 56 (1941): 120–40.

Chambers, A. B. 'Goodfriday, 1613. Riding Westward: The Poem and the Tradition'. *ELH* 28 (1961): 31–53.

Bibliography

Gardner, Helen. 'Notes on Donne's Verse Letters'. *Modern Language Review* 41 (1946): 318–21.

Leishman, J. B. 'The Sermons of John Donne'. *Review of English Studies* 8 (1957): 434–43.

Moloney, M. F. 'Donne's Metrical Practice'. *PMLA* 65 (1950): 232–9.

Nellist, B. F. 'Donne's *Storm* and *Calm* and the Descriptive Tradition'. *Modern Language Review* 59 (1964): 511–15.

Ong, W. J. 'Ramus: Rhetoric and the pre-Newtonian Mind'. *English Institute Essays* (1952): 138–70.

Quinn, Dennis. 'Donne's Christian Eloquence'. *ELH* 27 (1960): 276–97.

Raspa, A. 'Theology and Poetry in Donne's *Conclave*'. *ELH* 32 (1965): 478–89.

Roberts, D. R. 'The Death Wish of John Donne'. *PMLA* 62 (1947): 958–76.

Simpson, E. M. 'John Donne and Sir Thomas Overbury's Characters' *Modern Language Review* 18 (1923): 410–15.

'A Note on Donne's Punctuation'. *Review of English Studies* 1928: 295–300.

Sloan, T. O. 'The Rhetoric in the Poetry of John Donne'. *Studies in English Literature* 3 (1963): 31–44.

Sparrow, John. 'John Donne and Contemporary Preachers'. *Essays and Studies of the English Association* 16 (1930): 144–78.

Stein, Arnold. 'Donne and the Couplet'. *PMLA* 57 (1942): 676–96.

'Donne's Obscurity and the Elizabethan Tradition'. *ELH* 13 (1946): 98–118.

Shapiro, I. A. 'The Burley Letters'. *TLS* Sept. 12 (1952): 597.

'The Text of Donne's *Letters to Severall Persons.*' *Review of English Studies* 7 (1931): 291–301.

Umbach, Herbert H. 'The Rhetoric of Donne's Sermons'. *PMLA* 52 (1937): 354–8.

'The Merits of Metaphysical Style in Donne's Easter Sermons'. *ELH* 12 (1945): 108–29.

Wall, John N. 'Donne's Wit of Redemption: The Drama of Prayer in the *Holy Sonnets*'. *Studies in Philology* 73 (1976): 189–203.

Wallerstein, Ruth. 'Rhetoric in the English Renaissance: Two Elegies'. *English Institute Essays* (1948): 153–78.

Index

𝕊𝕊𝕊𝕊𝕊𝕊

Bible,—*contd.*
229; Isaiah, 144; Job, 48, 221, 229,
243; John, 157; Jonah, 52;
Leviticus, 48; Luke, 137, 143-4,
148, 201, 206; Pauline Epistles, 10,
63, 90, 105, 115, 148, 153, 179,
196, 217, 237; 2 Peter, 135;
Proverbs, 120, 182, 225, 232, 242;
Psalms, 10, 79, 105, 109, 135, 198,
212, 215-16, 236, 242-3; Revelation, 105, 120, 132, 140, 147, 167,
192, 206, 216; Song of Songs, 124,
225, 236; Wisdom Books, 243.
Versions: 'Complutence' (polyglot
bible), 212; Douai, 135; Geneva,
192, 211; Great Bible, 192; Greek
Testament, 148; Hebrew, 124, 211;
King James (Authorised Version),
135, 148, 153, 183, 190-92, 206,
211, 215, 225, 231; Rheims, 192;
Septuagint, 192, 211; Tyndale, 192;
Vulgate, 115, 135, 192, 211, 221;
Wyclif, 140, 179, 192. Book of
Life, The, 167, 201. symbolic
language of, 115
Bilson, Bishop Thomas, *The Per-
petual Government of Christ's Church*,
199
Blake, William, 211; *Morning*, 145
Bonaventura, St, *Illuminationes in
Hexaëmeron*, 124
Boniface III, Pope, 167
Book of Creatures, The, 167, 192,
201-2, 205
Boswell, James, *Life of Johnson*, 224
Botticelli, Sandro, *Primavera*, 103
Bottrall, Margaret, *Every Man a
Phoenix*, 200, 205
Brahe, Tycho, 64, 106, 111, 167, 169
Brooke, Christopher, 51
Brooks, Cleanth, *The Well Wrought
Urn*, 239
Browne, Thomas, 190; *Urn Burial*,
193
Browne, William, *Britannia's Pas-
torals*, 119
Browning, Robert, 69, 149, 151, 156
Bunyan, John, *Pilgrim's Progress*, 227
Burton, Robert, *Anatomy of Mel-
ancholy*, 106, 156, 242
Butler, Charles, *English Grammar*, 27
Buxton, John, *Elizabethan Taste*,
67, 69

Cadence, in poetry, 24, 157; in prose,
186, 198, 203; internal, 198;
phrasal, 199
Caesar, Sir Julius, 145-6
Calvin, John, 44, 192
Capgrave, John, 108
Carew, Thomas, *Elegie upon the death
of the Deane of St. Pauls*, 16
Carlyle, Thomas, *Frederick the Great*,
177
Carr (or Ker), Robert, Earl of
Somerset, 98, 122, 125
Castiglione, Baldassare, *Il libro del
cortegiano*, 95, 238
Catullus, 50
Casaubon, Isaac, Lectures on Persius,
37
Cave, John, 10
Caxton, William, 89
Chapman, George, 56, 151, 158;
Ovids Banquet of Sence, 22
Chaucer, Geoffrey, 120, 186, 195;
Canterbury Tales, 90; *Nun's Priest's
Tale*, 140-1; *Romaunt of the Rose*,
177; *Treatise on the Astrolabe*, 194
Chillingworth, William, *The Religion
of Protestants*, 90
Christian Platonists, 101, 103, 238
Chrysostom, John, 214
Cicero, 18, 121, 192, 194, 198; style
of, 165
Classical quantitative measures, in-
fluence on prose, 198
Coleridge, Samuel Taylor, *Biographia
Literaria*, 79
Colloquial contractions, 17, 24, 29,
38, 65
Columbus, Christopher, 166
Common Prayer, Book of, 140
Conceits (*concetti*), 50, 55-6, 68, 72,
79, 86, 88, 92, 95, 101, 125, 132,
135, 137, 142-3, 147, 220, 236, 239
Constitutions and Canons of the Angli-
can Church, 205
Copernicus, 69, 106, 142, 166-7;
Copernican cosmology, 104, 135,
234; *De Revolutionibus Orbium Co-
elestium*, 169
Corkine, William, *Second Book of
Ayres* (1612), 66
Coryate, Thomas, *Crudities*, 24
Court masques, 124
Coverdale, Miles, 194

Index